EVERYONE'S
MONEY BOOK

ON FINANCIAL PLANNING

JORDAN E. GOODMAN

Dearborn™
Trade Publishing
A **Kaplan Professional** Company

Vice President and Publisher: Cynthia A. Zigmund
Editorial Director: Donald J. Hull
Senior Managing Editor: Jack Kiburz
Interior Design: Lucy Jenkins
Cover Design: Design Alliance, Inc.
Typesetting: the dotted i

Published by Dearborn Trade Publishing, A Kaplan Professional Company

Printed in the United States of America

02 03 04 05 06   10 9 8 7 6 5 4 3 2 1

Library of Congress Cataloging-in-Publication Data

Goodman, Jordan Elliot.
   Everyone's money book on financial planning / Jordan E. Goodman.
       p.   cm.
   Includes index.
   ISBN 0-7931-5377-8 (pbk.)
   1. Finance, Personal. 2. Investments. I. Title.
   HG179 .G6752 2002
   332.024—dc21

                         2002009279

Contents

List of Figures vii
Preface ix

1. **Giving Yourself a Financial Checkup 1**

   Determining Your Net Worth 1
   How to Set Up a Recordkeeping System 10
   Defining Your Financial Goals 11
   Analyzing Your Cash Flow 15
   Creating a Budget That Works 30
   Points to Remember 32
   Resources 35

2. **Assembling a Long-Term Financial and Investing Plan 37**

   Setting Up an Investment Strategy 39
   Tracking Your Investments 45
   Assessing Your Risk Tolerance 47
   The Investment Risk Pyramid 50
   Points to Remember 52
   Resources 55

3. **Financing Your Needs Part One: Housing, Cars, and Credit 57**

   Housing 57
   Car/Vehicle Purchases 65
   Credit Management/Debt Planning 70

Points to Remember 77
Resources: Credit 78
Resources: Real Estate 78
Resources: Vehicles 80

4. **Financing Your Needs Part Two: Insurance, Employee Benefits, and College Financing 82**

Your Insurance Needs 82
Maximizing Your Employee Benefits 93
Financing College and Continuing Education 100
Points to Remember 106
Resources: Insurance 107
Resources: Employee Benefits 109
Resources: College Financing 110

5. **Retirement and Estate Planning 111**

The Basics of Retirement Planning 112
The IRA Option 120
The Basics of Estate Planning 120
Writing and Executing a Will 121
Funeral and Burial Arrangements 125
Points to Remember 126
Resources 126

6. **Basic Tax Planning 129**

Highlights of Recent Tax Changes 130
Filing a Tax Return 132
Tax Rates 134
Legal Deductions 137
Tax Credits 139
Capital Gains and Losses 140
Alternative Minimum Tax 140
Strategies to Cut Your Taxes 141
If You're Audited 142
Points to Remember 142
Resources 142

7. **Getting Financial Advice 144**

Who Can You Trust? 144
Finding an Accountant and Tax Preparer 146

The Right Banker 147
Getting Reliable Legal Advice 148
Financial Planners 152
Choosing an Insurance Agent 156
Settling on a Real Estate Advisor 157
Finding Money Managers and Brokers 159
Choosing a Stockbroker 162
Points to Remember 165
Resources 165

8. Smart Money Strategies for Every Age and Situation 168

Your 20s and 30s—Establishing Your Financial Foundation 168
Your 40s and 50s—The Peak Earning Years of Middle Age 172
Your 60s and Up—The Retirement Years 174
When You're Single 178
When You're Married 179
When You're Divorced or Widowed 182
Conclusion 187
Resources 187

Index 189

List of Figures

Figure	Title / Page
Figure 1.1	NYSE Web Site 3
Figure 1.2	Assets Worksheet 5
Figure 1.3	Liabilities Worksheet 8
Figure 1.4	Short-Term Goals Worksheet 13
Figure 1.5	Medium-Term Goals Worksheet 14
Figure 1.6	Long-Term Goals Worksheet 15
Figure 1.7	Goal-Tracking Worksheet 16
Figure 1.8	Determining the Monthly Savings Needed to Reach a Goal 17
Figure 1.9	Cash-Flow Analysis Worksheet 18
Figure 1.10	Annual Budgeting Worksheet 33
Figure 1.11	Monthly Budgeting Worksheet 34
Figure 2.1	CNNMoney Web Site 38
Figure 2.2	1925–2001: Chart of Stocks, Bonds, Bills, and Inflation 43
Figure 2.3	Investment Risk Pyramid 51
Figure 2.4	Risk Tolerance Quiz 53
Figure 3.1	Interest Rates 60
Figure 3.2	ASHI Web Site 62
Figure 3.3	Leasing Costs Worksheet 66
Figure 3.4	Car Loan Worksheet 67
Figure 3.5	Time Is Money: Time and Interest to Pay Off $1,000 Card Balance 71
Figure 3.6	Equifax Sample Credit File 74
Figure 4.1	Auto Insurance Pricing Worksheet 85

Figure 4.2   Auto Insurance Discount Worksheet 86
Figure 4.3   Disability Income Worksheet 88
Figure 4.4   Amount Saved by Funding an FSA 94
Figure 4.5   Tax Savings from a Salary Reduction Plan 95
Figure 4.6   College Board Web Site 101
Figure 4.7   College Costs and Savings Needs Worksheet 102
Figure 4.8   Money Accumulated by Investing $100 Per Month 103
Figure 5.1   Retirement Expenses Worksheet 113
Figure 5.2   Capital Accumulation Worksheet 115
Figure 5.3   Annual Savings Worksheet 116
Figure 5.4   mPower Café Web Site 117
Figure 6.1   Complete Tax Web Site 135
Figure 6.2   2002 Tax Rates and Brackets 136
Figure 7.1   Lawyers.com Web Site 150
Figure 7.2   Financial Planner Disclosure Form 153
Figure 8.1   Kiplinger.com Web Site 169

Preface

Congratulations. By opening this book, you are taking your first step toward financial fitness. It all starts with your recognition of the importance of planning for your financial future, no matter what your age or financial situation. Even if you just won the lottery or inherited a cool million, your future financial comfort would depend on putting together a long-term money management strategy.

Consider the numbers: If it takes $4,000 a month—$48,000 a year—to live comfortably today, with inflation of just 3 percent a year, in just 15 years you would need more than $6,600 a month, or almost $80,000 annually, to maintain your lifestyle. But don't be intimidated. You do not have to live paycheck to paycheck, and you do not have to be rich to achieve financial independence or to look forward to a comfortable retirement. You *do* have to take charge of your finances and understand how to make your money work for you. This book is your starting point to help you plan and chart your right financial course, so that your money doesn't manage you. The sooner you get started, the quicker you and your family will reap the financial rewards of your efforts.

Many people ignore financial planning because they think they don't have enough money to make it worthwhile, or they figure they don't need it or can't afford it. Chances are you have more than you think—both in assets and financial knowledge. And if you still aren't sure you are capable of understanding enough about money to take charge, there is plenty of free or low-cost information or help available in print, online, or in person—all of which you will find out about in this book.

I know that many people and organizations in the money business have a vested interest in keeping financial knowledge as mysterious as possible. I disagree wholeheartedly with this approach. By spending a little time learning about money, you can understand all the major aspects of financial planning and acquire enough confidence to make solid financial decisions. After all, even if you have a half-dozen financial advisors at your beck and call, the final decisions on what to do with your money are ultimately yours to make.

This book is loaded with easy-to-use worksheets and a plethora of resources, including books, magazines, newsletters, trade associations, government agencies, and Web sites. With a connection to the Internet and a few mouse clicks, you can get the latest financial news; search for price quotes; buy stocks, bonds, mutual funds, and insurance policies; find the cheapest credit cards; locate grants and scholarships for your child's college education; or learn about any area of personal finance. Many Web sites offer search tools and calculators to make it easy to personalize the information to your situation. If you would like a copy of Everyone's Money Software, which offers all of the worksheets in this book in an interactive format, log on to <www.moneyanswers.com> or call 888-201-6300.

If you don't like exploring the Web on your own, there also are sites that search for you to find what you need. Many of these sites are listed in the "Resources" section of each chapter. A note of caution when it comes to the online world: As in the real world, consumers need to beware of fraud, whether it is get-rich-quick schemes, identity theft, or some other scam. With the pervasive aspect of the Internet, privacy issues surface, too. So when you use the Web to gather or share information or make a transaction, be sure you are dealing with reputable organizations. They will usually display a seal from a trustworthy organization, such as BBBOnline <www.bbbonline.com> (the Better Business Bureau's online arm), TRUSTe <www.trustee.org>, or VeriSign <www.verisign.com>. Do not provide personal information unless you know a Web site is secure. Generally, you can tell a site is secure if there is a small icon of a locked padlock or key (depending on your browser) on your screen. If the site is not secure, the padlock will be unlocked, indicating the data is not encrypted when it travels across cyberspace.

If you are not computer savvy, there are still many resources to help you improve your financial situation. There are dozens of financial periodicals, books, pamphlets, and toll-free consumer help lines and organizations in this book to help you on your way to financial fitness.

With all this in mind, get ready to take control of your financial destiny. It starts now. No one will ever care about your personal financial situation as much as you do. This is your chance to make the best of your financial potential.

Everyone's Money Book on Financial Planning would not have been possible without the extremely hard work of finance writer Susan J. Marks, who expertly pulled together the threads of this book into a wonderful and comprehensive resource on financial planning. I also want to thank Mark A. Luscombe, principal analyst for the federal and state tax group of Riverwoods, Illinois–based CCH Incorporated, for his invaluable help on taxes.

CHAPTER 1

Giving Yourself a Financial Checkup

To figure out a financial plan of action tailored to meet your financial needs and goals, you must first take stock of where you are now. That means you must assess your net worth, a task that sounds more ominous than it really is. Calculating your net worth is like weighing in before the championship fight. To find out what you weigh financially, you add up the total value of what you own—your assets—and subtract the amount of debt you owe—your liabilities. This bottom line is your *net worth*. Don't be discouraged if your net worth is negative. Recognizing that you owe more than you own is the first step toward charting a path to financial health.

Your net worth is a snapshot in time, good only for the moment you calculate it. Even if you are just starting out, consider this the first photo in a lifelong album of financial achievements, a benchmark to compare yourself against as your net worth grows over the years.

Determining Your Net Worth

By doing this exercise, you will be able to see clearly how your assets and liabilities match or don't match. Then, as you find ways to control your spending, pay off your debts, and increase your savings and investment assets, you can watch your net worth grow and, in turn, reach your financial goals. If you are making all the wrong moves—like increasing your debt and depleting your savings—your net worth statement will clearly show the deterioration. I would advise you to assess your net worth at least once a year, perhaps around New Year's Day or soon after April 15 after you've filed your taxes and all your financial papers are at hand.

Calculating your net worth also is important, because it lets you easily see whether you are accumulating enough assets to support yourself comfortably in retirement and how much you will have to pass on to your heirs. A current net worth statement also will come in handy when you apply for loans, because lenders require you to show your assets and liabilities on the application.

Assets

There are five classes of assets, each distinguished by its liquidity—how quickly it can be turned into cash. The more liquid an asset, the easier it is to value. For instance, you know exactly what the $102.55 in your checking account is worth, but you would probably have to ask a local real estate agent or appraiser to give you the current worth of your house or dwelling. Here is a look at the classes of assets.

Current assets. These are easily convertible into cash and include bank accounts, money-market mutual funds, and Treasury securities. For each bank account, list the name of the bank where the asset is held and the current *yield*. Also list the yield on Treasury bills, which mature in a year or less, and U.S. savings bonds, which you can cash in any time without penalty as long as you have held them for at least six months. If you have overpaid your taxes and are due a refund from the Internal Revenue Service (IRS) or your state tax department, you should also count that as a current asset. If you are owed a bonus or commission within the next few months, that counts as current, too.

Securities. These include publicly traded stocks, bonds, mutual funds, futures contracts, warrants, and options. To find the security's current market value, check online at financial or brokerage Web sites, stock market sites like NYSE.com (New York Stock Exchange), or information sources like Hoover's Online <www.hoovers.com>. You can also find its current value in most major newspapers, particularly *The Wall Street Journal* (<www.wsj .com>), and from your broker. For each security, list your purchase price, the number of units held (like shares of stock), the percentage yield it pays (a dividend for a stock or interest for a bond), and when it matures (for a bond, a futures contract, or an option).

Real estate. Real estate includes first and second homes, condominiums, cooperatives, rental properties, and real estate limited partnerships. The current worth of all real estate should be based on appraisals from knowledge-able local experts like appraisers or real estate agents. Remember to subtract all selling costs such as real estate agency commissions. For partnerships, list the general managing partner who is running the operation, the yield being

Figure 1.1   Web sites like this one from the New York Stock Exchange <www.nyse.com> can keep you up-to-date on financial markets.

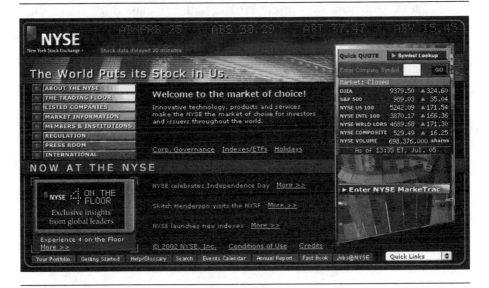

Source: Reprinted with permission from the New York Stock Exchange.

paid to you, if any, and the year you expect the partnership to be liquidated and proceeds paid out to you. Also include any mortgage loans that may be due you, such as on a house you sold on which you granted a loan.

Long-term assets. These include the cash value of life insurance policies; the worth of annuities, pensions, and profit-sharing plans; IRAs and Keogh plans; any long-term loans due you; any long-term royalties due you from writing a book or having patented an invention that is still selling; and any interests you have in an ongoing business. Your life insurance company can provide the current value of policies and annuities. Your employer can tell you what your pension and profit-sharing plans would be worth if you left the company now. To value your interest in a closely held business, ask your partners what they would be willing to pay if you wanted to cash in your share, or ask a specialized business broker.

Personal property. Personal property such as cars, jewelry, collectibles, and home furnishings should be valued at whatever you think they could sell for now in their present condition. Try to be realistic. For instance, check used-car ads in your newspaper or online at various sites to see what your car's model and year is now worth. (See Chapter 3 on car/vehicle purchases.) Bring any rare coins or stamps into a reputable dealer for an appraisal. For antiques or other collectibles, contact a local member of the American Society of Appraisers (555 Herndon Parkway, Suite 125, Herndon, VA 20170; 703-478-2228; <www.appraisers.org>).

In the Assets Worksheet in Figure 1.2, make a detailed list of not only which assets you have, but also who holds the titles to them. Some assets, like a securities portfolio for a child, may be held in a trust for which the parents are responsible until the child turns 18. If you need more space for any category as you fill out these worksheets, copy that page and attach it to your worksheet.

Liabilities

Liabilities should be divided into short-term and long-term categories, just as assets are. That's because some debts need to be paid very soon, like current bills or credit cards, while others, like mortgages or college loans, take years to repay. In the Liabilities Worksheet in Figure 1.3, list to whom you owe money, the interest rate you are paying, when the loan comes due if there is a maturity date, and how much money you owe.

You should use the following four main categories for listing your liabilities.

Current liabilities. These are debts you must pay within the next six months. That includes utility bills (telephone, electric, and gas), medical providers, home repair contractors, retail stores, and other short-term creditors. You also should include regular alimony or child-support payments, if these apply to you. If you owe money to a relative or friend, include that debt as well in this category.

Unpaid taxes. These taxes may be due either April 15 or as part of your quarterly estimated tax payments to both the IRS and your state tax department. They include income taxes and any capital gains taxes you owe on an asset you have sold for a profit. You also should include local property taxes. If you owe any sales taxes on purchases you have made recently, list that as well. Finally, if you are self-employed, you must also account for Social Security self-employment taxes.

Real estate debt. This category of debt includes both first and second mortgages on your primary residence, on any other residences you have, and on any rental properties that are producing income. On a separate line, list any home equity loans outstanding on your first or second home.

Installment debt. Installment debt covers all loans you have committed to pay off over a period of time. If you have lost a lawsuit and there is a liability judgment against you, that should be considered part of the installment debt you owe.

Figure 1.2   Assets Worksheet

Assets	Date Purchased	Original $ Value	Current Date	Current $ Value
1. Current Assets				
Bonuses or Commissions (due you)	_____	$ _____	_____	$ _____
Certificates of Deposit	_____	_____	_____	_____
	_____	_____	_____	_____
Checking Accounts	_____	_____	_____	_____
	_____	_____	_____	_____
Credit Union Accounts	_____	_____	_____	_____
Money-Market Accounts	_____	_____	_____	_____
	_____	_____	_____	_____
Savings Accounts	_____	_____	_____	_____
	_____	_____	_____	_____
Savings Bonds	_____	_____	_____	_____
	_____	_____	_____	_____
Tax Refunds (due you)	_____	_____	_____	_____
Treasury Bills	_____	_____	_____	_____
	_____	_____	_____	_____
TOTAL CURRENT ASSETS		$ _____		$ _____
2. Securities				
Bonds (type of bond)				
_____	_____	$ _____	_____	$ _____
_____	_____	_____	_____	_____
_____	_____	_____	_____	_____
_____	_____	_____	_____	_____
Bond Mutual Funds				
_____	_____	_____	_____	_____
_____	_____	_____	_____	_____
Individual Stocks				
_____	_____	_____	_____	_____
_____	_____	_____	_____	_____
_____	_____	_____	_____	_____
_____	_____	_____	_____	_____
_____	_____	_____	_____	_____

Figure 1.2   Assets Worksheet (continued)

Assets	Date Purchased	Original $ Value	Current Date	Current $ Value
Stock Mutual Funds				
_____	_____	$ _____	_____	$ _____
_____	_____	_____	_____	_____
_____	_____	_____	_____	_____
_____	_____	_____	_____	_____
Futures	_____	_____	_____	_____
Warrants and Options	_____	_____	_____	_____
TOTAL SECURITIES		$ _____		$ _____

3. Real Estate

Assets	Date Purchased	Original $ Value	Current Date	Current $ Value
Mortgage Receivable (due you)	_____	$ _____	_____	$ _____
Primary Residence	_____	_____	_____	_____
Rental Property	_____	_____	_____	_____
Real Estate Limited Partnerships	_____	_____	_____	_____
Second Home	_____	_____	_____	_____
TOTAL REAL ESTATE		$ _____		$ _____

4. Long-Term Assets

Assets	Date Purchased	Original $ Value	Current Date	Current $ Value
Annuities	_____	$ _____	_____	$ _____
IRAs	_____	_____	_____	_____
Keogh Accounts	_____	_____	_____	_____
Life Insurance Cash Values	_____	_____	_____	_____
Loans Receivable (due you)	_____	_____	_____	_____
Pensions	_____	_____	_____	_____
Private Business Interests	_____	_____	_____	_____
Profit-Sharing Plans	_____	_____	_____	_____
Royalties	_____	_____	_____	_____
Salary Reduction Plans (401(k), 403(b), 457 plans)	_____	_____	_____	_____
TOTAL LONG-TERM ASSETS		$ _____		$ _____

Figure 1.2   (continued)

Assets	Date Purchased	Original $ Value	Current Date	Current $ Value
5. Personal Property				
Antiques	_____	$_____	_____	$_____
Appliances (washing machines, dishwashers, vacuum cleaners, etc.)	_____	_____	_____	_____
Automobiles	_____	_____	_____	_____
Boats, etc.	_____	_____	_____	_____
Campers, Trailers, etc.	_____	_____	_____	_____
Clothing	_____	_____	_____	_____
Coin Collections	_____	_____	_____	_____
Computers, etc.	_____	_____	_____	_____
Furniture	_____	_____	_____	_____
Furs	_____	_____	_____	_____
Home Entertainment Equipment (CD players, stereos, televisions, VCRs, etc.)	_____	_____	_____	_____
Home Furnishings (drapes, blankets, etc.)	_____	_____	_____	_____
Jewelry	_____	_____	_____	_____
Lighting Fixtures	_____	_____	_____	_____
Motorcycles, etc.	_____	_____	_____	_____
Paintings and Sculptures	_____	_____	_____	_____
Pools, etc.	_____	_____	_____	_____
Stamp Collections	_____	_____	_____	_____
Tableware (glasses, plates, silverware, etc.)	_____	_____	_____	_____
Tools, etc.	_____	_____	_____	_____
Other	_____	_____	_____	_____
TOTAL PERSONAL PROPERTY		$_____		$_____
TOTAL ASSETS		$_____		$_____

Figure 1.3   Liabilities Worksheet

Liabilities	To Whom	Interest Rate %	Due Date	Amount Due $
1. Current Liabilities				
Alimony	_____	_____ %	_____	$ _____
Bills				
Electric & Gas	_____	_____	_____	_____
Home Contractor	_____	_____	_____	_____
Home Contractor	_____	_____	_____	_____
Oil Company	_____	_____	_____	_____
Physician & Dentist	_____	_____	_____	_____
Retail Stores	_____	_____	_____	_____
Telephone	_____	_____	_____	_____
Other	_____	_____	_____	_____
Child Support	_____	_____	_____	_____
Loans to Individuals	_____	_____	_____	_____
TOTAL CURRENT LIABILITIES				$ _____
2. Unpaid Taxes				
Income Taxes				
Federal	_____	_____ %	_____	$ _____
State	_____	_____	_____	_____
Capital Gains Taxes				
Federal	_____	_____	_____	_____
State	_____	_____	_____	_____
Property Taxes	_____	_____	_____	_____
Sales Taxes				
Locality	_____	_____	_____	_____
Social Security Taxes (self-employed)	_____	_____	_____	_____
TOTAL UNPAID TAXES				$ _____
3. Real Estate Liabilities				
Home # 1				
First Mortgage	_____	_____ %	_____	$ _____
Second Mortgage	_____	_____	_____	_____
Home Equity Loan	_____	_____	_____	_____

Figure 1.3   (continued)

Liabilities	To Whom	Interest Rate %	Due Date	Amount Due $
Home # 2				
First Mortgage	_____	_____ %	_____	$ _____
Second Mortgage	_____	_____	_____	_____
Home Equity Loan	_____	_____	_____	_____
Rental Property				
First Mortgage	_____	_____	_____	_____
Second Mortgage	_____	_____	_____	_____
TOTAL REAL ESTATE LIABILITIES				$ _____

4. Installment Liabilities

Liabilities	To Whom	Interest Rate %	Due Date	Amount Due $
Automobile Loans	_____	_____ %	_____	$ _____
Bank Loans for Bill Consolidation	_____	_____	_____	_____
Credit Cards	_____	_____	_____	_____
Education Loans	_____	_____	_____	_____
Equipment and Appliance Loans	_____	_____	_____	_____
Furniture Loans	_____	_____	_____	_____
Home Improvement Loans	_____	_____	_____	_____
Liability Judgments	_____	_____	_____	_____
Life Insurance Loans	_____	_____	_____	_____
Margin Loans Against Securities	_____	_____	_____	_____
Overdraft Bank Loans	_____	_____	_____	_____
Pension Plan Loans	_____	_____	_____	_____
TOTAL INSTALLMENT LIABILITIES				$ _____
TOTAL LIABILITIES				$ _____

Finally, if you have borrowed against your 401(k) retirement plan at work, you normally are obligated to pay it back by payroll deduction over five or ten years. This obligation should also be counted as installment debt. Credit card charges on which you owe at least the minimum payment should also be noted in this category, because you control when you will pay off the outstanding balance.

Now, for the moment of truth: Take your total assets from the Assets Worksheet and subtract your total liabilities from the Liabilities Worksheet. This determines your net worth.

Total Assets $ _____

(Minus) Total Liabilities   (_____)

Equals Positive (or Negative) Net Worth $ _____

First, is your net worth positive or negative? If it's positive, you have been doing a good job at building assets and lowering liabilities. Now that you know where you stand, you are in a good position to see your net worth grow even more in coming years.

If your net worth is negative, do not despair. Knowing that you owe more than you own is the first step towards improving your situation. Clearly, you have accumulated too much debt for the amount of assets you have assembled so far. But remember, this is only a snapshot of your current situation. Hopefully, the next time you calculate your net worth, it will be a more "positive" experience.

After you calculate your net worth each year, you should compare it to your calculations for the past five years to see how you have been progressing. Use this simple form to keep records:

Year	Net Worth	Percentage Increase/Decrease
This year	_____	_____
Last year	_____	_____
Two years ago	_____	_____
Three years ago	_____	_____
Four years ago	_____	_____
Five years ago	_____	_____

HOW TO SET UP A RECORDKEEPING SYSTEM

Filling out the worksheets in this book, online or as part of financial planning software, will be much easier if you don't have to dig through boxes of financial statements and old tax returns.

The best way to get started is to set up a filing system separate from the rest of your household files. Also, set up a separate file for each of the categories and be sure to note the location of all your important documents and other details like account numbers, names of brokers, insurance agents, and other people who know about your accounts. Many a widow or heir tells the story of total financial chaos when a husband or parent dies suddenly, and the records are scattered throughout the house and in various bank safe-deposit boxes. Even worse, if both you and your spouse die together, it will be extremely difficult for your children or other beneficiaries to reassemble your financial records.

Create a worksheet that consolidates all your important data in one place. You should organize your file system using the exact same categories, which are arranged alphabetically.

DEFINING YOUR FINANCIAL GOALS

Now that you know where you stand financially, you must figure out where you want to go. Setting specific financial objectives and putting them in writing—listing dollar amounts and noting exactly when you will need the money—will motivate you to achieve your goals. Because setting goals is really another way of defining priorities, the process helps you make sure that your limited resources and income are used most effectively to attain your highest priorities.

Don't think that goal setting is too hard; you have been doing it for most of your life. When you last started a diet, you set a specific goal for how many pounds you would trim. As you went through school, you set a goal of a certain grade-point average or maybe a goal of doing well enough to enter college or a particular graduate school. All you are doing now is applying the same discipline to your personal finances.

Everyone's Goals Differ

Individual financial goals differ because people are brought up with different values. For some, providing the finest education for their children is the top priority. For others, buying the best big-screen TV or hottest new car is a more important goal. No matter the goal, it is important that the decision to spend the money be a conscious one.

Setting a goal is not just about allocating the money to achieve it. It is also about allocating the time needed to attain what you want, which can determine the amount of money you earn. If you share finances with a spouse or partner, goal setting must be done mutually. To avoid friction, it's important for you to reach agreement with your spouse or significant other on which goals get the highest priority.

The goal-setting exercises in Figures 1.4 through 1.8, like the Net Worth exercise in the previous section, do not represent once-in-a-lifetime events. As you accomplish certain goals during your life, you must constantly be setting new ones.

Three Kinds of Goals

There are three different kinds of goals: short term, medium term, and long term. Within each of these three categories are not only goals but also priorities for those goals. Because you probably will not have enough money to achieve all your goals over the next year, you have to allocate some resources on an ongoing basis to each of the three categories so you have some chance of accomplishing the goals over time. The longer you delay starting to accumulate the money for longer-term goals like buying a home or funding retirement, the more difficult the realization of those goals becomes.

This section provides a worksheet for each of the three kinds of goals. After you locate one of your goals on the worksheet, note the amount of money you will need to pay for it, what priority it has compared with other goals, and when you would like to achieve it.

Short-term goals. Short-term goals are those you would like to achieve within the next year (see Figure 1.4). These might include paying off your credit cards; buying certain large items like a television, a car, or furniture; or taking a long-needed vacation.

Medium-term goals. Medium-term goals are items for which it takes between two and ten years to accumulate the money (see Figure 1.5). These may include building a down payment for a first or second home, creating a college fund for children older than eight years, or saving up to take a dream trip.

Long-term goals. Long-term goals take more than ten years to fulfill (see Figure 1.6). The most common long-term goal is a financially secure retirement, which takes a lifetime of financial discipline. Other long-term goals include paying for extensive travel, starting your own business, going back to school to receive a higher degree of education, and buying a vacation home. Another long-term goal is to make sure you can afford medical attention in your later years.

Tracking goals. Once you have determined and prioritized your goals, use the worksheet in Figure 1.7 to track your progress. That way, you will know exactly where you stand and what it will take to achieve what you set out to accomplish financially.

To figure out how much cash you will need to save or invest to reach the goal you analyzed in the Goal-Tracking Worksheet, use the table in Figure 1.8. The left column shows the number of years you have until you need the money for your goal. The next four columns show the divisors for four dif-

Figure 1.4   Short-Term Goals Worksheet

Goal	Priority	Date to Accomplish	$ Amount Needed
Build Up Emergency Reserve (worth three months' salary)	_____	_____	$_____
Buy Adequate Insurance			
Auto	_____	_____	_____
Health	_____	_____	_____
Home	_____	_____	_____
Life	_____	_____	_____
Contribute to Charity Name _____	_____	_____	_____
Fund IRA or Keogh Account	_____	_____	_____
Increase Contribution to Company Benefit Plan	_____	_____	_____
Join a Health/Sports Club	_____	_____	_____
Make Major Home Improvements	_____	_____	_____
Make Major Purchases	_____	_____	_____
Pay Off Bills	_____	_____	_____
Pay Off Credit Cards	_____	_____	_____
Save for Christmas Gifts, Birthdays, etc.	_____	_____	_____
Take Vacation	_____	_____	_____
Other (specify)			
_____	_____	_____	_____
TOTAL $ AMOUNT NEEDED			$_____

ferent rates of return that you can safely assume it is possible to earn, on average, over a long period of time. These rates of return assume you have adjusted for the effects of inflation and taxes and are known as real after-tax yields. The higher the rate of return, the more risk you have to take in your investment choices to achieve your goal.

To use the table, take the amount of money you will need to pay for your goal and pick an assumed rate of return. Then find the divisor for the number of years you have allocated to reach the goal. Simply divide your dollar goal

Figure 1.5   Medium-Term Goals Worksheet

Goal	Priority	Date to Accomplish	$ Amount Needed
Create College Fund for Children			
Child 1 _____	_____	_____	$ _____
Child 2 _____	_____	_____	_____
Save Down Payment for First Home	_____	_____	_____
Save Down Payment for Second Home	_____	_____	_____
Finance Special Occasions (weddings, bar mitzvahs, etc.)	_____	_____	_____
Help Child Finance Home	_____	_____	_____
Pay Off Education Debt	_____	_____	_____
Save for Next Child	_____	_____	_____
Take Overseas Trip	_____	_____	_____
Take Time Off to Pursue an Interest	_____	_____	_____
Other (specify)			
_____	_____	_____	_____
TOTAL $ NEEDED			$ _____

by the divisor, and you have figured out the monthly amount of savings needed to reach that goal. The divisor automatically calculates the effect of compounding of interest, which can become quite a powerful force over time.

For example, say you want to accumulate a $100,000 nest egg for your retirement in 20 years. If you assume a real after-tax yield of 8 percent, when you look down the 8 percent column to the 20-year line, the divisor is 592. Divide $100,000 by 592 to get the $168.92 a month you will have to save to meet your goal.

Here's an example for a shorter-term goal. Say you need $2,000 in two years to buy furniture for your living room. Assuming a 6 percent rate of return, divide $2,000 by the divisor of 25.4 to come up with a monthly savings target of $78.74.

With your net worth statement in hand and short-term, medium-term, and long-term goals clearly defined, you should be feeling better already.

Figure 1.6   Long-Term Goals Worksheet

Goal	Priority	Date to Accomplish	$ Amount Needed
Buy Retirement Home			$
Buy Vacation Home			
Continue Education			
Do Community or Charity Work			
Establish Long-Term Health Care for Self and/or Spouse			
Establish Retirement Fund			
Help Older Parents			
Make a Charitable Bequest			
Pay Off Mortgage Early			
Start a Business			
Start a Second Career			
Travel Extensively			
Other (specify)			
TOTAL $ NEEDED			$

Now it's time to analyze your cash flow to see where your money is coming from and where it is going on a monthly and annual basis.

ANALYZING YOUR CASH FLOW

Now that you know how much you are worth and what your financial goals are, it's time to do a detailed cash flow analysis that will allow you to trace your sources and uses of money.

Even though it is a simple exercise, most people never get around to it, and they anxiously wait for their next paycheck so they can pay their bills. By doing a cash flow analysis, you will know exactly how much income you can expect to receive as well as nearly all the expenses you plan to cover with that income. (Don't plan on any sudden windfalls like winning the lottery, but you should anticipate a few surprise expenses.)

Figure 1.7   Goal-Tracking Worksheet

Goal (identify) _____

Date in the Future You Will
  Need the Money _____

How Many Years until You
  Need the Money _____

Amount of Money Needed
  to Accomplish This Goal _____

Money Already Accumulated
  for This Goal _____

Rate of Return (%) Assumed
  for Accumulated Money _____

Money Remaining to Be
  Accumulated for This Goal _____

Money Needed to Be Saved Each
  Year at Assumed Rate of Return _____

Monthly Amount to Be Saved
  (previous line divided by 12) _____

The Cash Flow Analysis Worksheet presented in Figure 1.9 should be filled out on an annual basis. Some income, such as bonuses or capital gains distributions made by mutual funds, is received only at certain times of the year (in December, for example). Similarly, many expenses such as tuition payments, fuel oil bills, or quarterly tax bills occur only during certain months of the year. By totaling all your annual income and expenses, you will get a sense of how your overall cash flow looks for the year.

It is also important to do a more short-term cash flow analysis, because sometimes your expenses are due before the income arrives, causing a cash squeeze. The same Cash Flow Analysis Worksheet can be filled out on both a monthly and a quarterly basis.

With your bank, brokerage, insurance, and other statements; last year's tax return; your last year-end paycheck; and other records you have accumulated for the past six months, fill in the real numbers on the worksheet. This is not an exercise in wishful thinking; this is a document that will show you, for better or worse, how you actually are earning and spending your money now. It's no use inflating the income and lowballing the expenses, because you're the only one who will be hurt by not knowing the truth.

Figure 1.8   Determining the Monthly Savings Needed to Reach a Goal

	Divisors (By Rate of Return)			
Years to Goal	2%	4%	6%	8%
1	12.1	12.2	12.3	12.4
2	24.5	24.9	25.4	25.9
3	37.1	38.2	39.3	40.6
4	49.9	51.9	54.1	56.4
5	63.1	66.2	69.8	73.6
6	76.5	81.1	86.4	92.1
7	90.2	96.6	104.1	112.3
8	104.2	112.7	122.8	134.1
9	118.4	129.5	142.7	157.7
10	133.0	146.9	163.9	183.4
11	147.8	165.1	186.3	211.1
12	163.0	184.0	210.1	241.2
13	178.5	203.6	235.4	273.7
14	194.2	224.0	262.3	309.0
15	210.4	245.3	290.8	347.3
16	226.8	267.4	321.1	388.7
17	243.6	290.4	353.2	433.6
18	260.7	314.3	387.3	482.2
19	278.2	339.2	423.6	534.9
20	296.1	365.1	462.0	592.0
21	314.2	392.1	502.9	653.8
22	332.8	420.1	546.2	720.8
23	351.8	449.3	592.2	793.4
24	371.2	479.6	641.1	872.0
25	390.9	511.2	693.0	957.2

Sources of Income

The income side of the Cash Flow Analysis Worksheet is broken into six categories: earned, self-employment, family, government, retirement, and investment income. The following is a brief guide to the kinds of income that fall into each category. (For each of the six categories, we have provided a line on the worksheet to subtotal the income, which will make it easier to add up your total income at the end of the worksheet.)

Figure 1.9   Cash Flow Worksheet

Annual Income	$ Amount	$ Total

1. Earned Income
Salary after Deductions $ _____
Bonuses   _____
Commissions   _____
Deferred Compensation   _____
Overtime   _____
Stock Options   _____
Tips   _____
Other   _____

TOTAL EARNED INCOME $ _____

2. Self-Employment Income
Freelance Income $ _____
Income from Partnerships   _____
Income from Running a Small
   Business   _____
Rental Income from Real Estate _____
Royalties   _____
Other   _____

TOTAL SELF-EMPLOYMENT INCOME $ _____

3. Family Income
Alimony Income $ _____
Child Support Income   _____
Family Trust Income   _____
Gifts from Family Members   _____
Inheritance Income   _____
Other   _____

TOTAL FAMILY INCOME $ _____

4. Government Income
Aid to Families with Dependent
   Children Income $ _____
Disability Insurance Income _____
Unemployment Insurance Income _____
Veterans Benefits   _____
Welfare Income   _____
Workers' Compensation Income _____
Other   _____

TOTAL GOVERNMENT INCOME $ _____

Figure 1.9   (continued)

	$ Amount	$ Total
5. Retirement Income		
Annuity Payments	$ _____	
Social Security Income	_____	
Pension Income	_____	
Income from IRAs	_____	
Income from Keogh Accounts	_____	
Income from Profit-Sharing Accounts	_____	
Income from Salary Reduction Plans		
(401(k), 403(b), 457 plans)	_____	
Other	_____	
TOTAL RETIREMENT INCOME		$ _____
6. Investment Income		
Bank Account Interest		
CDs	$ _____	
Money Market Accounts	_____	
NOW Accounts	_____	
Savings Accounts	_____	
Bonds and Bond Funds		
Capital Gains	_____	
Dividends	_____	
Interest	_____	
Other	_____	
Limited Partnerships (real estate,		
oil, gas)	_____	
Money Funds and T-Bills		
Taxable Funds	_____	
Tax-Exempt Funds	_____	
T-Bills	_____	
Stock and Stock Funds		
Capital Gains	_____	
Dividends	_____	
Interest	_____	
Other	_____	
Other	_____	
TOTAL INVESTMENT INCOME		$ _____
7. Other Income (specify)		
_____	$ _____	
TOTAL OTHER INCOME		$ _____
TOTAL ANNUAL INCOME		$ _____

Figure 1.9   Cash Flow Worksheet (continued)

Annual Expenses	$ Amount	$ Total
1. Fixed Expenses		
Automobile-Related		
Car Payment (loan or lease)	$ _____	
Gasoline or Oil	_____	
Other	_____	
Total		$ _____
Family		
Alimony	_____	
Child Support Payments	_____	
Food and Beverage	_____	
School Tuition	_____	
Other	_____	
Total		_____
Home-Related		
Cable Television Fees	_____	
Mortgage Payments Home #1	_____	
Mortgage Payments Home #2	_____	
Rent	_____	
Total		_____
Insurance		
Auto	_____	
Disability	_____	
Dental	_____	
Health	_____	
Homeowners	_____	
Life	_____	
Other	_____	
Total		_____
Savings and Investments		
Bank Loan Repayment	_____	
Emergency Fund Contributions	_____	
Salary Reduction Plans	_____	
Contributions (401(k), 403(b),		
457 plans)	_____	
Other	_____	
Total		_____
Taxes		
Federal	_____	
Local	_____	
Property	_____	
Social Security (self-employed)	_____	

Figure 1.9   (continued)

	$ Amount	$ Total
State	$	
Other		
Total		$
Utilities		
Electricity		
Gas		
Telephone		
Water and Sewage		
Other		
Total		
Other (specify)		
_____		
Total		

TOTAL FIXED EXPENSES $ _____

2. Flexible Expenses

Children		
Allowances	$	
Babysitting		
Books		
Camp Fees		
Day Care		
Events (parties, class trips, etc.)		
Toys		
Other		
Total		$
Clothing		
New Purchases		
Shoes		
Upkeep (cleaning, tailoring, dry cleaning, etc.)		
Total		
Contributions and Dues		
Charitable Donations		
Gifts (Christmas, birthdays, etc.)		
Political Contributions		
Religious Contributions		
Union Dues		
Other		
Total		
Education		
Room and Board		

Figure 1.9   Cash Flow Worksheet (continued)

	$ Amount	$ Total
Books and Supplies (parents and/or children)	$ _____	
Tuition (parents and/or children)	_____	
Other	_____	
Total		$ _____
Equipment and Vehicles		
Appliance Purchases and Maintenance	_____	
Car, Boat, and Other Vehicle Purchases and Maintenance	_____	
Computer Purchases, etc.	_____	
Consumer Electronics Purchases	_____	
Licenses and Registration of Cars, Boats, etc.	_____	
Parking	_____	
Other	_____	
Total		_____
Financial and Professional Services		
Banking Fees	_____	
Brokerage Commissions and Fees	_____	
Financial Advice	_____	
Legal Advice	_____	
Tax Preparation Fees	_____	
Other	_____	
Total		_____
Food		
Alcohol	_____	
Foods and Snacks away from Home	_____	
Restaurant Meals	_____	
Tobacco	_____	
Other	_____	
Total		_____
Home Maintenance		
Garbage Removal	_____	
Garden Supplies and Maintenance	_____	
Home Office Supplies	_____	
Home Furnishings	_____	
Home or Apartment Repairs and Renovations	_____	
Home Cleaning Services	_____	
Home Supplies	_____	
Lawn Care and Snow Removal	_____	
Linens	_____	

Figure 1.9   (continued)

	$ Amount	$ Total
Uninsured Casualty or Theft Loss	$	
Other		
Total		$
Medical Care		
Dentist Bills		
Drugs (over the counter)		
Drugs (prescriptions)		
Eyecare and Eyeglasses		
Hospital (uninsured portion)		
Medical Devices (wheelchairs, canes, etc.)		
Medical Expenses (parents, etc.)		
Nursing Home Fees (parents, etc.)		
Personal Beauty Care (hair stylist, manicurist, etc.)		
Personal Care (cosmetics, toiletries, etc.)		
Physician Bills		
Unreimbursed Medical Expenses		
Other		
Total		
Miscellaneous		
Mystery Cash		
Postage and Stamps		
Recurring Nonrecurring Expenses		
Unreimbursed Business Expenses		
Other		
Total		
Recreation and Entertainment		
Animal Care		
Books		
Club Dues		
Cultural Events		
Health Club Memberships		
Hobbies		
Lottery Tickets		
Magazine and Newspaper Subscriptions		
Movie Admissions		
Music Admissions		
Photography (cameras, developing, film, etc.)		
Play Admissions		

Figure 1.9   Cash Flow Worksheet (continued)

	$ Amount	$ Total
Recreational Equipment (games, sports, etc.)	$	
Sporting Events Admission		
Videotape Rentals		
Other		
Total		$
Savings and Investments		
Bank Savings Contributions		
Stock, Bond, and Mutual Fund Contributions		
IRA Contributions		
Keogh Account Contributions		
Other		
Total		
Travel and Vacations		
Bus Fares		
Subway Costs		
Tolls		
Train Fares		
Travel Expenses (other than vacations)		
Unreimbursed Business Travel Expenses		
Vacations (airfare)		
Vacations (car rental)		
Vacations (food)		
Vacations (hotel)		
Vacations (other)		
Other		
Total		
Other (specify)		
_____		
Total		
TOTAL FLEXIBLE EXPENSES		$
TOTAL ANNUAL EXPENSES		$
TOTAL ANNUAL INCOME (MINUS)		$
TOTAL ANNUAL EXPENSES EQUALS		(_____)
TOTAL NET ANNUAL POSITIVE (OR NEGATIVE) CASH FLOW		$

Earned income. The most common and largest source of income for most people, of course, is their salary from a job. You should note on the worksheet your net take-home pay, after deductions.

Other sources of earned income include commissions paid to salespeople, bonuses for extraordinary performance, overtime, and tips. You may also be entitled to stock options, which give you the right to buy your company's stock at a preset price and to sell the shares for a profit. There are also many forms of deferred compensation based on your performance or in accordance with a contract. If you expect to exercise stock options or receive deferred compensation in the next year, you should note this on the worksheet.

Self-employment income. If you work for yourself or a closely held partnership, most of your income will come from this income category. Because taxes or other deductions are not normally withheld from freelance income, you will have to pay income and self-employment taxes on this money on a quarterly basis through estimated tax filings. Finally, if you are a writer, musician, painter, or inventor, you may be getting regular royalty income from sales of your books, music, paintings, or inventions.

Family income. If you are lucky enough to come from a family that has put money in a trust for you, this can be a significant source of regular income. You should list on the worksheet the income produced from the assets you inherited or the assets in a trust for you. If you receive regular (or even irregular) gifts from family members, the total amount should also be listed here. Finally, if you are divorced and receive alimony or child support, that income should be entered on the worksheet.

Government income. You might qualify to receive regular checks from the federal or state government like welfare, disability, or workers' compensation payments. If you had a job but were laid off, you are entitled to unemployment insurance for several months. Note these amounts on the worksheet.

Retirement income. There are several sources of income once you have retired, assuming you have built up retirement assets. You can receive a monthly payment from an annuity issued by an insurance company based on your lifelong contributions to the annuity. Alternatively, you can take your lump sum pension plan and buy an annuity from an insurance company to ensure a fixed monthly income for the rest of your life. Similarly, starting at age 59½, you can take money out of your IRA or Keogh account without penalty. (You must pay a 10 percent penalty if you withdraw from these accounts sooner, although there are specific exceptions.) If you worked at a company that offered a profit-sharing plan, a salary reduction plan, or a pension plan, you can have the earnings paid to you in monthly installments. Finally, as long as Social Security was keeping track of how many years you worked and what you were earning, you will get monthly Social Security checks as well.

Investment income. This category offers the most possibilities, because there are so many kinds of bank instruments, bonds, stocks, mutual funds, and limited partnerships designed to throw off income. Among bank products, you can earn regular interest income from certificates of deposit (CDs), money-market deposit accounts, NOW accounts on which you can write checks, and other savings accounts such as passbook accounts. Two additional kinds of short-term interest-bearing accounts are money-market mutual funds, which come in both taxable and tax-exempt varieties, and Treasury bills, which come in three-month and six-month maturities.

Among income-producing bonds, your options include corporate bonds, convertible bonds, Treasury notes maturing in up to ten years, Treasury bonds maturing in up to 30 years, municipal bonds, and foreign bonds. In addition, you may be counting on income produced from selling any of these kinds of bonds for a profit, listed on the worksheet as capital gains from bond sales. Similarly, you can produce regular income by investing in bond mutual funds that buy any of these taxable or tax-exempt bonds.

Stocks also give you several options for producing regular income. Many individual stocks pay quarterly dividends. Many mutual funds investing in stocks also are designed to pay a significant monthly dividend to income-oriented investors. Plus, most mutual funds make a yearly payout of all the capital gains they have accumulated during the year, known as a capital gains distribution. If you plan to sell some of your stocks or stock funds to realize a profit, that should be entered on the worksheet as income from capital gains.

Limited partnerships also provide a viable vehicle for producing regular income. Partnerships can invest in rental real estate, oil and gas wells, or the leasing of equipment such as airplanes or computers, all of which provide a monthly stream of income. If you have any interests in such partnerships, enter the annual income you expect from them on the worksheet.

Next, total the income you expect to receive in all six categories and add any other income sources as well to create your grand total annual income.

Expenses

Now you're going to figure out where all of that income disappears to every year. Your expenses can be divided roughly into two categories: what is fixed, meaning it must be paid on an annual or a monthly basis, and what is flexible, meaning you have more control over whether and when you spend it. By filling out the expense portion of the worksheet in these two categories, you will be able to see what percentage of your income fixed expenses take up. This will give you a clearer idea of how much money you have left over for discretionary spending.

There are seven categories that should be considered fixed expenses: automobile-related expenses, family expenses, home-related expenses, insurance, savings and investments, taxes, and utilities. Many are discussed in further detail in Chapters 3 and 4.

Automobile-related expenses. Most people either lease their car from the dealer or buy it with an auto loan. In either case, you will have to make a monthly payment until the lease is up or the loan is paid off. To keep the car running, of course, you will need gasoline in the tank and oil under the hood and regular maintenance.

Family expenses. Food and beverages are part of your regular fixed expenses. If you have children and they attend a school that charges tuition, this also goes in the fixed-expenses column. If you are divorced and still supporting your spouse and children, count alimony and child support as fixed expenses.

Home-related expenses. You have to live somewhere, and if you own or rent, certain expenses are impossible to avoid. And if you want cable television or high-speed Internet connections, make an allowance in your budget for these charges.

Insurance. The most common forms of insurance that you need to have—and pay for—are auto, disability, dental, excess liability (also known as an "umbrella" policy), health, homeowners, and life insurance.

Savings and investments. Finally, here is an expense category that lets you feel you are not spending money that you will never see again. It may seem hard to think of saving and investing as fixed expenses, but it's the only way to accumulate funds. The easiest way to invest is through some kind of automatic savings plan, such as your salary reduction plan (called a 401(k) in companies, a 403(b) in nonprofit institutions, and a 457 in government agencies). If you are self-employed, you can save regularly at your bank, credit union, or brokerage. And even though you may not think of repaying debt as savings, it's one of the best savings moves you can make. Not many investments out there can guarantee you the instant 18 percent tax-free return you earn for paying off credit card debt.

Taxes. If you do not have enough withheld from your paycheck or have a great deal of freelance income, you must make quarterly estimated payments to both the IRS and your state. Also, the freelancer should make regular Social Security self-employment tax payments as well. If you own your home, your city or county government expects you to pay property taxes, though often those taxes are actually paid by the bank that holds your mortgage and has set up your tax escrow account.

Utilities. If you want to keep the lights on, your electric utility gets its share of your budget. The same holds true for the gas company or oil dealer, if you want to stay warm. If you want to talk on the telephone, you must ante up each month to that utility. And don't forget water, sewage, or trash removal services either.

What's Left? Flexible Expenses

These seven categories include most of what you absolutely have to pay every year. The typical American spends about 70 percent of his or her income on fixed expenses. With some good planning, you will have about 30 percent of your income left for more discretionary purchases, known by financial professionals as flexible spending.

There are many more ways to spend money when you have some choice in the matter, so I've broken flexible expenses into 13 categories.

Children. The joys of parenthood don't come cheap. Even many older children often continue to need financial help until they get a job and become established. So depending on their age, you should count on spending on allowances, babysitting, day care, books, toys, and school supplies.

Clothing. Set aside money not only for new clothes and shoes but also for the upkeep of your clothes, such as for dry cleaning, tailoring, and pressing. All those trips to the dry cleaner may seem insignificant, but those bills can really add up over a year.

Contributions and dues. The amount you give to charities, religious institutions, and political candidates is up to you. You may be able to deduct some or all of your contributions, which will give you a bit of a tax break. For the most part, though, give because you believe in the cause, not to get the write-off. If you are a member of a union, dues are normally not so voluntary. Also, include in this category dues to other professional organizations.

Education. If you or your children plan on going to a school that charges tuition, it's never too early to start budgeting not only for tuition but also for room and board, books, software, and supplies. And don't forget to budget for those sports or music lessons.

Equipment and vehicles. Cars, boats, motorcycles, and motor homes all need maintenance, registrations, licenses, and a place to park. Computers, televisions, videotape recorders, CD players, DVD players, and other consumer electronics need videotapes, CDs, and DVDs, along with occasional repairs. The same holds true for all of life's other conveniences, whether buying a Cuisinart or a washing machine.

Financial and professional services. Some areas of finance are too complicated for the average person, which makes it worthwhile to pay an expert for advice. That can be particularly true with tax, legal, and investment matters (see Chapters 7 and 8 for more on finding the right advisors). Banks and financial institutions also charge various fees that you need to allow for.

Food. In addition to food you buy to serve at home, you should allow for food outside the home, including both restaurant meals and on-the-go snacks. Count any purchases of alcohol and tobacco in this food category.

Home maintenance. The bigger your house or apartment, the more expensive it is to maintain. You should expect a certain amount of repairs and outside maintenance every year, along with ongoing cleaning and household expenses.

Medical care. Health insurance these days comes with out-of-pocket expenses like partial premiums, deductibles, and copayments. In some cases, reimbursements also are limited. Budget for over-the-counter medicines, personal care items, and toiletries, as well as haircuts, manicures, and pedicures if they are part of your routine.

Miscellaneous. There are always going to be some expenses that just don't fit into any other category. Unreimbursed business expenses and postage are two that come to mind. Quite frequently these are the recurring nonrecurring expense hits. Generally, each of these happens only once, but a new one seems to occur every month or so. By assuming that such recurring nonrecurring expenses will pop up, you can budget for them.

And then there is always that big hole in your budget I like to call "mystery cash," because you have no idea what happened to it once you took it out of the ATM.

Recreation and entertainment. You may like pets, books, movies, music, photography, plays, sports, sporting events, or sewing, all of which can become expensive hobbies. Nothing is wrong with any of these, but they cost money.

Savings and investments. Although you should put aside a certain amount of money as part of your fixed expenses to keep your emergency fund solvent, you should also try to invest in bank instruments, stocks, bonds, and mutual funds that will provide you with the wherewithal to reach the financial goals you set. If you don't start investing for these goals, the money will never be there when you need it. While some of the investments should be in a regular taxable bank, brokerage, or mutual fund account, some of the money should be compounding tax deferred in an IRA or a Keogh account.

Travel and vacations. There are two kinds of travel—business or pleasure. You should set aside money for both. For business, you will spend money to commute to work, whether that means driving (paying tolls and parking your car) or taking a bus, subway, or train. In addition, there are often expenses you incur while on the road for your business that your company might not reimburse. Vacations are all on you, and you should be realistic about the cost, including acquiring souvenirs.

The Bottom Line

As you fill out the Cash Flow Analysis Worksheet, only certain sections may apply to you right now. Some day, you probably will use those sections you cannot use now. For the moment, feel free to skip those categories that do not apply.

After you have filled out both the income and expense sides of this worksheet, it will be time to get down to the bottom line. Subtract your expenses from your income, and you have your annual cash flow. If you are taking in more than you are spending, congratulations. You have a positive cash flow. Your next job is to figure out the best places for your extra cash—probably savings vehicles and investments, after you have set aside your emergency reserve.

On the other hand, if your expenses total more than your income—not an unlikely situation—you are in negative cash flow, and it's time to start scrutinizing your expenses. Just because you have negative cash flow does not mean you are in trouble. You still may be putting away money in your company savings plan, so you are investing more than you remember. But if the reason you are spending more than you are taking in is excessive debt, it's time to take notice. This exercise is your wake-up call, and the time to mend your ways is now!

CREATING A BUDGET THAT WORKS

Now you know your assets and liabilities, have clearly prioritized your financial goals, and have analyzed how your income matches up with your expenses. Using this information as a base, you now must project into the future to create a budget that works for you.

If the word *budget* sounds too ominous or constricting, you can call it a spending or money plan or even a financial road map. Look at a budget as a friend that gives you control over your finances in a way that lets you decide what is most and least important to you. A budget is an intensely personal plan, because there is probably no one you know who has exactly the same priorities as you. If you find it important to include in your budget a lavish ski vacation to the Alps every winter, so be it—as long as the numbers tell you that you can afford it.

Putting *You* in Control

A budget is a living, breathing document that expands or contracts as your circumstances and priorities change. Think of it as a road map, allowing you to know the direction you want to go but giving you several options on how to get there.

A budget will tell you what mortgage payment you can afford. It also lets you know ahead of time if you have enough cash to meet quarterly tax payments or monthly debt. Buying those holiday gifts won't mean fretting about where to find the money either, if you properly budgeted for it ahead of time. And down the road at retirement, you will know if your Social Security and pension income will be enough to live on to maintain your current lifestyle.

These kinds of issues will continue through the different stages of your life, but your budget worksheet information will allow you to make rational, informed decisions.

Creating a written budget communicates your priorities in black and white and will motivate you to take charge of your financial life. As the year goes on, you will feel in control of your money, because you will know whether you are spending more or less than you expected in each category of spending. And at the end of the year, you will be able to evaluate how you did based on accurate information, making next year's budget even more useful.

Your Annual Budget

There are two kinds of budgets—annual and monthly. The annual plan takes thought, because you probably can't do a good job of forecasting all your income and expenses in an afternoon. Plan to do it in several sessions over about a week's time. Try several different scenarios and do your first few rounds of budgeting in pencil, so you can erase until all the numbers add up.

And keep in mind some common sense approaches that can help ensure the success of a budget.

Involve everyone. Work out a budget with everyone who will be affected by it. It should be discussed with your spouse or significant other, as well as your kids. Everyone needs to feel involved in the plan, because you will have a much better chance of meeting your targets than if they had no input.

Be realistic and specific to your situation. You should not count on levels of spending or income that you only wish you had; that will only frustrate the exercise. A budget, in itself, will not increase your income or cut your spending; it only allows you to see what is going on so you can improve it.

Priorities relate to your goals. When setting priorities, refer back to the "Defining Your Financial Goals" section, in which you went through the exercise of determining what is most and least important to you.

Don't sweat the dollars-and-cents details. Use round numbers in your budget planning. The goal, after all, is to help control your spending to meet your financial goals. It is not to drive yourself crazy by getting your spending down to the last penny. Do remember that often it is the little expenses that add up and can defeat your budgeting, however. For example, if you pick up a $2 latte from the corner espresso bar five mornings a week, in a year's time that adds up to $520.

Changes year to year. Don't automatically assume you will earn or spend the same amount in each category every year. Last year's figures should be a guide, not a straitjacket. Part of your budget is taking control of your finances, so move numbers on the expense side up or down, depending—to some extent—on what you would like to see happen in the next year.

In setting up your budget (see Figure 1.10), use the totals from the Cash Flow Analysis Worksheet from the previous section and add four columns to it. Label the first column, "Actual Last Year." In it, record what you actually earned and spent in each of the categories in the last year. This should be easy, because all you have to do is transfer the figures from the Cash Flow Analysis Worksheet.

Next, you want to project what you think you will earn and what you want to spend in each of the categories over the next year. Label this second column, "Budget This Year." As you proceed through the year, you will be keeping track of what you are actually earning and spending in each category. This should be entered in the third column, "Actual This Year." In the fourth column, you will calculate whether you are above or below what you projected in each category. Label this last column, "+/– Budget vs. Actual This Year" or "Difference."

With this design, you instantly can see whether your income and expenses are coming in over or under projections. When you total them, you can observe whether you are shooting above or below your total budget. If you are over-budget, the culprit category usually sticks out like a sore thumb. If you are underbudget, you might make a mid-course correction to determine where else to put some money, such as savings or investments or paying off debt.

Your Monthly Budget

In addition to doing an annual budget, you should keep a running tab of how you are doing on a monthly basis in at least the major categories. The Monthly Budget Worksheet in Figure 1.11 will let you compare your budgeted amount with your actual income and spending.

At the end of the worksheet, calculate whether you are overbudget or underbudget overall. Using this worksheet, you will be able to see month by month what kind of progress you are making toward meeting your budget, and what items are at greatest variance with your projections.

POINTS TO REMEMBER

- To figure out where you want to go, you first must know where you are, and that means assessing your net worth.

Figure 1.10   Annual Budget Worksheet

YEAR _____

Annual Income	Actual Last Year	Budget This Year	Actual This Year	+/(−) Budget vs. Actual This Year
Earned Income	$ _____	$ _____	$ _____	$ _____
Self-Employment Income	_____	_____	_____	_____
Family Income	_____	_____	_____	_____
Government Income	_____	_____	_____	_____
Retirement Income	_____	_____	_____	_____
Investment Income	_____	_____	_____	_____
Other Income	_____	_____	_____	_____
TOTAL ANNUAL INCOME	$ _____	$ _____	$ _____	$ _____
Expenses				
Fixed Expenses				
Automobile-Related	$ _____	$ _____	$ _____	$ _____
Family	_____	_____	_____	_____
Home-Related	_____	_____	_____	_____
Insurance	_____	_____	_____	_____
Savings and Investments	_____	_____	_____	_____
Taxes	_____	_____	_____	_____
Utilities	_____	_____	_____	_____
Other	_____	_____	_____	_____
Total Fixed Expenses	$ _____	$ _____	$ _____	$ _____
Flexible Expenses				
Children	$ _____	$ _____	$ _____	$ _____
Clothing	_____	_____	_____	_____
Contributions and Dues	_____	_____	_____	_____
Education	_____	_____	_____	_____
Equipment and Vehicles	_____	_____	_____	_____
Financial and Professional Services	_____	_____	_____	_____
Food	_____	_____	_____	_____
Home Maintenance	_____	_____	_____	_____
Medical Care	_____	_____	_____	_____
Miscellaneous	_____	_____	_____	_____
Recreation and Entertainment	_____	_____	_____	_____
Savings and Investments	_____	_____	_____	_____
Travel and Vacations	_____	_____	_____	_____
Other	_____	_____	_____	_____
Total Flexible Expenses	$ _____	$ _____	$ _____	$ _____
TOTAL EXPENSES	$ _____	$ _____	$ _____	$ _____
TOTAL INCOME LESS TOTAL EXPENSES	$ _____	$ _____	$ _____	$ _____

Figure 1.11   Monthly Budget Worksheet

MONTH _____   YEAR _____

Income	Budget	Actual	YTD Budget	YTD Actual
Earned Income	$	$	$	$
Self-Employment Income				
Family Income				
Government Income				
Retirement Income				
Investment Income				
Other Income				
TOTAL INCOME	$	$	$	$
Expenses				
Fixed Expenses				
Automobile-Related	$	$	$	$
Family				
Home-Related				
Insurance				
Savings and Investments				
Taxes				
Utilities				
Other				
Total Fixed Expenses	$	$	$	$
Flexible Expenses				
Children	$	$	$	$
Clothing				
Contributions and Dues				
Education				
Equipment and Vehicles				
Financial and Professional Services				
Food				
Home Maintenance				
Medical Care				
Miscellaneous				
Recreation and Entertainment				
Savings and Investments				
Travel and Vacations				
Other				
Total Flexible Expenses	$	$	$	$
TOTAL EXPENSES	$	$	$	$
TOTAL INCOME LESS TOTAL EXPENSES	$	$	$	$

- You should recalculate your net worth regularly, usually once a year or whenever there is a major change in your financial situation such as marital or job status.
- There is no right or wrong financial goal as long as it is a conscious decision on your part.
- Be honest with your income, expenses, and budgeting (your forecast of future income and expenses), because you're the only one who will be hurt by not knowing the truth.
- Think of a budget as a road map that allows you to know the direction you want to go but gives you several options on how to get there.

RESOURCES

Books

The Complete Idiot's Guide to Managing Your Money, Robert K. Heady and Christy Heady (Alpha Books, Macmillan Computer Publishing, A Prentice Hall Macmillan Co., 201 W. 103rd St., Indianapolis, IN 46290). Simple-to-follow money management basics and loaded with tips to save (and make) money.

Ernst & Young's Personal Financial Planning Guide, Robert J. Garner, Charles L. Ratner, Barbara J. Raasch, and Martin Nissenbaum (John Wiley & Sons, 1 Wiley Dr., Somerset, NJ 08875-1272; 732-469-4400, 800-225-5945; www.wiley.com). Covers fundamentals of financial planning and also looks at how major life events affect one's current financial picture.

Get in the Game: The Girl's Guide to Money & Investing, by Vanessa Summers (Bloomberg Press, 100 Business Park Drive, P.O. Box 888, Princeton, NJ 08542; www.bloomberg.com). A self-help personal finance book for Gen X women.

Investing 101, by Kathy Kristof (Bloomberg Press, 100 Business Park Drive, P.O. Box 888, Princeton, NJ 08542; www.bloomberg.com). A simple and straightforward approach to how to have enough money when you need it.

The Savage Truth on Money, by Terry Savage (John Wiley & Sons, 1 Wiley Dr., Somerset, NJ 08875; 800-225-5945; www.wiley.com). A guide to long-term financial independence and how technology can help.

Talking Dollars and Making Sense: A Wealth-Building Guide for African-Americans, by Brooke M. Stephens (McGraw-Hill, P.O. Box 545, Blacklick, OH 43004; 800-634-3961; www.pbg.mcgraw-hill.com). This book honestly examines the attitudes, beliefs, and behaviors of African Americans with regard to money.

A Woman's Guide to Investing, by Virginia B. Morris and Kenneth M. Morris. (Lightbulb Press, 112 Madison Ave., New York, NY 10016; 212-485-8800; www.lightbulbpress.com). Targeted to the specific investment needs of women and compiled in collaboration with the women and investing experts at Oppenheimer Funds Inc.

Publications/Web Sites

Financial Electric Library. The ultimate source of information to answer whatever question you have about personal finance; draws on hundreds of magazines, books, wire services, newspapers, and broadcast transcripts. <www.elibrary.com>

Kiplinger.com (The Kiplinger Washington Editors, Inc., 1729 H St., NW, Washington, DC 20006-3938; 888-419-0424; www. kiplinger.com). Full of useful personal finance tips and ideas on college financial issues, retirement, banking, checking, ATMs, all types of insurance, and tax software.

Fool.com (The Motley Fool, 123 N. Pitt St., Alexandria, VA 22314; 703-254-1999). Offers advice and many resources on investment strategies. <www.fool.com>

The Money Page. A source of links to personal finance information, including consumer credit, electronic money, investor's guide, money talk, money forums, banking, ATMs, insurance, real estate, retirement, Social Security, and travel. <www .moneypage.com>

Software

Everyone's Money Software (888-201-6300; www.moneyanswers.com). Offers all the worksheets in this book and the even-more-comprehensive *Everyone's Money Book,* so that the software does all the calculations and recordkeeping for you.

Microsoft Money Deluxe (Microsoft Corp., One Microsoft Way, Redmond, WA 98052; 800-426-9400; www.microsoft.com). Covers all the bases of personal finance in a logical, easy-to-navigate style. Microsoft Money was designed to work with Windows software, and it does so very elegantly.

Quicken Deluxe (Intuit, 2535 Garcia Ave., Mountain View, CA 94043; 650-944-6000; www.intuit.com). From Intuit, the most comprehensive, in-depth program in personal finance.

CHAPTER 2

Assembling a Long-Term Financial and Investing Plan

Although budgeting is crucial to balancing your income and spending over the coming months and years, you also must take steps to project how your needs will evolve during the rest of your life (see Chapters 3 and 4). Here is where long-term financial planning fits in. This process not only helps you avoid, or at least prepare for, financial surprises and disasters, it also helps those in good financial shape become even better prepared for the future. As you get older, certain financial events inevitably are bound to occur, and the more prepared you are for them, the easier they will be to handle. The relatively small amount of time you spend on long-term planning will pay off enormously for the rest of your life—in terms of dollars and cents and in the security of knowing you will be able to deal with almost any twist or turn of your financial fate.

As you found out in the "Defining Your Financial Goals" section in Chapter 1, there are short-, medium-, and long-term dimensions to your financial life. Although budgeting is aimed at satisfying your short-term goals, you might never get to the medium- and long-term objectives without a comprehensive financial plan. Many of the aspects of long-term planning will be discussed in more detail later in this book. What follows is a brief introduction to some of the elements you will need to consider in setting up your strategy for long-term success.

Figure 2.1   *Money* magazine and CNN, along with America Online, bring you a personal finance Web site loaded with the ins and outs of handling your money.

Source: Reprinted with permission from Cable News Network, LP, LLLP.

SETTING UP AN INVESTMENT STRATEGY

Your financial plan will outline how much capital you will need to accumulate to meet certain long-term goals, such as paying for your children's college education, buying or upgrading a home, or providing for a secure retirement. Part of the investment strategy is assembling a portfolio of stocks, bonds, mutual funds, and bank instruments that will get you where you want to go. One of the main risks you must overcome in a long-term plan is the slow but steady erosion of the worth of a dollar because of inflation. A good investment strategy will keep your dollars growing faster than inflation, so that when you need to spend them, you will have enough. Another element of investing is finding a level of risk with which you feel comfortable.

You have plenty of choices to match your short- or long-term investment needs. Beginners at investing tend to start out with most of their money in cash instruments. These are investments that are safe from loss of principal— checking, savings, and certificate of deposit (CD) accounts at banks, savings and loans, and credit unions; money-market mutual funds; and Treasury bills (T-bills).

Putting your money away in the bank is an admirable practice, but putting some of it into investments such as stocks and bonds can offer higher rates of return—with more risk. If inflation is high and rising and the Federal Reserve pushes up interest rates to try to cool off the economy, interest rates on your cash will climb as they did in the early 1980s. On the other hand, if the Fed cuts interest rates to stimulate spending as they did in the early 2000s, rates can drop, so that your cash only earns 1 or 2 percent interest. Keep in mind, however, that whatever investments you make, it always is important to have some cash available to meet everyday living expenses as well as unplanned emergencies. The rule of thumb is to always have at least three months of living expenses easily available. Here are a few investment options, starting with what to do with your cash on hand.

Savings and Checking Accounts

Financial institutions offer different types of accounts, including passbook savings accounts. These generally pay low interest rates of 1 to 2 percent, and unless you do not have enough money to meet minimum balance requirements on higher yielding accounts, they are not a very attractive investment. NOW (negotiable order of withdrawal) and super-NOW accounts are interest-bearing checking accounts that often require minimum balances to avoid fees. They also pay about 1 to 2 percent interest. Before you sign up, see whether you typically keep enough in your checking account to earn more in interest than you will pay in fees.

An attraction of these accounts is their security. Each different account you have registered at a bank, savings and loan, or credit union is insured up to $100,000 by an agency of the federal government:

- *Banks.* Federal Deposit Insurance Corp., 550 17th Street NW, Washington, DC 20429-9990; 877-275-3342; <www.fdic.gov>
- *Credit unions.* National Credit Union Administration; 1775 Duke St., Alexandria, VA 22314; 703-518-6300; <www.ncua.gov>
- *Savings and loans.* Office of Thrift Supervision, 1700 G. Street, NW Washington, DC 20552; 202-906-6000; <www.ots.treas.gov>

Many banks today also offer their services over the Internet, so you don't have to limit yourself to a local bank. With the help of Web sites like Banx-Quote.com and Bankrate.com, seek out the best deals anywhere. Other sites that can help you pick an online bank include Gomez.com (610 Lincoln St., Waltham, MA 02451; 781-768-2100; www.gomez.com), which rates online banks, and Netbanker.com, from Financial Insite, publishers of Online Banking Report (4739 University Way NE, Suite 1002, Seattle, WA 98105; 206-517-5021).

Some things to consider when choosing a financial institution include the following:

- *Check the institution's safety.* Individual financial statements are available free online from the National Information Center of the Federal Reserve System <www.ffiec.gov/nic>. Also, Veribanc, Inc. can provide risk analysis and bank safety ratings (P.O. Box 461, Wakefield, MA 01880; 800-VERIBANC; <www.veribanc.com>).
- *What are the minimum deposit levels required to avoid monthly service charges and other fees?*
- *How is account interest compounded?* The fastest compounding is continuous as opposed to daily or monthly.

A credit union, which is a financial cooperative of individuals with a common affiliation, also is an alternative. To find one near you that you are eligible to join, contact the Credit Union National Association (CUNA, P.O. Box 431, Madison, WI 53701; 800-356-9655; <www.cuna.org>).

Asset Management Accounts

Offered by brokerage firms, these accounts have check-writing privileges, debit and credit cards, and margin loan capacity. The latter allows you to borrow against the value of your securities. If you have stocks, bonds, and mutual funds and enough money to make it worthwhile, this asset management account may offer the highest return on your cash and the greatest convenience. Typically, the annual management fee is $25 to $100. Assets in the accounts also are insured against the bankruptcy of the brokerage for up to $500,000 in securities, including $100,000 in cash by the Securities Investor Protection Corporation (SIPC, 805 15th St. NW, Suite 800, Washington, DC 20005; 202-371-8300; <www.sipc.org>). Such an account automatically sweeps all interest and dividend income distributed by your securities into a money-market fund until you decide what to do with the money.

Money-Market Deposit Accounts (MMDAs)

This type of account pays the highest interest of any readily accessible product a bank offers—typically 1 to 3 percent—but your access to an MMDA is somewhat restricted. Federal banking law stipulates that you only can write three checks of any amount and make three electronic transfers a month. Your best strategy is to make three large transfers a month into your checking account, from which you can write as many checks as you want. This way, most of your money will be earning higher interest for a longer period of time. These accounts generally require a minimum $1,000 deposit and are FDIC insured.

Money-Market Mutual Funds

These are not the same as MMDAs. Money-market mutual funds are run by fund management companies and buy short-term securities that offer the best yields available in the marketplace at that time. The FDIC or any other government agency does not insure them, but there has never been a default or even a near-default in a money-market mutual fund. Unlike MMDAs, they usually impose a minimum amount on checks that ranges from $100 to $500. Unlike an MMDA, the money-market fund comes in taxable and tax-free varieties.

Treasury Bills (T-bills)

Backed by the full faith and credit of the U.S. government, T-bills provide the ultimate in safety and liquidity. Any Treasury security that is issued with a maturity of one year or less is known as a Treasury bill. Generally, the longer you commit your money, the higher the yield. Yields on Treasury bills tend to be lower than yields on money-market mutual funds because of the extra security of the T-bill.

You can buy a T-bill directly from any Federal Reserve Bank or branch, or by mail with no fee. (Check out the Fed's Web site, <www.federalreserve .gov>, for online links to the various institutions.) You also can buy bills through the Treasury Direct program, or through brokers or banks.

Certificates of Deposit (CDs)

These are bank, savings and loan, or credit union instruments that allow you to lock in an interest rate for a specific period of time. If you withdraw your money before the CD matures, you face an early-withdrawal penalty set by each bank—often three months' interest. The most popular CDs mature in three months, six months, and one year, although banks offer some with up to five-year maturities and various other customized and designer CDs. Banks do not charge fees to buy a certificate. All interest from CDs is taxable in the year it is received, even if it is reinvested. Remember to calculate the effect of those taxes when comparing potential CD returns against other alternatives like tax-free money funds or municipal bonds.

Stocks

When you buy shares of common stock in a company, you actually are becoming a part owner, and as such, hold a piece of equity in that company. That's why stocks often are referred to as equities. If you look over the past few decades, prices of good-quality companies' stock invariably have moved higher, rewarding their shareholders. As a device to increase your net worth so you can achieve your financial goals, stocks or stock mutual funds are your best investment over the long run (see Figure 2.2). The three major U.S. stock markets are the New York Stock Exchange (NYSE), the American Stock Exchange (AMEX), and the Nasdaq National Market System (formerly known as the over-the-counter market).

When it comes to selecting stocks, remember that despite the endless predictions by market gurus that this or that stock is about to soar or plunge, no one really knows what will happen to stock prices in the short term. So, for the most part, don't pay much attention to the prognosticators, and certainly it is not necessary to pay for their advice. For every expert who forecasts something one way, chances are you can find an equally qualified expert who offers the exact opposite forecast. Here are other suggestions when it comes to stock picking:

- Invest for the long term.
- Buy stocks systematically.
- Invest in what you know.
- Research your choices carefully.
- Monitor the company after you have bought the shares.
- Don't be pressured to buy or sell just because everyone else is doing so.
- Consider transaction costs before you buy.
- Have a selling target price in mind when you buy a stock.

Figure 2.2 1925–2001 Chart of Stocks, Bonds, Bills, and Inflation

From 1925 to 2001

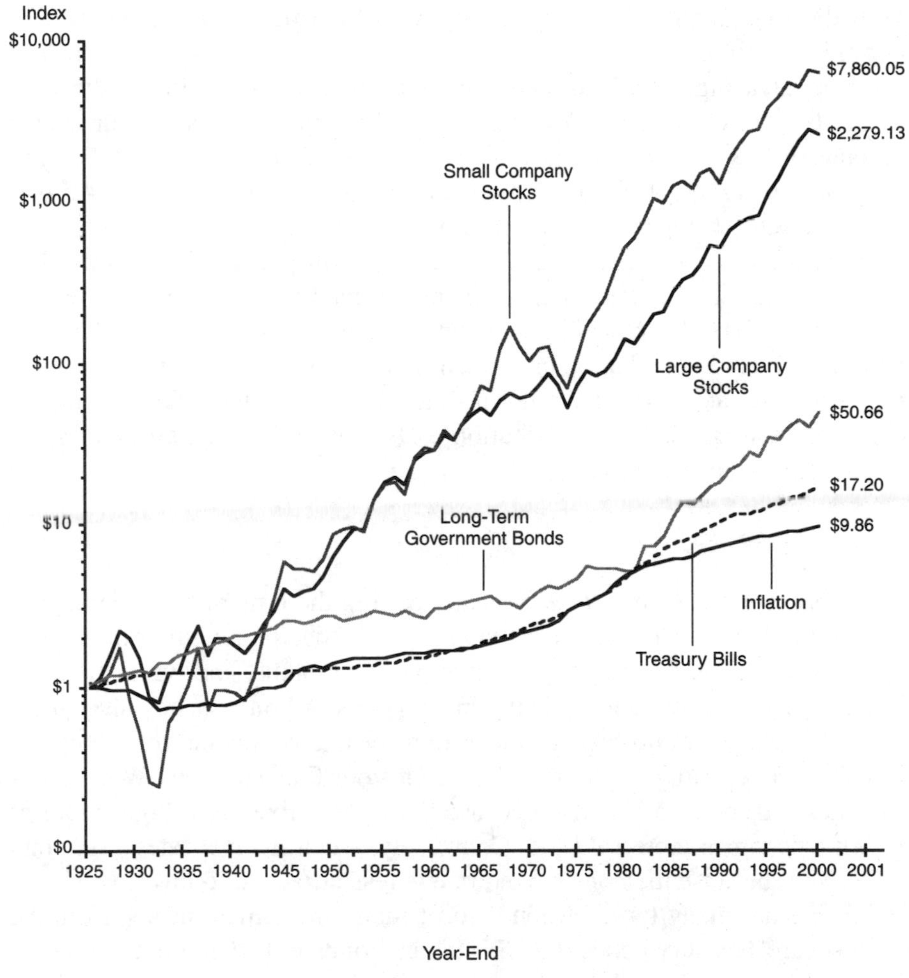
Index
$10,000
$1,000
$100
$10
$1
$0
$7,860.05
$2,279.13
Small Company Stocks
Large Company Stocks
$50.66
$17.20
$9.86
Long-Term Government Bonds
Inflation
Treasury Bills
1925 1930 1935 1940 1945 1950 1955 1960 1965 1970 1975 1980 1985 1990 1995 2000 2001
Year-End

Source: (c) *Stocks, Bonds, Bills, and Inflation 2002 Yearbook*™, Ibbotson Associates, Chicago (annually updates work by Roger G. Ibbotson and Rex A. Sinquefield).

Mutual Funds

A popular alternative to individual stocks is a stock mutual fund, a pool of money that a fund manager invests in stocks to achieve a specific objective. Among a fund's advantages are instant diversification, and there is a fund to meet most every financial goal and risk-tolerance level. The two basic kinds of mutual funds are load and no-load, differentiated by the method by which they are sold. A load is a commission paid to a salesperson, financial planner, or broker when you buy the fund. You deal directly with the mutual fund company to buy a no-load fund, and so there is no commission to pay.

The advantage of a load fund is that you receive professional advice on which fund to choose. The disadvantage is that the commission reduces the amount of money you have at work in the fund. Thus, for every dollar you sink into the fund, only 95.5 cents will earn money if you pay the full 4.5 percent load. Over a longer time period, however, if the load fund performs better than the no-load fund, the up-front charge will pale in significance. But even no-load funds charge a management fee that both types of funds levy— from as little as 0.2 percent of your assets to as much as 2 percent. Other possible fees include dividend reinvestment loads, exchange fees if you opt for one fund over another in a family of funds, and 12b-1 fees. The latter, generally to be avoided, cover distribution costs like advertising, promotion, literature, and sales incentives.

Bonds

When you invest in a *bond,* you are loaning the issuer of that bond your money in return for a fixed rate of interest for a specific length of time. Normally, you receive interest payments every six months, and when the bond matures, you receive your original principal back. A bond is a key investment vehicle, because it allows you to lock in a set rate of income for a long period of time, creating a solid foundation for your financial plan. When interest rates fall, bond prices rise because the bond—fixed at a higher rate of return—becomes more valuable. Conversely, when interest rates rise, bond prices fall, because the bond's fixed rate is less attractive to investors.

There are many types of bonds to fit many investment needs, from the ultra secure Treasury bonds or U.S. savings bonds issued and backed by the U.S. government, to slightly more speculative government agency securities. The latter includes issues from agencies like the Farmers Home Administration (FmHA), Federal Home Loan Mortgage Corp. (Freddie Mac), and even the U.S. Postal Service. Though they do not carry the full faith and credit of the U.S. government behind them, you can be fairly certain that Congress would make sure these agencies don't default on their debt

Going up the risk ladder are mortgage-backed securities; then municipal bonds issued by states, cities, counties, towns, villages, and taxing authorities of many types; corporate bonds; foreign bonds; zero-coupon bonds; convertible bonds; and the most speculative of all, high-yield or junk bonds. If the process of choosing individual bonds seems too complicated, bond mutual funds might be right for you.

Precious Metals

Since 3000 BC, gold has been recognized as the ultimate medium of exchange. It is rare, in continuous demand, portable, and an asset in its own right. Gold is an investment that prospers when the economy suffers, a hedge against inflation and international tensions. Its last great run-up was in the late 1970s, when interest rates and inflation soared into double digits, Arab oil embargoes fueled skyrocketing oil prices, and the former Soviet Union invaded Afghanistan. Gold peaked at $875 an ounce in January 1980.

Over the past few years, gold has lost some of its luster as inflation remains relatively under control. Even after the horrific events of September 11, 2001, when terrorists destroyed the World Trade Center in New York City and part of the Pentagon in Washington, D.C., and the United States declared war on terrorism, the price of gold rose just a bit over $300. Nonetheless, gold still may have a place in your portfolio. Studies show that over the long term, portfolios containing gold are more stable and have higher returns than gold-free portfolios, because gold tends to move in the opposite direction of paper assets like stocks and bonds. The same holds true for other precious metals, though to a lesser degree. Investors also use silver and platinum as inflation hedges, but neither are viewed as the ultimate store of value like gold.

Higher-Yielding CDs

When it comes to bank instruments like CDs, you don't have to restrict your search for high yields to your neighborhood or even your state. Many banks accept out-of-state deposits by wire or mail. The highest yields around the country are publicized constantly in major financial newspapers as well as on Web sites from companies like Bankrate, Inc. (<www.bankrate.com>). Or you can subscribe to their newsletter, *100 Highest Yields* (11811 U.S. Highway 1, Suite 101, North Palm Beach, FL 33408; 800-243-7720, ext. 506).

TRACKING YOUR INVESTMENTS

You can follow your individual investments in the newspapers, in financial publications like the *Wall Street Journal,* and online. Public companies' Web sites usually have an investor relations Web page. (See "Resources" at the end of this chapter.) Here are the most commonly quoted indexes.

AMEX Composite Index

This index tracks the average of stocks traded on the American Stock Exchange, which tend to be medium- and small-sized growth stocks. The index is weighted by the market capitalization of its component stocks, meaning that stocks with a larger number of shares outstanding and with higher stock prices affect the index more than smaller companies with lower prices.

Dow Jones Industrial Average

The most commonly quoted average tracks the movement of 30 of the largest blue chip stocks traded on the NYSE. The Dow Jones is the price-weighted average, so it is more affected by the movement of higher-priced shares than by lower-priced ones, no matter how many shares are outstanding. Dow Jones and Co., which maintains the average, also tracks utilities (electric and gas) in the Dow Jones Utilities Average, and transportation stocks (airlines, railroads, and truckers) in the Dow Jones Transportation Average. The combined industrial, utilities, and transportation averages are called the Dow Jones Composite Average.

Nasdaq Composite Index

This index tracks the movement of all companies traded on the Nasdaq National Market System. These stocks are, for the most part, smaller and less established than the blue chips in the Dow Industrial Average or the S&P 500. The Nasdaq Composite is market-value weighted, which gives more influence to larger and higher-priced stocks.

NYSE Composite Index

This is the index for the trading of all NYSE stocks. It is market-value weighted and expressed in dollars and cents. When commentators say, "The average share lost 15 cents on the New York Exchange today," for example, this is the index to which they are referring.

Standard & Poor's 500 Index

The S&P 500 is the benchmark against which most portfolio managers compare themselves. It is composed of 500 blue chip stocks, separated by industry. The index always tracks 400 industrial company stocks, 60 transportation stocks, and 40 financial stocks, like banks or insurance companies. The S&P 500 is the fairest yardstick against which you can measure the performance of your stocks.

Wilshire 5000 Equity Index

The broadest measure of all indexes, the market-value-weighted Wilshire, includes all major NYSE, AMEX, and Nasdaq stocks and gives a good indication of the overall direction of all stocks, large and small.

Foreign Indexes

The key indexes used to track stock prices in other countries include the CAC-40 in France; the DAX in Germany; the Financial Times 100 (known as the Footsie) in the United Kingdom; the Hang Seng Index in Hong Kong; the Nikkei 225 Index in Japan; the Toronto 300 Index in Canada, and the Zurich Index in Switzerland.

ASSESSING YOUR RISK TOLERANCE

Unfortunately, for many people, the word *risk,* just like the word *budget,* has a negative connotation. Why would you want to risk your hard-earned money? The answer: If you take no risks with your assets, you will be unlikely to earn a return high enough to achieve your financial goals—"no risk, no return" is how the saying goes.

Now, we're not advocating that you take enormous risks with all of your money. Not every risky investment will earn a high return; if it did, it wouldn't be risky. By diversifying your assets carefully among high-risk, medium-risk, and low-risk investments, you will end up with a larger pool of assets over time than if you keep all of your money in low-risk, low-return choices. In general, the further in the future a return is expected, the greater the risk. Because it is tricky enough to predict what is going to happen over the next few months, it is even more difficult to know what the long-term future holds. Therefore, under normal circumstances, the longer you commit yourself to an investment, the more risk you are taking. But because you are taking more risk, you should be compensated in the long run by a higher return.

As you determine your tolerance for risk, you should understand several types of risk. There are ways to control and minimize each of these risks, but before we get to that, here are the most important risks you will face.

Currency Risk

Although most of your assets will probably be in dollar-denominated investments, you should be aware of the risk of currency movements if you own stocks or bonds denominated in other currencies. When you buy an individual stock or bond in another country, or a mutual fund that invests in foreign securities, the value of your investment fluctuates based on how many dollars it takes to buy a unit of the foreign currency. Currency movements, which swing day to day based on each country's economic and political conditions, can therefore hand you substantial gains or losses.

Deflation Risk

If prices are falling sharply because of a severe economic contraction, you face the risk that the value of your assets will drop just as sharply. This is what happened during the Great Depression of the 1930s, when stock prices, real estate prices, and prices of just about everything else plummeted. The key to sidestepping deflation risk is to make sure you do not have too much of your wealth in assets that could get hit by a deflationary wave. Treasury bonds provide a good haven from deflation.

Lack of Diversification Risk

If all your assets are in one kind of investment, like stocks or CDs, you are not protected if that asset falls sharply in value. Even more dangerous is to keep most of your money in just one stock, bond, or CD, because if something happens to it, you have no alternate assets to fall back on. Many people make the biggest financial mistake having too much of their net worth tied up in their own company's stock. Instead, lower your risk by spreading your holdings among different kinds of assets as well as among several individual investments within each kind of asset.

Inflation Risk

Even if prices are rising at about 5 percent a year, the value of your dollars is steadily eroding over time. Sometimes you don't notice inflation risk until you are hit with sticker shock from a major purchase like a car or home, when you see how much prices have risen.

Interest Rate Risk

Over the past two decades, interest rates on bonds, money-market accounts, mortgages, and all other types of interest-sensitive financial instruments have been extremely volatile. In the early 1980s, the prime rate reached as high as 21½ percent, and rates on bonds, CDs, and mortgages also soared into double digits. By the 2000s, rates had plunged to the low single digits.

Interest rate risk can therefore cut both ways. If you lock into a fixed-rate instrument like a bond or CD when rates are low and then rates rise sharply, the value of your investment will plunge if you have to resell it. On the other hand, if you set your lifestyle according to the high yields you can earn in an environment of soaring interest rates, you will endure a painful shock when rates fall and your lifestyle suffers.

Lack of Liquidity Risk

There are times when you need to sell something, but the market for it has dried up temporarily. That leaves you with two options: You can hang on to what you had wanted to sell, or you can sell it even if you must accept an artificially low price. In general, the more aggressive an investment is, the more subject it is to the risk of holding an illiquid asset. Stocks of small companies and junk bonds, for example, are relatively easy to buy and sell under normal circumstances. But when bad news hits these markets or investors become nervous, the ability to sell at a fair price temporarily disappears.

Playing It Too Safe Risk

If you keep all your money in supersafe CDs, money-market funds, and Treasuries, you run the risk of outliving your assets, because your return has not kept current with inflation. This risk is not frequently recognized, but it is probably the biggest risk that people take.

Political Risk

If you invest in countries where the political structure is not as stable as in the United States, you run the risk of a change in government, which will dramatically devalue the worth of your holdings. A milder form of political risk is the change in U.S. government policy that can favor one industry over another.

Repayment Risk

There are two kinds of repayment risk. The most common, also known as credit risk, is the chance that you will not get repaid what you are owed when it is due. The second risk is the opposite: you are repaid before you want or expect to get your money back. You are taking credit risk whenever you buy a bond, because your ability to collect on that obligation is only as good as the issuer's ability to repay it.

The other kind of repayment risk entails getting your money back faster than you expect. For example, if you lock in a 10 percent yield on a bond and the going rate falls to 6 percent, you will not be able to replace that bond with a new one at the same yield. Most bond issuers have the right to redeem, or call, a bond a certain number of years after it has been issued.

Mortgage-backed securities—pools of thousands of individual mortgages packaged for sale—run the same risk. When mortgage rates fall sharply and homeowners rush to refinance their loans, holders of mortgage-backed securities lose, because the securities repay most of their principal quickly, and as with bondholders, they can't replicate the high rates they thought they had locked in for years.

Volatility Risk

This risk happens when an investment swings wildly in value in a short period of time. Of course, volatility gives you a greater chance to profit if you buy when the price is low and sell when it is high. But that's easier said than done. Just because an investment is volatile in the short run doesn't mean you should avoid it altogether. Keep in mind that you enter into the investment with the hope of a long-term gain.

THE INVESTMENT RISK PYRAMID

In assembling a portfolio that achieves your financial goals and still allows you to sleep comfortably at night, think of your entire mix of assets in the form of an investment pyramid (see Figure 2.3).

At the top of your pyramid are the riskiest assets, which offer the greatest potential for high returns as well as big losses. The high-risk apex includes collectibles, foreign investments, futures contracts, junk corporate and municipal bonds, new stock issues, oil and gas limited partnerships, options, raw land, small growth stocks, tax shelters, unfinished real estate construction, venture capital, and warrants.

The next tier of the pyramid, the moderate-risk sector, includes stock and bond mutual funds, income-oriented limited partnerships, mortgage-backed securities, individual growth stocks, corporate bonds, and rental real estate.

The third tier of the pyramid, called the low-risk sector, consists of annuities, blue chip stocks, Treasury bonds, life insurance contracts, municipal bonds with high credit ratings, short-term bond funds, utility stocks, and zero-coupon bonds.

The base of the pyramid is composed of investments where there is almost no chance of losing your principal. This includes bank CDs, cash, checking accounts, money-market mutual funds, and guaranteed investment contracts (GICs) found in salary reduction plans, savings accounts, and Treasury bills. However, remember that the risk of investments that are too safe is that your investments earn low yields and do not allow you to keep up with inflation.

No matter what your age or situation, you should probably have some of your assets in each of the four sectors of the pyramid at all times. What should change over time is how much you invest in each sector. You might be young and able to take more risk, so more of your money should be in the high-risk apex. Or you may be retired and need to live off your investments. More of your money should then be in low-risk and base investments. But even the young person should have a cash reserve in base investments, and the retiree should have a small amount of money in apex investments, so they both can stay ahead of inflation.

Figure 2.3 Investment Risk Pyramid

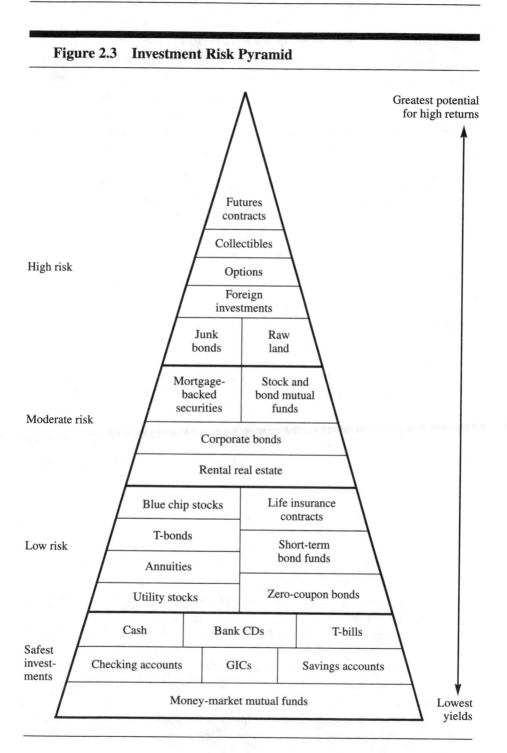

A Quiz to Determine Your Risk Tolerance

Even though by now you should realize that you have to take some calculated risks to attain your financial goals, this doesn't mean you will be comfortable doing it. The quiz in Figure 2.4 will give you some insight into how much risk you feel able to take on. Answer each of the questions, giving yourself one point for answer one, two points for answer two, and up to four points for answer four. Then add up the points to see what kind of risk taker you are.

Keep your risk score in mind as you read through the rest of the book. If you are a diehard conservative, you should resist the temptation to put much money in riskier investments, even though they may sound promising. Keep the investment pyramid in mind, though; you don't want to have all your assets in only the safest bets. If you are a moderate-risk investor, put more of your money in the middle and top sectors of the investment pyramid, as long as you carefully gauge the level of risk you are taking. For high-risk investors, allocate more of your money to the apex of the investment pyramid but don't neglect the pyramid base. You should be careful not to become so enthusiastic about an investing idea that you put too much of your capital at risk in something that goes bust.

Wherever you stand on the risk spectrum, keep in mind that dealing with your personal finances in general and investing in particular are not only about maximizing the amount of dollars in your pocket. Finding your financial comfort zone is also important, so that you feel psychologically secure about the decisions you are making. It's no use becoming rich if you die from the stress of attaining your wealth (even though your heirs might disagree!).

For more detailed information on Investment Strategies, see *Everyone's Money Book on Stocks, Bonds, and Mutual Funds.*

POINTS TO REMEMBER

- Think of a financial plan as a way to help avoid or at least prepare for financial surprises and disasters.
- Your investments should take into account the level of risk you are willing to accept comfortably.
- Don't be afraid or uncomfortable to look beyond your neighborhood or even your state for the best yields when it comes to banking, CDs, or investing.
- The Internet is a great information tool when it comes to tracking down the best deal or researching an investment.

Figure 2.4   Risk Tolerance Quiz

A. If someone made me an offer to invest 15 percent of my net worth in a deal he said had an 80 percent chance of being profitable, the level of profit would have to be

1. No level of profit would be worth that kind of risk.
2. seven times the amount I invested.
3. three times the amount I invested.
4. at least as much as I have invested in the first place.

Points: _____

B. How comfortable would I be assuming a $10,000 debt in the hope of achieving a $20,000 gain over the next few months?

1. Totally uncomfortable—I would never do it.
2. Somewhat uncomfortable—I would probably never do it.
3. Somewhat comfortable—I might do it.
4. Very comfortable—I would jump at the chance to do it.

Points: _____

C. I am holding a lottery ticket that has gotten me to the finals, where I have a one in four chance of winning a $100,000 prize. The least I would be will to sell my ticket for before the drawing is

1. $15,000.
2. $20,000.
3. $35,000.
4. $60,000.

Points: _____

D. I have spent more than $150 on one or more of these activities: professional sports gambling, recreational betting on poker or basketball games I participate in, casino gambling.

1. I have never participated in any of these activities.
2. I have participated in these activities only a few times in my life.
3. I have participated in one of these activities in the past year.
4. I have participated in two or more of these activities in the past year.

Points: _____

E. Whenever I have to decide where to invest a large amount of money, I

1. delay the decision.
2. get somebody else (like my broker) to decide for me.
3. share the decision with advisors.
4. decide on my own.

Points: _____

Figure 2.4   Risk Tolerance Quiz (continued)

F. If a stock I bought doubled in the year after I bought it, I would

1. sell all my shares.
2. sell half of my shares.
3. not sell any shares.
4. buy more shares.

Points: _____

G. Which of the following describes how I make my investment decisions?
1. Never on my own
2. Sometimes on my own
3. Often on my own
4. Always on my own

Points: _____

H. My luck in investing is
1. terrible.
2. average.
3. better than average.
4. fantastic.

Points: _____

I. My investments are successful mainly because
1. God is always on my side.
2. I was in the right place at the right time.
3. when opportunities arose, I took advantage of them.
4. I carefully planned them to work out that way.

Points: _____

J. I have a high-yielding certificate of deposit that is about to mature, and interest rates have dropped so much that I feel compelled to invest in something with a higher yield. The most likely place I will invest the money is
1. U.S. savings bonds.
2. a short-term bond fund.
3. a long-term bond fund.
4. a stock fund.

Points: _____

TOTAL SCORE: _____

How to score yourself:

0–16 points: You are a conservative investor who feels uncomfortable taking any risk.

17–29 points: You are a moderate investor who feels comfortable taking moderate risks.

30–40 points: You are an aggressive investor who is willing to take high risks in search of high returns.

RESOURCES

Books

Barron's Business Keys, Keys to Understanding the Financial News, 2d ed., by Nicholas G. Apostolou and Larry Crumbley (Barron's Educational Series, Inc., 250 Wireless Blvd., Hauppage, NY 11788; www.barronsedu.com).

Charles Schwab's Guide to Financial Independence: Simple Solutions for Busy People, by Charles R. Schwab (Three Rivers Press, Random House, Order Dept., 400 Hahn Rd., Westminster, MD 21157; 800-733-3000; www.randomhouse.com). Basic book for people who recognize the importance of investing but know little or nothing about how to do it.

Consumer Information Center, Pueblo, CO 81009. Write them to request the following pamphlets: *Get the Facts on Saving and Investing, I Bonds Investor's Guide,* and *U.S. Savings Bonds Investor Information.*

Savings Bonds, When to Hold, When to Fold and Everything In-Between, by Daniel J. Pederson (Sage Creek Press, 121 E. Front St., 4th Floor, Traverse City, MI 49684; 800-927-1901).

Organizations

Bureau of the Public Debt (Customer Service, Parkersburg, WV 26106; 800-722-2678; www.publicdebt.treas.gov). A branch of the U.S. Department of Treasury with lots of information on Treasuries.

Consumer Federation of America (1424 16th St., NW, Suite 604, Washington, DC 20036; 202-387-6121). A consumer-oriented group that offers advice and information on a broad range of finance issues.

Federal Reserve banks and branches. To find the location of your nearest Federal Reserve bank or branch, check your local telephone book under Federal Government, or contact the Federal Reserve, Board of Governors (20th Street and Constitution Avenue, NW, Washington, DC 20551; 202-452-3000; www.federalreserve.gov).

Treasury Direct (800-722-2678; www.treasurydirect.gov). To purchase Treasury securities or get more information on buying and selling Treasuries.

Web Sites

America Online. Features extensive information on investing and personal finance <www.aol.com> through its link with CNNmoney <www.cnnfn.com>.

BusinessWeek Online. Features articles, quotes, charts, quarterly and annual scoreboards, portfolio tracking, analysis, calculators, and more. <www.businessweek .com>

CBS MarketWatch.com. Features articles, news headlines, top performers, quotes and charts, analysis, and more on personal finance and investing.<www .cbsmarketwatch.com>

Closed-End Fund Investor. A comprehensive site (some information is free) focusing on closed-end funds that provides profiles, charts, holdings, and reports on hundreds of funds. <www.icefi.com>

FirstGov for Consumers. A resource for consumer information from the federal government; topics include banking, buying, identity theft, and investor information. <www.consumer.gov>

MSN Money. Microsoft teams with CNBC for a one-stop shop for information, research, and help about all aspects of personal finance and money. <www .moneycentral.msn.com>

NYSE.com. The site for the New York Stock Exchange with online equivalent of the Big Board's ticker, though like many sites prices are delayed slightly. <www .nyse.com>

Charles Schwab. Includes quotes, charts, research, and how-to information on investing, retirement planning, and personal finance issues; also offers online tutorials. <www.charlesschwab.com>

Yahoo! The Yahoo! Finance part of the Web site is one of the most comprehensive search engines for information on all kinds of investments. <www.yahoo.com>

CHAPTER 3

Financing Your Needs
Part One: Housing,
Cars, and Credit

Your financial plan is designed to satisfy your needs, whether short, medium, or long term. It is important to determine fairly and accurately what those needs are. As is the case with creating a budget, not honestly expressing your needs achieves nothing and will only end up hurting you and your family. What follows is a brief look at strategies for coping with three of your major needs—housing, transportation, and credit. More major needs—insurance, financing education, and maximizing employee benefits—are addressed in Chapter 4.

HOUSING

Whether figuring how to put together a down payment on a first home, adding to your existing home, or planning a move to a retirement community, long-term housing needs are expensive and take planning. The planning entails deciding what kind of housing you would like at each stage of your life and then considering the different financial strategies to pay for it. In some circumstances, it might make more sense to rent than to buy. In other cases, a 15-year mortgage might be better than a 30-year one.

Some advantages of home ownership include:

- Tax breaks
- Property value appreciation
- Pride of controlling where you live

• Living free and clear of mortgage payments after the loan is paid off

On the other hand, some advantages of renting include:

• No effect of eroding real estate prices
• A smaller bite out of your household budget
• Ability to invest any money saved in stocks, bonds, and mutual funds that may have more appreciation potential than real estate
• No risk of higher mortgage payments as could be the case if you owned a home and had an adjustable-rate mortgage
• Less hassle if you relocate frequently

The buy-versus-rent decision also involves expectations for your future lifestyle. A number of Web sites, including MSN's Home Advisor at <www .homeadvisor.msn.com>, have handy calculators to help with the financial end of the buy-versus-rent decision.

If You Decide to Rent

If you plan to rent, the following tips can help you get the most for your money:

• Before beginning your search, refer back to the budget exercise in Chapter 1 to determine how much rent you can afford. Ideally, your rent (including utilities) should absorb no more than 30 percent of your gross income or 25 percent of your net income.
• Before settling on a neighborhood, tour it extensively during the day, at night, on weekdays, and weekends. You want to get a feel for noise levels in the neighborhood and what your neighbors are like, among other factors.
• You can avoid real estate agent fees if you find your apartment or rental home yourself and deal directly with a landlord or renter who offers a sublease.
• Don't rent the first home or apartment you see. Usually, the more time you take, the better the deal you will find.
• When looking at apartments or rental homes, check all appliances and facilities. Inquire about parking facilities, security procedures, pest control, and grounds maintenance, if applicable. Determine which utility costs are included and which excluded from your rent.
• Once you've found a place that meets your needs, lock in as low a rent as possible for as long as possible. Have written references from your employer or past landlords ready in case your landlord asks for them.
• Landlords will also require at least a month's security deposit and possibly two months' rent. In many states, landlords are required to put

that money in an escrow bank account and credit you with any interest it earns.

- If you plan on staying at least a year, insist on getting a year-long renewable lease that requires the landlord to maintain the basic facilities at an acceptable standard.
- Ask the landlord whether your lease grants you the right to sublease to another renter, and under what conditions you can get out of your lease before it officially terminates.
- If you like your apartment or rental home so much that you want to own it someday, ask the landlord whether he or she would apply some or all of your rent toward a down payment on the purchase of the property.

If You Decide to Buy

You now must determine how much house you can afford, what kind of house to buy, where you want to live, how to find the best deal, how to make an offer that is accepted, and how to finance your home with a mortgage. After you've done all of this, you must maintain the home and possibly remodel it to fit your needs.

To qualify for a home loan, you must pass certain tests that all banks will impose. If you make a 10 percent down payment on a home, banks will approve a loan only if your monthly real estate obligation—which includes mortgage principal and interest payments, real estate taxes, and homeowners insurance (and maintenance costs for a cooperative or condominium)—is 28 percent or less of your gross monthly income. In addition, all of your debt should not total more than 36 percent of your gross monthly income. Web sites like Quicken.com at <www.quicken.com> have online calculators that do this for you. Lately, some banks have been stretching these traditional limits to allow a higher percent of your income to be devoted to housing costs, but this makes both banks and homeowners nervous.

Figure 3.1 will help you determine how large a mortgage you can afford. It shows monthly payments at different interest rates and mortgage amounts. All these payments are calculated for a 30-year fixed-rate mortgage and include both principal and interest repayment. It is safe to assume that closing costs, which include points, legal fees, title searches, transfer taxes, and other charges, will amount to about 2 to 4 percent of your mortgage amount. You should deduct all of these closing costs from the cash you have available for a down payment.

Most sellers and lenders require at least a 10 percent down payment, though some will accept 5 percent. If you can make a down payment of 20 percent or more of the home's purchase price, you will not only save thousands of dollars of interest over the mortgage's life, but you also can avoid

Figure 3.1   Interest Rates

Mortgage Amount	5%	5.5%	6%	6.5%	7%	7.5%	8%	8.5%	9%	9.5%
$ 50,000	$268	$284	$300	$316	$333	$350	$367	$384	$402	$420
75,000	403	426	450	474	499	524	550	577	603	631
100,000	537	568	600	632	665	699	734	769	805	841
125,000	671	710	749	790	832	874	917	961	1006	1051
150,000	805	852	899	948	998	1049	1101	1153	1207	1261
175,000	939	994	1049	1106	1164	1224	1284	1346	1408	1471

Source: Vectra Bank Colorado.

the cost of private mortgage insurance (known as PMI). Your loan will likely be approved much more readily as well. Private mortgage insurance protects the lender if you default on your loan payments.

The down payment. Buying a home depends on your ability to put together a down payment. Here are a few suggestions:

- Borrow the money from your parents or other relatives.
- Put securities or bank deposits in escrow to act as your down payment. With the Merrill Lynch Mortgage 100 program (866-275-6522; http://askmerrill.ml.com), if you place 130 percent of a home's purchase price (the extra is a cushion against market fluctuations) in escrow in the form of stocks, bonds, mutual funds, and certificates of deposit, Merrill will lend you 100 percent of your home's purchase price. A caution: If the value of the securities pledged as collateral decreases below a certain level, you may have to deposit more or liquidate some assets.
- Take out a loan against the equity in your employer's profit sharing, thrift, or 401(k) plan, usually up to a maximum of $50,000 and repayable in up to 10 years.
- Make savings a priority by setting up an automatic saving plan with your bank, brokerage firm, or mutual fund company.
- Get a Federal Housing Administration (FHA) or Department of Veterans Affairs (VA) loan, both of which require lower or in some cases no down payments.

- Obtain private mortgage insurance with your lender, thus reducing the required amount of your down payment because your lender is now protected against your default.
- Buy a foreclosed home. Local lenders, as well as the FHA and VA, will usually accept low down payments to induce buyers to buy homes on which the lenders have foreclosed.

More tips. Here are a few other things to keep in mind when it comes to buying a home:

- Cooperatives and condominiums assess monthly fees and often must approve any buyer.
- First-time buyers should consider hiring a buyer's broker, who then works exclusively to get them the best possible deal. One excellent resource to find a buyer's broker is the Buyer's Home Finding Network at 800-500-3569 or <www.finderhome.com>.
- Whether renting or buying, as you evaluate various properties, write in a notebook the location, layout, features, and financial details of each place to help you keep track of the various properties.
- If you're buying, you will need to have the property professionally inspected. The American Society of Home Inspectors can help you locate an inspector near you (932 Lee St., Suite 101, Des Plaines, IL 60016-6546; 847-759-2820, 800-743-ASHI; www.ashi.org). There also is a free locator tool on their Web site (see Figure 3.2).
- You also will need an independent appraisal of the property. You can locate a qualified appraiser through the National Association of Master Appraisers (P.O. Box 12617, 303 W. Cypress St., San Antonio, TX 78212-0617; 800-229-6262; www.masterappraisers.org) or the Appraisal Institute (550 W. Van Buren St., Suite 1000, Chicago, IL 60607; 312-335-4100; www.appraisalinstitute.org).

Choosing the Best Mortgage

The entire process of uncovering and qualifying for a mortgage is crucial to making the most of your real estate dollar. The Internet can help in your search for the most competitive mortgage rate. The first step is to identify loan sources. The following are the most likely lenders:

- Savings and loans
- Savings banks
- Commercial banks
- Credit unions

Figure 3.2   The American Society of Home Inspectors, like many professional organizations, has a tool on its Web site to help you find a home inspector in your area.

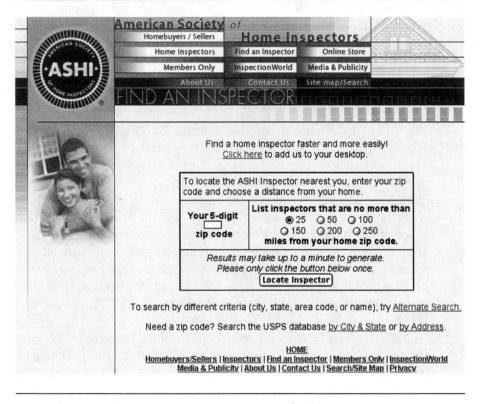

Source: Reprinted with permission from the American Society of Home Inspectors®, Inc.

- Mortgage bankers
- Mortgage brokers
- Sellers

In addition to traditional home loans, most of these lenders will make loans guaranteed by the FHA or VA. When you shop for a mortgage, compare not only the interest rate but also the closing costs (points and other fees) that can add to your total cost significantly. A few services, such as the Home Buyer's Mortgage Kit run by HSH Associates (1200 Route 23N, Butler, NJ 07405; 800-873-2837; www.hsh.com), can give you, for a small fee, a current comparison of rates and terms for lenders in your area.

The most common types of mortgages include:

- *Fixed-rate.* The traditional 30-year variety is the industry standard, because it offers long-term predictability. If you want to prepay your mortgage, make sure that you will not be assessed any prepayment penalties. Making biweekly payments on a 30-year loan will speed up your payment of the loan, though it will not be quite as fast as a 15-year mortgage.
- *Adjustable-rate (ARM).* Instead of offering an interest rate fixed for the life of the loan, an adjustable-rate mortgage features an interest rate that moves up and down with prevailing rates.
- *Automatic rate cut (ARC).* This is a variation on the adjustable-rate mortgage. The rate starts off slightly higher than current mortgage rates, but every time mortgage rates fall by a quarter point or more every 120 days, the rate automatically adjusts downwards with no closing costs, points, or fees for the borrower. The best part is that the rate never rises after it has fallen. (For more information, call 888-ARCLOAN or log on to <www.arcloan.com>.)
- *Convertible.* A convertible mortgage is an ARM that can be changed to a fixed-rate mortgage at a specified rate. This gives you the opportunity to start with a low adjustable rate and then lock in a low fixed rate for a long time.
- *Balloon.* A balloon mortgage requires a series of equal payments, then a large payment (balloon) at the loan's termination. Usually, balloon mortgages are offered at fixed rates, though some adjustable-rate balloons also are available.
- *Growing equity (GEM).* A growing equity mortgage, often known as a rapid payoff loan, offers a fixed rate and a changing monthly payment. Formally, the loan is for 30 years but may be paid off in 15 years or less because your payments reduce the outstanding principal quickly.
- *Shared appreciation (SAM).* With this loan, you pay a below-market interest rate on your mortgage and, in return, offer the lender between 30 and 50 percent of the appreciation, or increased value of your home, when you sell it in a specified number of years. If that day comes and you do not want to sell, you must pay the lender its share of the property's appreciation.
- *Buy-down.* If you buy a home from a developer, it may offer a buy-down, or mortgage subsidy, to help you afford the property.

Refinancing a Mortgage

It generally can pay off to refinance a mortgage if the difference between your loan rate and a newer loan is one percentage point or less, depending on closing costs and how long you plan to stay in your home. A good way to determine whether refinancing makes sense and what refinancing options are best for you is to analyze your situation using calculators available on numerous Web sites, including Quicken's Mortgage Tools at <http://quickenloans.quicken.com/>.

Reverse Mortgages

Another way to tap the equity in your home, particularly if you are retired and own your home free and clear, is to assume a *reverse mortgage.* Instead of borrowing against your equity and paying interest, you contract with a bank to convert some of your home equity to cash while you retain ownership. These are called reverse mortgages, because the bank makes payments to you, which is the opposite of traditional mortgages. You can use the money for anything you want, though it is prudent to use it for living expenses such as taxes, insurance, heat, or food.

With a reverse mortgage, you can take your proceeds in a lump sum, in monthly checks, or through a line of credit you can tap whenever you want. The amount you can borrow depends on your age, the value of the equity in your home, and the interest rate charged by the lender. Some loans charge a fixed rate of interest, while others charge a variable rate. The reverse mortgage comes due when you die, sell the home, or move permanently. At that point, you or your heirs must pay off the loan, or the bank will take title to your home.

All payments you receive from a reverse mortgage (technically, they are loan advances) are considered nontaxable income. Therefore, they do not lower your Social Security or Medicare benefits. On the other hand, the interest you pay on reverse mortgages is not tax deductible until you pay off all or part of your total reverse mortgage debt.

A related technique to tap your home's equity when you retire is to assume a reverse annuity mortgage (RAM). With this plan, you use the proceeds generated by a mortgage on your home to buy an annuity from an insurance company. The insurer pays the interest on your mortgage and sends the rest of the money to you in monthly installments. Upon your death, the insurer usually sells your home and repays the mortgage balance. Remaining funds are passed on to your heirs through your estate.

For more information on reverse mortgages, contact the National Center for Home Equity Conversion (360 N. Robert, Suite 403, St. Paul, MN 55101; 651-222-6775; www.reverse.org). It publishes several books on the topic, including *Home-Made Money,* which you can get for free by calling 800-209-8085 or by going to <www.aarp.org/revmort>.

Selling Your Home

When the time comes to sell your home, you must do just as much homework as you did when you bought the property. Here are a few tips:

- Before you show your home, make sure it is in tip-top shape. Add a fresh coat of paint. Locate plants and flowers strategically. Mow the lawn. Spruce up the exterior. Clean every room thoroughly. Remove excess clutter and furniture to maximize the appearance of living space.
- Distribute a one-page fact sheet listing your home's selling points and illustrating the layout. If you're located in an active real estate market, you might be able to sell within a few weeks.
- Many states require you to disclose all of your home's problems in writing to prospective buyers. If the buyer signs this sales disclosure form acknowledging that he or she has been informed of the home's problems, the buyer has little right to sue you later if any problems crop up.

Investment Real Estate

Investing in real estate for profit is tricky and can take a great deal of time and expertise. When seeking advice about it, make sure that you know who to listen to. The field is rife with self-promoters promising instant riches for no money down. Their so-called seminars are, in fact, high-pressure sales pitches.

If you wish to invest legitimately in real estate, you have several principal ways to do so: real estate mutual funds, real estate investment trusts (REITs), real estate limited partnerships, rental real estate, vacation homes, and raw land. Timeshares, often sold as real estate investments, are in fact not investments at all. When you purchase a timeshare, you own a specific block of time at a particular place, and your timeshare units are not liquid. Also be careful about buying raw land. It is usually difficult to sell, and unless you rent the land to someone, the property produces no income. Meanwhile, you incur expenses, such as maintenance and property taxes.

For an in-depth look at real estate, see *Everyone's Money Book on Real Estate.*

CAR/VEHICLE PURCHASES

Depending on how you use a car and how long you keep it, there are different financial strategies to consider in obtaining a vehicle. You might compare leasing versus buying. (Completing the worksheets in Figures 3.3 and 3.4 can help you from a financial standpoint.) You should also weigh the merits of buying a new versus a used car.

Figure 3.3   Leasing Costs Worksheet

	Leasing Costs
Security Deposit	$
First Lease Payment	
Last Lease Payment	
Monthly Lease Payment	
Down Payment	
Sales Taxes	
Registration Fees	
Title Fees	
License Fees	
Insurance Premiums	
Dealer-Provided Maintenance Costs	
Default Charges	
Excess Mileage Charges	
Excess Wear-and-Tear Charges	
Final Disposition Charges	
Balloon Payments	
TOTAL LEASING COSTS	$

The Web is a good place to start. Dozens of sites offer information on the cost or value of all kinds of vehicles, financing options, insurance, warranties, and more. Some, like <www.edmunds.com>, even link you to dealerships selling the vehicle of your choice. Some ways to find sites include typing "car" into a search engine like Google.com or clicking on the "auto" link on America Online or Yahoo! More resources also are at the end of this chapter. Many sites disclose the wholesale cost for a particular car, but this does not necessarily represent the actual cost to the dealer because of dealer incentives, holdbacks, and bonuses.

The process of buying a car involves two separate but related steps: (1) determining your transportation needs and the vehicle that best suits them, and (2) then figuring out how to pay for the car, whether dealer or bank financing, leasing, or paying cash.

Determining Your Needs

Before you visit a dealer's showroom or look at car reviews in magazines, carefully evaluate your transportation needs. By writing down the fea-

Figure 3.4   Car Loan Worksheet

	Car Loan Costs
Down Payment	$ _____
Monthly Interest Costs	_____
Sales Taxes	_____
License Fees	_____
Registration Fees	_____
Insurance Premiums	_____
Estimated Maintenance Charges	_____
Trade-in Allowances	_____
TOTAL CAR LOAN COSTS	$ _____

tures you want in a car and how much you are willing to spend, you can avoid making a hasty decision you will regret later. Also, don't forget to consider the safety of the neighborhoods where you will park the car. (If the vehicle will not be in a garage and may be parked in a high crime area, you may want special antitheft devices or perhaps a less expensive car.) You may also want to consider how much you can afford to spend annually for gasoline. (Check out the Department of Energy's Web site on fuel economy for various vehicles at <www.fueleconomy.gov>.)

Finding and Making a Deal

After you know what you want in a car, to further narrow your options set a general target price or price range, such as under $10,000, $10,000 to $15,000, $25,000 to $30,000, and so on. Then consult magazines like *Motor Trend, Consumer Reports,* and *Car and Driver* to learn what they say about the models that interest you. Again, don't overlook the Internet. But a word of caution: What you read online may differ from reality. A dealer may list a vehicle's mileage, for example, but in reality it may be substantially higher. So proceed carefully.

For a complete, unbiased write-up of all cars, consult the April auto issue of *Consumer Reports* or its *New Car Buying Guide* (Consumer Reports Books, P.O. Box 10637, Des Moines, IA 50336; 515-237-4903; 800-500-9760). The Web site <www.consumerreports.org> also has plentiful, objective information on their test results. For free data on injury records and collision and theft loss by make and model, contact the Highway Loss Data Institute (1005 N. Glebe Rd., Suite 800, Arlington, VA 22201; 703-247-1600; www.highwaysafety.org).

Once you've selected a few cars, test-drive them. Try the car on different roads, check the radio's reception, and notice how well the car blocks out street noise. You also may want to bring a heavy coat to be sure the car still is comfortable when you are wearing it. If you fall in love with the car, swoon in private and you will save a lot of money.

Be sure to ask about the car's warranty coverage. Think twice about an extended warranty or service contract. Most are not good deals, can be quite expensive, contain many exclusions, and require a deductible each time you bring in your car for repair.

To get the best price, start by knowing the dealer's cost from organizations like CarBargains and LeaseWise at <www.checkbook.org>, or from Consumer Reports Auto Price Service (101 Truman Ave., Yonkers, NY 10703; 800-203-5454; www.consumerreports.org). You should bargain from the dealer's cost upward, not the sticker price downward. Typically, the dealer will settle for a profit margin from 3 to 7 percent more than the dealer's cost if the car is not in great demand. That might amount to $200 to $500 more than the dealer paid. The suggested retail price might build in a profit margin as high as 12 percent. Even if you opt for a "no-haggle" dealership, there's room to negotiate with the price of your trade-in.

If you hate to haggle, you might consider an auto broker or a buyer's service to obtain a good price. You can locate them through the Yellow Pages or national groups like Nationwide Auto Brokers (29623 Northwestern Highway, Southfield, MI 48034; 800-521-7257, 248-354-3400; www.nationwide-auto.com), the American Automobile Association (check your local phone book or visit their Web site, www.aaa.com), or CarQ: Your New Car Source (P.O. Box 513, Kentfield, CA 94914-3123; 800-517-2277; www.carQ.com).

When negotiating to buy a new car, limit the conversation to the car's price until you agree on a deal. Do not discuss trade-in allowances for your existing car, rebates, or financing options until the price is firm. To get an idea of your trade-in's value, a few sources are the National Automobile Dealers Association's *N.A.D.A. Official Used Car Guide, Retail Edition,* published quarterly (NADA, 8400 Westpark Dr., McLean, VA 22102; 800-248-6232); *Edmund's Used Car Prices,* available on most newsstands or free at <www.edmunds.com>; or *The Kelley Blue Book Used Car Guide, Consumer Edition, Used Car and Truck Retail Values,* available at most bookstores or free at <www.kbb.com>.

Most of the advice about buying a new car also pertains to buying a used car. When you've located a car that interests you, examine it yourself or have a mechanic you trust examine it, test drive it, and then bargain with the seller as you would with the salesperson at a new-car dealership.

Financing a Vehicle

The monthly loan payment includes loan fees, the fee the lender paid to obtain your credit report, and charges for credit life insurance. Credit life insurance will pay off the auto loan for you if you die with a balance. Most financial advisors recommend against credit life coverage, because it is very expensive and your regular life insurance should pay your bills if you die prematurely.

When shopping for the best loan, here are some things to consider:

- Look at the annual percentage rate (APR), the interest rate you pay each year on that unpaid loan balance.
- How much of a down payment is required? Most lenders ask for 10 to 20 percent of the value of the car.
- Dealers generally offer financing through the captive finance arm of the automaker, but those interest rates usually are higher than those available at local banks or credit unions.
- If a company offers 0 percent financing, beware of any strings attached, such as you must pay a higher price for the car than if you financed it through another source or paid cash.

To find low loan rates, consult Bank Rate Inc. (11811 U.S. Highway 1, Suite 101, North Palm Beach, FL 33408; 800-243-7720; www.bankrate .com). Also consider insurance companies as a loan source. Many auto insurance companies offer attractive rates, and most life insurance companies provide loans on the cash value in your policy.

When deciding on a financing package, determine how much you can afford to pay each month. One way to lower your monthly payment is to increase your down payment or opt for a longer loan term.

The Leasing Option

Leasing contracts can be tricky, but you often come out ahead by leasing instead of financing a car. There are two kinds of leases. The first is a closed-end lease, which also is called a walk-away lease. It allows you to return the car in good condition when the agreement expires, and as long as the mileage is within the amount allotted, you can walk away without further expense. (If you go over the mileage, however, you can get hit with penalties of around $0.15 a mile.)

The other type of lease is an open-end one that usually gives the leasing company the right to sell the car when the lease expires if you don't want to buy the vehicle yourself. According to most leases, if the company receives less than the residual value for the car, you must make up the difference. If the car's value is equal to or greater than the residual value, you owe nothing. Depending on your contract, you may even receive a refund if the appraisal value is considerably more than the residual value.

CREDIT MANAGEMENT/DEBT PLANNING

There are times in your life when it makes sense to borrow and other times when it is better to pay off debt. A young couple buying and furnishing their first home should expect to borrow to cover these enormous costs, while someone nearing retirement should already have his or her mortgage paid off (in an ideal world) and have as little debt as possible. When you do borrow, you must decide among various repayment alternatives in order to pay the lowest interest and still provide yourself with repayment flexibility. Think of interest as rent on money that you borrow from a lender, whether that lender is a bank, credit union, savings and loan, or retail store.

Categories of Credit

The two basic categories are open-end or revolving credit, in which required monthly payments are less than the total amount due, and closed-end credit, which provides a fixed amount of money to finance a specific purchase for a specific period of time.

Open-end credit. When shopping for this kind of credit, compare the following elements of one loan to another:

- *Annual percentage rate (APR).* Some lenders charge a fixed APR, while others levy a finance charge that rises and falls based on the movement of an underlying index like the prime rate.
- *Finance charge calculations.* Lenders use varying methods to determine your *average daily balance* on which finance charges are calculated. Look for one that calculates the balance based on the current billing cycle and that excludes new purchases.
- *Grace period.* This is the amount of time a lender allows before charging interest on the loan, which is typically 20 to 25 days.
- *Annual fees.* Generally, the lower the interest rate, the higher the fee. Check online at Bank Rate Inc. at <www.bankrate.com> or CardWeb at <www.cardweb.com> and its affiliate CardTrak at <www.cardtrak .com> for a few of the no-fee cards.
- *Minimum payment.* Depending on your credit record and the lender's policy, the minimum amount you must pay each month will vary.
- *Late fees.* Most lenders charge a set fee of $10 to $20, but watch out for those that nick you for lots more.

Figure 3.5   Time Is Money: Time and Interest to Pay Off $1,000 Card Balance

	Rate	Time	Lifetime Interest Paid
Making minimum	12%	11.5 yrs	$ 696
monthly payments	15	14.3	1,122
of 2% ($20)	18	19.25	1,931
Doubling payments	12%	6.25 yrs	$ 289
to 4% per month	15	6.7	392
	18	7.25	515

Source: Oppenheimer Funds <www.oppenheimerfunds.com>.

- *Transaction fees.* Some banks charge pesky little fees every time you make a purchase or get a cash advance. Those fees, though small, can add up quickly.

For a list of all the best credit card rates, lowest fees and interest rates, and most generous rebates and rewards programs, obtain a Credit Card Optimizer Kit at 877-666-6399 for $5.95.

Closed-end credit. Like their open-end counterparts, these lenders must disclose every loan's APR and finance charge in accordance with the Truth-in-Lending Act, as well as any other fees like appraisal fees, service charges, credit insurance premiums, and processing fees.

Closed-end loans can have either fixed or variable interest rates. If you are considering a variable-rate loan, be careful if the index to which the adjustable-rate loan is tied is particularly volatile like the prime rate or yields on Treasury bills. You could expose yourself to far more risk than if it is tied to the average mortgage rate or long-term Treasury bonds. Also, the less frequently the loan rate can change, the less risk you assume. Finally, consider whether you could afford the adjustable-rate loan if it soars to its lifetime cap. If that level would drain your income or savings, a variable-rate loan probably isn't a good idea.

Secured versus Unsecured Credit

A secured loan is backed by a particular asset—known as collateral—that the lender can seize, or repossess, if you stop payments on your loan. Secured credit cards also are available. You deposit a certain amount of cash with a credit card issuer in return for a credit line of the same size. For instance, you might deposit $1,000 with a bank to qualify for a $1,000 credit line. If you don't yet have any credit cards or have had past credit problems, this is one way to re-establish a good credit history. Check out CardWeb .com/CardTrak (800-344-7714; www.cardtrak.com) for a good deal. Unsecured credit generally offers a lower interest rate and does not require that a specific asset be pledged.

Truth-in-Lending Rules

No matter what kind of credit you pursue, the federal Truth-in-Lending Act requires that lenders provide certain information so that you can compare one loan to another. A few of the facts lenders must provide include:

- Company providing the loan or credit line
- Size of the loan or credit line in dollars
- Finance charge in dollars and as an APR
- Expected repayment schedule
- Annual fees
- Grace period, if any
- Prepayment penalties, if any, and how they are calculated
- Late payment feeds, if any, and how they are calculated

Types of Loans

Here are a few of the most common forms a loan will take.

Credit card. When you select a provider, look not only at the interest rates and fees, if any, but also at benefits and services. Also, don't confuse a credit card with a debit card. The latter is accepted by merchants just like a credit card, but the amount you're spending is immediately withdrawn from your bank checking account.

Home equity loans. In effect, a home equity loan is a second mortgage on your home. You usually get a line of credit up to 70 or 80 percent of the appraised value of your home, minus whatever you still owe on your first mortgage. You will qualify for a loan not only on the value of your home but also on your creditworthiness. If you opt to finance a car purchase this way, remember that your house is on the line if you can't pay the money back.

Installment loans. Usually these loans are designed to help pay for a particular item with a set number of payments over a specified period of time. Compare terms and rates available from the product's manufacturer or the retailer selling the product against a loan from a local bank, credit union, or savings and loan. Often such a lender offers better rates than the manufacturer or retailer. Installment loan contracts must state whether there is a penalty for early payoff of the loan.

Life insurance loans. If you have built up cash value in your life insurance policy, you may consider borrowing against that asset. Insurance companies will lend cash up to the full cash value of your policy at a below-market interest rate, and depending on circumstances, it could end up being interest-free.

Margin loans. Borrowing against the value of your stocks, bonds, mutual funds, and other securities held by your broker can save you thousands of dollars in interest costs. In the early 2000s, margin loans typically charged about 6 to 8 percent versus the 10 to 20 percent charged on installment and credit card debt. But if the market value of your securities goes down, you may have to put up more cash to compensate, or the lender will sell your securities to meet the margin call.

Mortgage loans. These are secured loans, allowing the lender to repossess your home if you fail to meet your payments. Most mortgages require that you invest a certain amount of money as a down payment. The lender then calculates how much of your gross income the monthly payments will absorb. (For more on mortgages, see the real estate section in this chapter.)

Retirement plan loans. If you have built up equity in a retirement plan, such as a 401(k) salary reduction plan, a Keogh account, or an individual retirement account (IRA), you may be able to borrow at attractive rates as long as you follow certain rules.

IRS rules on rollovers enable you to withdraw from your Keogh or IRA without penalty for up to 60 days once a year. If you miss the deadline, though, you owe taxes on the money plus a 10 percent penalty.

Service loans. Though you may not think of it as credit, you receive many interest-free loans each month to pay for services like utilities or doctor bills. To smooth out your monthly payments, many utilities offer a level-payment plan in which you remit the same amount each month over a year's time.

Qualifying for and Building Credit

When lenders size you up to determine how much credit, if any, to grant you, they count on the three Cs:

1. *Character.* How responsibly will you handle your credit obligations?
2. *Capacity.* What is your financial ability to assume a certain amount of debt?
3. *Capital.* What financial assets are at your disposal to pay off debts?

If any or all three aspects of your credit are lacking, it's still possible to improve your credit record. Start by applying for a department store or gasoline company credit card—both of which are relatively easy to qualify for—and then pay your bills on time. Take out a secured credit card by depositing

Figure 3.6   Equifax Sample Credit File

How to Read Your Credit File

Please address all future correspondence to: Credit Reporting Agency
Business Address
City, State 00000

SAMPLE CREDIT FILE

This section includes your name, current and previous addresses and other identifying information reported by creditors.

Personal Identification Information

Your Name   Social Security #:   123-45-6789
123 Current Address   Date of Birth: April 10th, 1940
City, State 00000

Previous Address(es)
456 Former Rd. Atlanta, GA 30000
P.O. Box XXXX Savannah, GA 40000

Last Reported Employment: Engineer, Highway Planning

This section includes public record items obtained from local, state and federal courts.

Public Record Information

Lien Filed 03/93; Fulton CTY; Case or Other ID Number-32114; Amount-$26667; Class-State; Released 07/93; Verified 07/93

Bankruptcy Filed 12/92; Northern District Ct; Case or Other ID Number-673HC12; Liabilities-$15787; Personal; Individual; Discharged; Assets-$780

Satisfied Judgment Filed 07/94; Fulton CTY; Case or Other ID Number-898872; Defendant-Consumer; Amount-$8984; Plaintiff-ABC Real Estate; Satisfied 03/95; Verified 05/95

This section includes accounts that creditors have turned over to a collection agency.

Collection Agency Account Information

Pro Coll (800) xxx-xxxx

Collection Reported 05/96; Assigned 09/93 to Pro Coll (800) XXX-XXXX Client - ABC Hospital; Amount-$978; Unpaid; Balance $978; Date of Last Activity 09/93; Individual Account; Account Number 787652JC

This section contains both open and closed accounts.

[1] The credit grantor reporting the information.
[2] The account number reported by the credit grantor.
[3] See explanation below.
[4] The month and year the credit grantor opened the account.
[5] Number of months account payment history has been reported.
[6] The date of last payment, change or occurrence.
[7] Highest amount charged or the credit limit.
[8] Number of installments or monthly payment.
[9] The amount owed as of the date reported.
[10] The amount past due as of the date reported.
[11] See explanation below.
[12] Date of last account update.

Credit Account Information

Company Name	Account Number	Whose Acct	Date Opened	Months Reviewed	Date of Last Activity	High Credit	Terms	Balance	Past Due	Status	Date Reported
[1]	[2]	[3]	[4]	[5]	[6]	[7]	[8]	[9]	[10]	[11]	[12]
Department St.	32514	J	10/86	36	9/97	$950		$0		R1	10/97
Bank	1004735	A	11/86	24	5/97	$750		$0		I1	4/97
Oil Company	541125	A	6/86	12	3/97	$500		$0		O1	4/97
Auto Finance	529778	I	5/85	48	12/96	$1100	$50	$300	$200	I5	4/97

Previous Payment History: 3 Times 30 days late; 4 Times 60 days late; 2 Times 90+ days late
Previous Status: 01/97 - I2; 02/97 - I3; 03/97 - I4

This section includes a list of businesses that have received your credit file in the last 24 months.

Companies that Requested your Credit File

09/06/97	Equifax - Disclosure	08/27/97 Department Store
07/29/97	PRM Bankcard	07/03/97 AM Bankcard
04/10/97	AR Department Store	12/31/96 Equifax - Disclosure ACIS 123456789

Whose Account	*Status Type of Account*	*The following inquiries are NOT reported to businesses:*
Indicates who is responsible for the account and the type of participation you have with the account. J = Joint I = Individual U = Undesignated A = Authorized User T = Terminated M = Maker C = Co-Maker/Co-Signer B = On behalf of another person S = Shared	O = Open (entire balance due each month) R = Revolving (payment amount variable) I = Installment (fixed number of payments) *Timeliness of Payment* 0 = Approved not used; too new to rate 1 = Paid as agreed 2 = 30+ days past due 3 = 60+ days past due 4 = 90+ days past due 5 = Pays or paid 120+ days past the due date; or collection account 7 = Making regular payments under wage earner plan or similar arrangement 8 = Repossession 9 = Charged off to bad debt	**PRM** - This type of inquiry means that only your name and address were given to a credit grantor so they could offer you an application for credit. (PRM inquiries remain on file for 12 months.) **AM or AR** - These inquiries indicate a periodic review of your credit history by one of your creditors. (AM and AR inquiries remain on file for 12 months.) **EQUIFAX, ACIS or UPDATE** - These inquiries indicate Equifax's activity in response to your request for either a copy of your credit file or a request for research. **PRM, AM, AR, Equifax, ACIS, Update and INQ** - These inquiries do not appear on credit files businesses receive, only on copies provided to you.

Form 102631-8-98 USA

Source: Reprinted with permission of Equifax Inc.

money with the issuing bank, and then make several charges and pay them in a timely manner, too. Another alternative is to persuade someone to cosign your application, and then you take care of the bills responsibly.

Remember that each person has his or her own credit report and is scored separately. That's especially important for women who work in their homes. Often when there is a divorce or a husband dies, these women find they have no credit history and have trouble getting credit. So no matter what your age, if you are married be sure you have at least one credit card in your own name—not Mrs. John Smith, but Mary Smith!

Credit bureaus generate credit reports about you, typically by acquiring information from major lenders that issue credit cards as well as car loans, airline credit cards, and any liens or legal actions pending against you. (See Figure 3.6 for a sample report.) Other debts like mortgages, utilities, and medical bills normally are not reported to a credit bureau unless you miss payments over an extended period of time. Many states stipulate that you are entitled to a free credit report annually. Also, you are entitled to a report if you are denied credit because of something in your financial background. The three major credit bureaus are:

1. **Experian** (National Consumer Assistance Center, P.O. Box 2002, Allen, TX 75013; 888-397-3742; www.experian.com)
2. **Equifax** (P.O. Box 740241, Atlanta, GA 30374; 800-685-1111; www.equifax.com)
3. **Trans Union** (P.O. Box 1000, Chester, PA 19022; 800-888-4213; www.transunion.com)

You have the right to correct mistakes or dispute items on your credit report. If a credit bureau agrees to correct your record, it must notify the credit grantor requesting the report. If the credit bureau finds its report accurate, you still can write a letter (maximum 100 words), which will become part of your record. Also be careful of so-called credit repair clinics. No matter what they say, they cannot "guarantee" to get rid of persistent creditors or delete negative items in your credit report. Use the money you might spend on these clinics to repay debts.

In addition to your credit record, you should be aware that you have a credit score, which combines all of these factors into one number that lenders look at when deciding whether or not to give you credit and at what interest rate. To see both your credit record and credit score, log on to <www.guardmycredit.com>, which is the Privista Web site. It is free for 30 days, and then Privista charges a nominal fee for you to be able to monitor your credit carefully on an ongoing basis.

Problems with Billing

You have certain legal rights to correct any errors in billing on open-end loans, particularly credit card loans. To do so, you must write a letter within 60 days of the statement's postmarked date explaining the error. No investigation begins until the company receives your letter. The letter should include:

- Name, address, and credit card account number
- An explanation of the error you think has been made
- The dollar amount in dispute
- The merchant involved
- The date of the error

Send the letter certified mail, return receipt requested, to the special address for billing disputes listed on your statement. Although the creditor investigates your complaint, you do not have to pay the charges in dispute or the finance changes that accrue on that amount. However, the dollar amount in dispute still will be applied against your credit limit. The creditor has 30 days to answer your complaint and 90 days to resolve it. If the creditor finds no error, you must pay the disputed amount, including finance charges during the time of the investigation.

Managing Your Credit Wisely

The best way to establish a solid credit rating is to handle your debt obligations prudently. Assess how much debt as a percentage of your income that you can afford, and limit your borrowing to that amount. If you are young and earn a stable or growing income, your debt percentage may be as high as 30 percent, though it is preferable to keep it under 20 percent. If you are older or earn a less reliable income, try to limit your debt to about 10 percent of your income.

If you are willing to invest a little time and effort, you can "surf" your credit card balance from one issuer to another to take advantage of issuers' low introductory rates. That way, you maintain a consistently lower interest rate than if you stayed with one credit card all the time. Some words of caution, however, with regard to credit card surfing and the Internet: If you surf your balance from one card to the next, make absolutely sure that you pay at least the minimum due on time, because otherwise the rate will jump up from the low single digits to the mid-20s and the credit card company will probably not bring the rate back down. Also, make sure that you do not accumulate too much debt capacity by jumping from one card to another by closing down accounts that are paid off. When on the Internet, be careful about giving out your personal information, including credit card numbers, unless you know you are dealing with a reputable organization and that the site is secure.

If Your Debt Gets out of Hand

If you find your debts are out of control, the worst thing you can do is to ignore them. Most lenders would rather help you work out a debt repayment schedule than seize your property or send a collection agency after you. If creditors assign collection agencies to your case, you still have certain rights under the federal Fair Debt Collection Practices Act. Among those rights, collection agencies must send a written notice telling you how much you owe, to whom, and what to do if you dispute the debt. If you send an agency a letter within 30 days saying that you do not owe the debt in question, the agency cannot contact you again unless it mails you proof of the debt, such as a copy of the bill that remains unpaid. Debt collectors also cannot use techniques to collect the money that are abusive, deceptive, or unfair. (For more on your credit rights, check out the FTC's Web site <www.ftc.gov>.)

If contacting your creditors about your problem does not work, you may want to contact the Debt Relief Clearinghouse to help find a credit counselor to consolidate your debts, so you can pay them off within a few years at much lower interest rates than you could ever get on your own (67 Hunt Street, Agawam, MA 01001; 800-779-4499; www.debtreleifonline.com).

The Last Resort: Bankruptcy

Declaring bankruptcy is not a decision to be taken lightly, because it will haunt your credit record for ten years. But its main advantage is that you obtain relief from many of your debts, and depending on the laws in your state, may be able to keep some or most of your assets. You still have to continue paying alimony, taxes, child support, and student loans.

The two types of personal bankruptcy are Chapter 13, which is a way to discharge a big chunk of your debt and set up a controlled payment schedule for the rest, and Chapter 7, which requires you to turn over almost all your assets to the bankruptcy court to liquidate them to raise cash for creditors.

For more on debt planning, see *Everyone's Money Book on Credit.*

POINTS TO REMEMBER

- Renting a home may make sense if you have the discipline to take the extra money you save and invest it in securities that gain value more quickly than real estate.
- If you're short on cash for a down payment on a home, look at creative options, including putting securities in escrow or borrowing from your parents or your 401(k).
- Everyone has his or her own credit record, so no matter your age or gender, be sure you have at least one credit card in your own name.

- When it comes to your credit, don't ignore your debts, because generally lenders would rather work with you than have to repossess your property.

RESOURCES: CREDIT

Books

Nolo Press (950 Parker St., Berkeley, CA 94710; 800-992-6656; www.nolo .com). Publishes a number of self-help books including:

- *Credit Repair,* by Robin Leonard and Deanne Loonin
- *How to File for Chapter 7 Bankruptcy,* by Stephen Elias, Albin Renauer, Robin Leonard, and Kathleen Michon
- *Chapter 13 Bankruptcy: Repay Your Debts,* by Robin Leonard
- *Money Troubles: Legal Strategies to Cope with Your Debts,* by Deanne Loonin and Robin Leonard
- *Take Control of Your Student Debt,* by Robin Leonard and Deanne Loonin

Organizations

American Financial Services Association (919 18th St., NW, Suite 300, Washington, DC 20006; 202-296-5544; www.americanfinsvcs.com). The trade group for consumer finance companies; will send you the *Consumer's Almanac* for a nominal fee.

Springboard Network (P.O. Box 5438, Riverside, CA 92517; 888-462-2227; www.ncfe.org). Nonprofit organization specializing in credit counseling.

Web Sites

Financenter.com. A wealth of information on how to finance major assets like homes and cars; site allows you to compare various borrowing alternatives (800-264-5399). <www.financenter.com>

Econsumer.gov (U.S. Federal Trade Commission, CRC-240, 600 Pennsylvania Ave., NW, Washington, DC 20580; 877-382-4357; www.econsumer.gov). An international effort to gather and share cross-border e-commerce complaints from more than a dozen countries.

RESOURCES: REAL ESTATE

Books

Home Buying for Dummies by Eric Tyson and Ray Brown (Hungry Minds Inc., 919 E. Hillsdale Blvd., Suite 400, Foster City, CA 94404; 800-762-2974; www .hungryminds.com). Expert advice and insights in an easy-to-read format.

The McGraw-Hill Real Estate Handbook, by Robert Irwin (McGraw-Hill, P.O. Box 543, Blacklick, OH 43004; 800-634-3961; www.mcgraw-hill.com). A comprehensive look at almost every aspect of real estate, including financing techniques, taxes, property management, real estate brokers, and investment opportunities.

The Mortgage Kit, by Thomas Steinmetz (Dearborn Trade, 155 N. Wacker Dr., Chicago, IL 60606; 800-245-2665; www.dearborntrade.com). Explains the intricacies of many of the latest financing options in great detail.

Renter's Rights (Quick & Legal Series), by Janet Portman and Marcia Stewart (Nolo Press, 950 Parker St., Berkeley, CA 94710; 800-992-6656; www.nolo.com). Covers tenant's rights in all 50 states.

Seller Beware: Insider Secrets You Need to Know about Selling Your House— From Listing through Closing the Deal, by Robert Irwin (Dearborn Trade, 155 N. Wacker Dr., Chicago, IL 60606; 312-836-4400; 800-245-2665; www.dearborntrade .com). Tells readers how to navigate safely around the problems that can arise from an undisclosed defect in a home.

10 Steps to Home Ownership: A Workbook for First-Time Buyers, by Ilyce R. Glink (Times Business/Random House, 201 E. 50th St., New York, NY 10022; 800-800-3246). An advice book geared toward pre-buyers, those who are three months to three years away from a purchase.

Organizations

Commercial Investment Real Estate Institute (430 N. Michigan Ave., Suite 600, Chicago, IL 60611; 312-321-4460; www.ccim.com). Represents those involved in commercial and investment-oriented real estate.

Domania (1360 Soldiers Field Road, Boston, MA 02135; 617-779-8900; www.domania.com). Intended to educate homebuyers, homesellers, and homeowners by providing free online access to public real estate data and information, including property tax information.

Federal National Mortgage Association (3900 Wisconsin Ave., NW, Washington, DC 20016; 202-752-7000; www.fanniemae.com). Creates a secondary market in mortgage-backed securities; also operates Homepath.com that has calculators on its Web site.

National Association of Home Builders (1201 15th St., NW, Washington, DC 20005; 202-822-0200; 800-368-5242; www.nahb.com). Represents single-family and multifamily homebuilders, remodelers, and others associated with the home-building industry.

National Association of REALTORS® (430 N. Michigan Ave., Chicago, IL 60611; 312-329-8200; 800-874-6500; www.realtor.com). The trade group for real estate agents.

Federal Government Regulators

Department of Housing and Urban Development (451 7th St., SW, Washington, DC 20410; 202-708-1112; www.hud.gov). The main regulatory agency overseeing housing and real estate issues.

Federal Reserve Board (20th St. and C St., NW, Washington, DC 20551; 202-452-3946; www.federalreserve.gov). Oversees bank and savings and loan mortgage lending.

RESOURCES: VEHICLES

Books

Car Buyer's and Leaser's Negotiating Bible, by W. James Bragg (Random House, Order Dept., 400 Hahn Rd., Westminster, MD 21157; 800-733-3000; www .randomhouse.com). Find the real dealer cost, determine the true wholesale value of your trade-in, and negotiate by phone or fax without going to the showroom.

The Complete Car Cost Guide and *The Complete Small Truck Cost Guide* (Intellichoice, Inc., 471 Division St., Campbell, CA 95008-6922; 408-866-1400; www.intellichoice.com). Annual editions; offers a wealth of information on the cost of owning specific vehicles.

Consumer Reports New Car Buying Guide and *Consumer Reports Used Car Buying Guide,* by the editors of Consumer Reports (Consumer Reports Books, P.O. Box 10637, Des Moines, IA 50336; 800-500-9760; www.consumerreports.org). Complete car pricing information; updated every year.

The Ultimate Car Book, by Jack Gillis (HarperCollins, P.O. Box 588, Dunmore, PA 18512; 800-331-3761; www.harpercollins.com). Includes reviews, ratings (value, fuel economy, insurance costs, complaints, crash tests, maintenance, etc.), safety features, and advice on warranties, lemon laws, reducing insurance costs, etc.

Organizations

Council of Better Business Bureaus (4200 Wilson Blvd., Arlington, VA 22201; 703-276-0100; www.bbb.org). Takes complaints about local car dealers and offers brochures.

National Vehicle Leasing Association (1900 Arch St., Philadelphia, PA 19103; 212-564-3484; www.nvla.org). The trade group for automotive leasing companies.

Federal Government Regulator

Federal Trade Commission (6th St. and Pennsylvania Ave., NW, Washington, DC 20580; 202-326-2222; www.ftc.gov). Has jurisdiction over car dealers and many auto-related issues.

Web Sites

More Web sites with information on buying and selling of new and used cars include:

- Autobytel.com <www.autobytel.com>
- Cars.com <www.cars.com>
- Carfax: Vehicle History Reports <www.carfax.com>
- CarQ: Your New Car Source <www.carQ.com>
- IntelliChoice Car Center <www.intellichoice.com>
- InvoiceDealers <www.invoicedealers.com>
- MSN Carpoint <www.carpoint.com>
- National Highway Safety Administration <www.nhtsa.dot.org>
- Carprice.com <www.carprice.com>
- Carloan.com <www.carloan.com>

CHAPTER 4

Financing Your Needs
Part Two: Insurance,
Employee Benefits,
and College Financing

Certain financial events and needs inevitably occur throughout your life, and the more prepared you are for them, the easier they will be to handle when they arrive. Spending a little time today looking at what those needs are will pay off both in terms of dollars and cents and in the security it gives you to know you are well prepared to meet them. In Chapter 3, we looked at housing, cars, and credit needs. Following is a brief look at successful strategies for coping with insurance, employee benefits, and college financing.

YOUR INSURANCE NEEDS

A key part of your long-term financial plan is to make sure you, your family, and your major possessions are protected in case something disastrous happens. That means finding the right kind of auto insurance, disability coverage, liability protection, health plans, homeowners policies, and life insurance.

Before you buy a policy from an insurance company or contact one of its sales representatives, have some idea of the firm's financial condition. Some of the independent firms that rate insurance companies' financial strength include A.M. Best, Moody's Investors Service, Standard & Poor's (S&P) Corporation, and Weiss Ratings. (For contact information, see "Resources" at the end of this chapter.) Ask your state insurance department if there are any problems with the company. The National Association of Insurance Commissioners has links to state insurance commissioners (2301 McGee St. #800, Kansas City, MO 64108; 816-842-3600; www.naic.org).

You also can hire an insurance advisor who makes no commission and is paid a flat rate to help you find the right policies. To find an advisor, contact INSurance INFOrmation (Cobblestone Court #2, 23 Route 134, South Dennis, MA 02660; 800-472-5800). Another good source of free information on all kinds of insurance is the nonprofit Insurance Information Institute (110 William St., 24th Floor, New York, NY 10038; 800-331-9146; 800-942-4242/ National Insurance Consumer Hotline; www.iii.org).

The Basics

Insurance is designed to distribute the risk of adverse events among a company's policyholders. When such an event occurs, whether it is a car accident, a heart attack, or a death, the insurance company calls it a loss. When that loss affects a policyholder directly, it is known as a first-person loss. When another person sustains the loss but the policyholder is liable, it is termed a third-party loss. In return for this protection, you must pay the insurance company what is known as a premium. The company then invests those premiums in stocks, bonds, real estate, and other vehicles that provide income and capital gains to the insurance company.

The first step in selecting any insurance policy is determining how much coverage you need and what you can afford. Start by identifying your potential losses; then determine how you could cope with those losses if you did not have insurance. For example, ask yourself whether your spouse could support your children if you died unexpectedly. If the answer is no, you need life insurance to cover that risk.

Next, calculate how much you can afford to pay for insurance premiums based on the budgeting exercise in Chapter 1. Prioritize your insurance needs by the size of the potential loss. The greater the risk, the higher priority the insurance. And make sure that you are covered against catastrophic losses. Then, look into discounts insurance companies offer to slash your premiums, such as raising your deductibles or taking preventive measures to minimize the likelihood of a claim.

Auto Insurance

The first principle of car insurance is that your policy covers a specific automobile. In addition to potential damage to your car or injuries caused by your car, your policy also insures the people who drive or ride in the vehicle. By accepting higher deductibles and lower coverage limits, you can reduce your premium. But don't limit your coverage or raise your deductibles so much that the policy won't protect you when you really need it.

Your auto insurance is really several kinds of coverage combined in one policy. The primary components of coverage are:

- *Bodily injury.* This pays for injuries if you cause an accident. Most states require minimum coverage, usually $15,000 to $25,000. If you have substantial assets, you should obtain at least $100,000 per individual and $300,000 for each accident.
- *Property damage.* States generally require a minimum of $5,000 to $25,000 coverage. You should probably obtain at least $25,000 worth, because car repair costs are so high.
- *Collision.* This covers the cost of repairing your car after an accident. The older your car, the less coverage needed. Try to obtain a policy that reimburses you for replacement cost, not the book value of your car.
- *Comprehensive.* This covers losses sustained by your car other than in collisions with cars or property, such as if your windshield is broken by a thief or for alternative transportation if your car is stolen.
- *Medical payments.* This pays hospital, doctor, and even funeral expenses as a result of injuries that you and your passengers sustain in a car accident. "Med pay," as it is called, also kicks in if you or a family member is hit by a car while a pedestrian or hurt when riding in someone else's car.
- *Personal injury protection.* In states with no-fault insurance laws, personal injury protection (PIP) covers a broader assortment of medical charges, including lost wages.
- *Uninsured or underinsured motorist.* This coverage protects you if you are involved in an accident with a driver who is uninsured or severely underinsured. It also protects you if you are injured by a hit-and-run driver.

The worksheets in Figures 4.1 and 4.2 summarize the elements of auto insurance. Use them to compare premium prices between companies. When choosing among polices with different deductibles, list all the alternatives on the worksheet but choose only one when you total the premiums.

Disability Insurance

If you miss work for a short time, your employer will probably provide short-term sick leave, and you may collect benefits from some other sources. But it still probably is not enough money to live comfortably. This is where individual long-term disability insurance becomes crucial, especially if you are self-employed. If you qualify, you can receive between 50 and 80 percent of your regular salary, depending on the policy, plus cost-of-living adjustments in some policies.

Figure 4.1   Auto Insurance Pricing Worksheet

	Amount of Coverage	Company 1 Premiums	Company 2 Premiums
Bodily Injury	$_____	$_____	$_____
Property Damage	_____	_____	_____
Collision (no deductible)	_____	_____	_____
With $100 Deductible	_____	_____	_____
With $500 Deductible	_____	_____	_____
With $1,000 Deductible	_____	_____	_____
Comprehensive (no deductible)	_____	_____	_____
With $100 Deductible	_____	_____	_____
With $500 Deductible	_____	_____	_____
With $1,000 Deductible	_____	_____	_____
Medical Payments	_____	_____	_____
Personal Injury	_____	_____	_____
Uninsured or Underinsured Motorist	_____	_____	_____
TOTAL BEFORE DISCOUNTS		$_____	$_____

Figure 4.2   Auto Insurance Discount Worksheet

Discount	Company 1 Discount	Company 2 Discount
Defensive Driving Course	$ _____	$ _____
	_____ %	_____ %
Good Driving Record	$ _____	$ _____
	_____ %	_____ %
Car Pool	$ _____	$ _____
	_____ %	_____ %
Limited Annual Mileage	$ _____	$ _____
	_____ %	_____ %
Antitheft Devices	$ _____	$ _____
	_____ %	_____ %
Antilock Brakes	$ _____	$ _____
	_____ %	_____ %
Passive Restraint Systems	$ _____	$ _____
	_____ %	_____ %
Nonsmoker	$ _____	$ _____
	_____ %	_____ %
Older than Age 50	$ _____	$ _____
	_____ %	_____ %
Good School Grades	$ _____	$ _____
	_____ %	_____ %
Total Discount Savings	$ _____	$ _____
TOTAL PREMIUM BEFORE DISCOUNTS (see Figure 4.1)	$ _____	$ _____
(MINUS) **TOTAL DISCOUNT SAVINGS**	$(_____)	$(_____)
EQUALS		
NET PREMIUM	$ _____	$ _____

Many clauses in disability contracts can be crucial in determining the benefits you receive if you are injured, so read the fine print, especially as it relates to the following:

- Definition of disability
- Cause of disability
- Exclusions
- Pregnancy
- Residual benefits
- Payment amount, method of payment, beginning and payment date, and payment caps
- Renewal

Make sure the coverage you buy cannot be cancelled and that it is renewable at the original premium price, or guaranteed renewable no matter what your health is.

The worksheet in Figure 4.3 will help you total your potential sources of disability income. Fill in the monthly amount you would receive from each policy, the waiting period before benefits begin, and the number of years you would receive benefits. By completing the Disability Income Worksheet when you are not disabled, you will have a better idea of how you might cope if such a tragedy ever occurred. By adding your potential sources of disability income, you can also calculate how much private insurance you need to buy, either through your employer or on your own.

Health Insurance

With the soaring cost of medical care and the resulting pressure on health insurance premiums, it is crucial to understand your health insurance options and maximize your benefits at the least possible cost. Read the policy's fine print, especially any references to whether preexisting medical conditions are covered. You might also consider contacting a health insurance agent or broker to help you find the policy that best suits your needs, or check a Web site like Quotesmith at <www.quotesmith.com> (800-556-9393).

Here is a brief look at the most common types of disability policies:

- *Fee-for-service indemnity policy.* The most expensive, this type of policy has two plans: one that reimburses for doctors' bills, drugs, outpatient surgical procedures, and other medical expenses up to a certain annual dollar limit; and the other plan that covers major medical, extended hospital visits, and other major medical procedures. Deductibles usually apply, after which coverage is 80 percent up to an annual limit and 100 percent over the limit.

Figure 4.3 Disability Income Worksheet

Disability Insurance Program	Monthly $ Amount	Waiting Period (Months)	Benefits for How Long (Years)
Government Programs			
Black Lung	$ _____	_____	_____
Civil Service	_____	_____	_____
Department of Veterans Affairs	_____	_____	_____
Medicaid	_____	_____	_____
Social Security	_____	_____	_____
Workers' Compensation	_____	_____	_____
Group Programs			
Employer	_____	_____	_____
Sick Leave	_____	_____	_____
Union	_____	_____	_____
Individual Programs			
Auto	_____	_____	_____
Credit Disability	_____	_____	_____
Individual Disability	_____	_____	_____
Mortgage Disability	_____	_____	_____
Other (while disabled)			
Savings and Investments	_____		
Spouse's Income	_____		
Other	_____		
TOTAL MONTHLY INCOME (while disabled)	$ _____		

- *Health maintenance organization (HMO).* The least expensive option, an HMO offers unlimited access to the organization's medical services and providers at their facilities for a flat annual fee. There also could be minimal copays. But unless it is an emergency, you must choose a provider from among their providers and only go to their facilities. Some HMOs have a reputation of discouraging medical tests to keep costs in line. For an evaluation of a managed care plan you may be considering, contact the nonprofit National Committee for Quality Assurance (2000 L St., NW, Suite 500, Washington, DC 20036; 202-955-3500; 800-839-6787; <www.ncqa.org>).
- *Point of service (POS).* Many HMOs offer an indemnity-type option known as a POS plan. The primary care doctors in a POS plan usually make referrals to other providers in the plan. But members can refer themselves outside the plan and still get some coverage. If the doctor makes a referral out of the network, the plan pays all or most of the bill.
- *Preferred provider organization (PPO).* PPOs are somewhere in the middle of the two previous plans in application and costs. Copays are required. Caregivers—you choose from among a much broader group compared with an HMO—receive a set monthly fee to provide services but can earn more if more care is given. If you wish to go outside the network, the insurance company still will reimburse you for the care but at a reduced percentage rate.
- *Medicare.* For those age 65 or older, Medicare provides substantial health insurance benefits, whether you are retired or still working. When you apply for Social Security benefits, you automatically apply for Medicare. If you plan to work past age 65, you should still apply for Medicare, then learn more about what is covered and what is not. For more details, call the Social Security Administration's Medicare hotline at 800-772-1213.

More options. For even more protection, you can buy excess major medical coverage to supplement a regular major medical policy with a low lifetime limit. Excess major medical policies, often called catastrophic policies, usually have a very high deductible of about $15,000 but can be vital if you need an expensive medical procedure.

If you are a particularly bad risk because of some health problem, try your state's health insurance risk pool, which is designed to offer coverage to those considered otherwise uninsurable. As you might suspect, however, the premiums for risk pool coverage are usually extremely expensive. Other types of medical insurance include:

- Long-term care policies that cover health costs of long-term custodial care either in a nursing home or at home. For more information on getting the best long-term care policy, contact Long-Term Care Quote (600 West Ray Street D4, Chandler, AZ 85225; 800-587-3279; www .searchltc.com).
- Medicare supplemental policies, known as Medigap or MedSup plans, pick up where Medicare leaves off, covering Medicare copayments and deductibles. As long as you enroll in Medicare Part B within six months after enrolling in Medicare Part A, you cannot be rejected when you apply for a Medicare supplement policy if you are at least 65 years old.
- Medical care repricing policies. Companies such as Care Entrée (800-464-2075) offer you, the individual consumer, the same low rates for all medical procedures that have been negotiated by the large insurance companies and HMOs. This applies to doctors, hospitals, veterinarians, dentists, vision and hearing care specialists, and drug prescriptions. Unlike health insurance, there are no limitations for preexisting health conditions, and the cost is extremely reasonable—usually $55 per month per family.

COBRA. The Congressional Omnibus Budget Reconciliation Act (COBRA) gives you the right to carry your group health insurance for up to 18 months after you have left an employer. (You do not receive this benefit if you are fired for cause or due to misconduct.) You must pay the full premium for the coverage, but at group rates that are far less expensive than buying a similar policy at individual rates.

If you will need COBRA benefits, fill out the appropriate forms from your employer's benefits department. If you take no action within 60 days of leaving a company, you will be denied continued coverage.

Homeowners Insurance

The process of buying insurance to protect your home and its contents is similar in many ways to buying auto, disability, or health insurance. Once you purchase a homeowners policy, you should keep it up-to-date and reassess its coverage as your home and lifestyle change.

Property damage. The primary reason to buy homeowners insurance is to compensate you for property damage or loss either from natural occurrences like earthquakes, fire, storms, and mudslides, or from man-made or equipment-made disasters like malfunctioning equipment, arson, burglary, electrical fires, explosions, riots, vandalism, and water pipe breaks. So be sure to buy enough insurance to replace most or all property at risk. If you cannot afford the premiums on full-replacement-cost insurance, the least you should settle for is 80 percent replacement cost. Cutting back from 100 to 80 percent will slash your premiums by as much as 25 percent. However, if you settle for less than 80 percent, you expose yourself to too much financial risk.

Insurers offer two policies to cover these risks: named-peril insurance and all-risk insurance. Named-peril coverage protects you against only the specific dangers spelled out in the insurance contract. All-risk insurance, on the other hand, covers almost every possible source of loss or damage except those specifically named, such as floods, earthquake, nuclear war, dry rot, termites and insect damage, and wear and tear. Because the all-risk policy is more comprehensive, its premiums are usually higher than those on a named-peril policy covering the same property.

In addition to your regular homeowners coverage, you might want to purchase special insurance, known as a rider or a floater, for particularly valuable artwork, collectibles, silver, furs, jewelry, electronics, or other items. And if you have a home-based business, you can get needed extra insurance protection for all your equipment.

Renter's and condominium insurance. If you rent, your landlord's insurance covers the building in which you live, but you should buy a separate policy to cover your possessions. The provisions of a renter's policy are nearly identical to those of homeowners coverage. If you own valuables, such as jewelry or a computer, you probably need a floater to provide coverage beyond the typical limits. As with homeowners insurance, it is best to buy replacement cost coverage rather than a policy based on cash value. Most renter's policies also provide liability insurance if someone claims injury due to your negligence. For example, bodily injury liability pays medical costs as well as your legal defense fees, if you injure or kill someone.

Insurance for condominium owners is similar to coverage available for renters. The condominium association buys insurance that protects the buildings, grounds, and common areas, while each owner must obtain special condominium coverage for the contents of their apartments, walls that are not shared with other apartments, and other things that are not commonly owned, as well as liability claims.

Taking inventory. Keeping those general guidelines in mind, determine how much homeowners insurance you need. First, take a household inventory to see what actually needs insuring. Walk around your home and list on an inventory sheet each item you own, what you paid for it, and how much it might cost to replace. Also note model and serial numbers. If you have no idea what things cost today, you might consider bringing in an appraiser to help you. Creating a list divided by rooms in your house will help you inventory the contents of your home.

In addition to listing your household possessions, photograph or videotape each room. Keep the pictures or tape somewhere other than your home, such as at work, so you will have access to it if your house is destroyed or damaged.

Liability coverage. In addition to reimbursing you for lost or damaged property, homeowners insurance protects you and members of your household against claims and lawsuits for injuries or property damage that you or your family members may have caused accidentally. To protect against a huge jury award, purchase extra liability coverage as part of your regular policy. This is generally known as *umbrella coverage,* and it usually extends your liability insurance to $1 million or more.

Life Insurance

If your family or other people depend on your income, you need life insurance to help them live without your support if you pass away. The insurance contract requires that the insurance company pay your beneficiaries a set amount, called the death benefit, if you should die for almost any reason. (Suicide is usually excluded for the first two to three years of a policy.) Your beneficiaries can receive the money in one lump sum, free of federal income taxes.

How much is enough? Each family is different, but a rule of thumb is five to ten times your annual income. These funds should be enough to replace the insured's paycheck, cover daily living expenses, college costs, retirement needs, and pay the insured's final medical bills and burial costs. Software like Microsoft Money or Quicken or a good insurance agent can help determine how much insurance you need.

Types of life insurance. You must decide what is best based on how much coverage you need, the premium you can afford, and whether you want insurance only for its death benefit or also for its savings potential. *Term insurance* merely pays off if you die. Whole life, universal life, and variable life insurance are versions of cash-value insurance, which combine a death benefit and an investment fund that grows tax-deferred.

Consider the four basic types of coverage:

1. *Term.* An inexpensive option; hundreds of companies offer it. You can obtain price quotes from any insurance agent, many direct mail insurers, banks, or online or phone quote services such as Accu-Quote, QuoteSmith, and others described in the "Resources" section at the end of this chapter. You can buy either annual renewable term for which the premium rises each year as you grow older or level-premium, where the premium stays the same for a number of years —typically at least ten years—and then jumps to a higher level if you choose to renew.

2. *Whole life.* While term starts with low premiums that rise over time and provides you with no investment reserves, whole life policies lock you into one premium rate for life based on your age when you buy the policy and provide an investment reserve where your cash value builds up tax-deferred until you withdraw it. You can also borrow against your policy's cash value at attractive interest rates and use the proceeds for whatever you want.

3. *Universal life insurance.* Also a cash-value fund, you can pay premiums at any time and in any amount you prefer, as long as certain minimum levels are met. Also, your amount of insurance protection can be increased or decreased easily to meet your current needs. As with whole life, you can borrow up to the full amount of your cash value at favorable interest rates.

4. *Variable life insurance.* This type of cash-value policy offers you the option of investing your cash value in stock, bond, or money-market funds managed by the insurance company. It is higher risk but offers juicier return potential. As with other cash-value policies, these returns compound tax-deferred until you withdraw your principal, and you can borrow against the cash value at attractive interest rates.

Annuities. Insurance companies also sell annuities, which pay a regular stream of income while you live, usually after you retire, in contrast to life insurance, which pays your beneficiaries a lump sum when you die. Annuities also provide the advantage of tax-deferred compounding on the investment portion of the account. There are two basic types: immediate and deferred. Immediate annuities are purchased with a lump sum—typically a rollover from a 401(k) or other pension plan—and they begin to generate an income stream immediately. Deferred annuities are bought by younger people who want to save tax-deferred for many years, then convert to a payout schedule once they retire. Annuities can either be invested in fixed-income securities like bonds or guaranteed investment contracts (known as fixed annuities) or in stocks and other growth-oriented assets (known as variable annuities) that offer more growth potential at higher risk. For more detail on fees and rankings of all kinds of annuities, consult the *Annuity Shopper* newsletter (8 Talmadge Dr., Monroe TWP, NJ 08831; 800-872-6684; www.annuityshopper.com).

MAXIMIZING YOUR EMPLOYEE BENEFITS

Your package of employee benefits is crucial in putting together your personal financial plan, so don't just toss that unopened employee handbook in the drawer when you start work at a new job. First, enroll in every available retirement savings program, including profit sharing and salary reduction plans. Within the plans, allocate most of your money to growth vehicles such as stocks if you are at least ten years from retirement, because stocks have the best chance of dramatic growth over the long term. Remember that you can usually borrow against your retirement savings if necessary.

Also, investigate the health insurance options your company offers to determine which plan will cost you the least in premiums and offer you the broadest coverage. Sign up for a flexible spending account (FSA) if your company offers one and if you think that you will have enough out-of-pocket health care or day care costs that will not be covered by your regular insurance plan. An FSA can save you on taxes, because you fund it with pretax dollars from your paycheck and reimburse yourself for health expenses that otherwise would not be covered (see Figure 4.4). If you are self-employed or work for a small company that offers no retirement plan, fund a traditional or Roth individual retirement account (IRA), a Keogh, or another qualified plan. Your employee benefits or human resources department will provide written information and frequently computer-based information that explains your benefits. You must take the initiative to read, understand, and enroll in these plans.

If your company offers a cafeteria plan, it is important to order your priorities and allocate your benefit dollars in a way that best suits your situation. If you are in your 20s or 30s, are healthy, and have young children, consider shifting more of your dollars into life insurance and dependent-care programs that can help pay for child care. If you are in poor health and nearing retirement, you might allocate more of your dollars to retirement savings plans and health insurance.

Figure 4.4   Amount Saved by Funding an FSA

	Using the FSA	Not Using the FSA
Income	$45,000	$45,000
Minus FSA Deposits	– 4,500	– 0
Taxable Income	$40,500	$45,000
Minus Federal Taxes (28% Tax bracket)	– 6,833	– 7,853
Take-Home Pay	$33,667	$37,147
Minus After-Tax Expenses	– 0	– 4,500
Spendable Pay	$33,667	$32,647
Tax Savings ("Using the FSA" minus not "Using the FSA")	$ 1,020	$ 0

Source: Reprinted with permission of Hewitt Associates, Lincolnshire, IL.

Pension and Retirement Savings Programs

The most financially significant wealth creation benefit employers offer their workers are plans that allow the employees to build substantial savings for retirement.

There are two classes of programs:

1. *Defined benefit.* The more traditional model in which an employer promises to provide a specified retirement benefit called a pension, and all the money comes from and is invested by the employer.
2. *Defined contribution.* This approach can take many forms, including employee stock ownership plan, profit sharing, or salary reduction 401(k) or 403(b) plans. The employer gives workers the chance to put aside money for their retirement, often on a pretax basis, and may or may not match some or all of the workers' contributions, depending on the plan. Usually the worker has to make investment choices between various stock, bond, and money-market funds, making them responsible for the outcome instead of the employer.

Defined benefit vesting rules. To qualify for defined pension benefits, you must work at a company long enough to become vested. Being vested means having enough years of service to give you the legal right to receive

---

Figure 4.5   Tax Savings from a Salary Reduction Plan

	With a Salary Reduction Plan	On Your Own
Annual Pay	$40,000	$40,000
Minus pretax investment	− 2,400	− 0
Taxable pay	$37,600	$40,000
Minus federal income tax (based on 28% tax bracket)	− 9,021	− 9,693
Take-home pay	$28,579	$30,307
Minus after-tax investment	− 0	− 2,400
Take-home pay (including investment)	$28,579	$27,907
Taxes saved ($28,579 − $27,907)	$ 672	$ 0
Plus company match (at 30% of $2,400)	+ 720	0
TOTAL SAVINGS	**$ 1,392**	**$ 0**

Source: Reprinted with permission of Hewitt Associates, Lincolnshire, IL.

some or all of your benefits when you reach retirement age, even if you no longer work for that employer.

Determining your payment. Most employers use one of three ways to determine your monthly pension benefit:

1. *Flat benefit formula plans* pay a flat dollar amount each month at retirement. The more years you worked at a company, the higher the monthly payment.
2. *Career-average formula plans* average the income you earned over your entire career at a company to determine your monthly payment. In some cases, you receive a percentage of your pay for every year you participated in the pension plan.
3. *Final-pay formula plans,* which generally produce the highest monthly payments, average your income for your last few years (typically five) at a company, when you probably earned your peak salary. Once you retire, you receive a payment based on a percentage of these average earnings multiplied by the number of years you worked at the firm.

Your retirement benefit is determined by one of these formulas and by your age when you retire. In general, the later you retire, the higher your monthly payment.

Method of payment. You have several options on how to receive the money at retirement. Normally, you must decide between an annuity, which pays a specific monthly sum for a particular period of time, and a lump sum, which pays you all the cash at once for you to invest on your own.

There are several types of annuities:

- *Ten-year term certain annuity,* which pays you a fixed amount for ten years and then stops. This is a risky choice, because you likely will live more than ten years after retirement.
- *Life annuity with ten-year term certain* pays a fixed monthly amount for the rest of your life. If you die before the annuity has paid you benefits for ten years, your beneficiary will receive your payments only for the remainder of the original ten years.
- *Joint and survivor annuity* can be a good idea if you are married or if someone depends on your income. This pays a fixed amount until both you and your spouse or dependent die. When you die, your spouse or dependent receives qualified joint and survivor annuity (QJSA) payments until he or she dies.
- *Lump sum* payouts can be rolled over into a tax-deferred account like an individual retirement account (IRA) or a Keogh account within 60

days, so that capital gains, dividends, and interest continue to compound tax-deferred until you begin withdrawing the money.

When a company goes bankrupt with an underfunded pension plan, a government agency—the Pension Benefit Guaranty Corporation (PBGC)—comes to the rescue. It is a guarantee fund, similar to the Federal Deposit Insurance Corporation (FDIC) for bank depositors, that guarantees basic benefits, including the monthly pension check, some early retirement and disability benefits, and some benefits for survivors of deceased beneficiaries. For more on how this agency can protect your pension payments, contact them at Pension Benefit Guaranty Corporation, 1200 K St., NW, Washington, DC 20005-4026; 202-326-4000; 800-400-7242; www.pbgc.gov.

Defined contribution pension plans. Several types of defined contribution plans exist. Following is a look at a few of the most common types:

- *Employee stock ownership plan.* The firm's and your contributions are invested in company stock, which gives you and other employees more incentive to work diligently and make the company prosper. Be careful with this option. You could end up with nothing if your company falters.
- *Money-purchase pension plan.* Your employer is obligated to contribute a set amount of your salary to the plan each year, no matter whether profits are up or down. When you retire from the company, your monthly benefit payment is based on the amount that has accumulated in the plan.
- *Profit-sharing plan.* Your company contributes a certain percentage of your salary to the plan each year, depending on the firm's profits. This may amount to as much as 15 percent to 20 percent of your income in an extremely profitable year or as little as nothing if the company lost money.
- *Salary reduction plan.* A salary reduction plan allows you to defer a certain percentage of your salary to a tax-deferred account in which you pick the investment allocation. When offered to employees of a corporation, the plan is called a 401(k); at a nonprofit organization it is a 403(b) plan; and for government workers it is a 457 thrift plan. These extremely popular programs, also known as CODAs (cash-or-deferred arrangements), allow you to contribute pretax dollars to a plan, and in many cases, your contribution is matched in whole or in part by the employer.
- *Stock bonus plan.* Such a plan is similar to a profit-sharing plan in that bonuses are given at the board's discretion when the company's prof-

its are high. When you retire under a stock bonus plan, however, your benefits are paid in stock rather than cash.

- *Thrift savings plan.* With a thrift savings plan, you as an employee can contribute a certain percentage of your salary (up to about 10 percent) on an after-tax basis to the plan.

Vesting rules. With a defined contribution plan, the amount of cash you invest is immediately vested, and you cannot lose it if you leave the company. You may lose some or all of the company's matching contributions if you leave the company, however.

Allocating your assets. Because your assets within a defined contribution plan grow tax-deferred, make maximum use of the tax shelter. It probably makes more sense to buy bonds, which pay taxable interest, in a defined contribution plan, where that interest compounds tax-deferred. Or you might invest in growth and income stocks so taxable dividends can be reinvested tax-deferred. When you buy growth stocks outside one of these tax-sheltered plans, you pay tax only when you sell shares for a capital gain. Therefore, if you hold onto stocks that pay little or no dividends for years, you do not need the tax shelter offered by the defined contribution plan. When deciding your asset allocation formula, factor in your risk tolerance level as determined in the Risk Tolerance Quiz in Chapter 1.

Payout options. Once you reach retirement age, you have three options as to how to collect your defined contribution benefits:

1. Take your money as a lump sum, known as a *cash out,* and roll the proceeds into another tax-deferred account like a rollover IRA.
2. Keep your funds in the defined contribution plan (though you cannot make further contributions).
3. Buy an annuity with the defined contribution plan assets.

Employees of Small Companies and the Self-Employed

If you run or work for a small business or if you are self-employed, you have three options for which contribution limits often change annually:

1. *Simplified employee pension (SEP) plan.* This is a simpler, small-company version of the defined contribution plan offered by larger employers. The IRS limits the total annual contribution to $40,000, or just over 13 percent of annual earnings for the self-employed (15 percent for employees).
2. *SIMPLE plans.* SIMPLE stands for Savings Incentive Match Plan for Employees. They can be set up as SIMPLE 401(k)s or SIMPLE IRAs,

and are allowed for companies with no more than 100 employees earning at least $5,000 a year. If a company offers the SIMPLE plan, it cannot offer other qualified retirement plans to its workers. The most that workers can contribute annually to a SIMPLE plan is $7,000.

3. *Keogh plans.* If you are self-employed on a full-time basis, or even if you earn extra income through freelance work, you can set up a Keogh retirement plan. It is the most complicated of the three types of plans, must be established before for the end of a tax year, and usually involves more than one person. The maximum contribution if you are self-employed is just over 13 percent of your AGI.

Even if you have other retirement plans, consider opening an IRA. The contribution may or may not be tax-deductible—the IRS rules are complex—but your earnings still will grow tax-deferred inside the IRA account. Even better is the Roth IRA, in which earnings compound completely tax-free as long as you keep the assets in the account for at least five years.

Health and Wellness Benefits

The benefits of good health coverage pay you back today and tomorrow. (See Chapter 3 for more on health care needs.) Some possible health/wellness benefits from employers include:

- Medical savings accounts (MSAs) that allow employees to put aside money out of their paychecks on a pretax basis to be used to pay health expenses or health insurance premiums (For more on MSAs, contact the Employers Council on Flexible Compensation, 927 15th St., NW, Suite 1000, Washington, DC 20005; 202-659-4300, 888-353-9672; www.ecfc.org.)
- Dependent care and child care benefits, including referral services
- Flextime that allows you to work hours that accommodate your child care responsibilities.
- Parental leave in accordance with the Family and Medical Leave Act (FMLA) of 1993 that grants you a maximum of 12 weeks for a new child, whether the child is natural, adopted, or in foster care.
- Adoption assistance of up to $2,000 to help cover the myriad costs of adopting a child.
- Employee assistance programs that include counseling on substance abuse, mental health and emotional issues, money, and legal problems.
- Education assistance in the form of tuition reimbursements.
- Access to legal services at substantial discounts
- Company-sponsored insurance programs that offer various types of insurance at cheaper group rates

FINANCING COLLEGE AND CONTINUING EDUCATION

College costs so much these days that many parents consider paying for it an almost unattainable goal. But don't despair. There are steps you can take today that promise you will be able to accumulate at least a good part of the money needed. It takes discipline, advance planning, and long-term saving, as well as an understanding of the qualifications for various kinds of student loan programs and scholarships. There literally are tens of thousands of scholarships available. The Internet is one of the best tools available to help find some of that free money for education.

Estimating the Costs

Start by projecting the estimated amount of money you will need. Even if your child is a toddler, consider whether he or she is more likely to attend a public university either in the state where you live or out-of-state, or a private university, and whether graduate school might be an option. Then check out college Web sites and other online sources to get a better idea of the cost. Sites like College Board in Figure 4.6 provide up-to-date numbers and even have online calculators to help you figure your needs (45 Columbus Ave., New York, NY 10023; 212-713-8000; www.collegeboard.com). The worksheet in Figure 4.7 will also help you estimate realistically how much you will need to accumulate to finance college and how much you will need to save to reach that goal.

Tax laws regarding education loans and deductions change constantly, so check with your tax specialist or the IRS at <www.irs.gov> for the most up-to-date regulations. A good source for information on the various savings plans is the College Savings Plans Network (877-277-6496; www.collegesavings.org) from the National Association of State Treasurers (P.O. Box 11910, Lexington, KY 40578; 859-244-8175; www.nast.net).

To give you an idea of how much money you will accumulate if you save $100 a month, see Figure 4.8. Find the number of years until your child enrolls in college in the left column. Across the top, you can see how your money will compound at different after-tax rates of return. If you save more than $100 a month, multiply these numbers by the appropriate multiple of $100. For example, if you save $400 a month, multiply these numbers by four.

Investing to Pay College Bills

Your college portfolio should be balanced among high-, medium-, and low-risk investments. As the tuition bills draw closer, you should be taking less risk, so that ideally all the money you need will be sitting in your money-

Figure 4.6 The College Board's Web site has a wealth of information on scholarship and college financing.

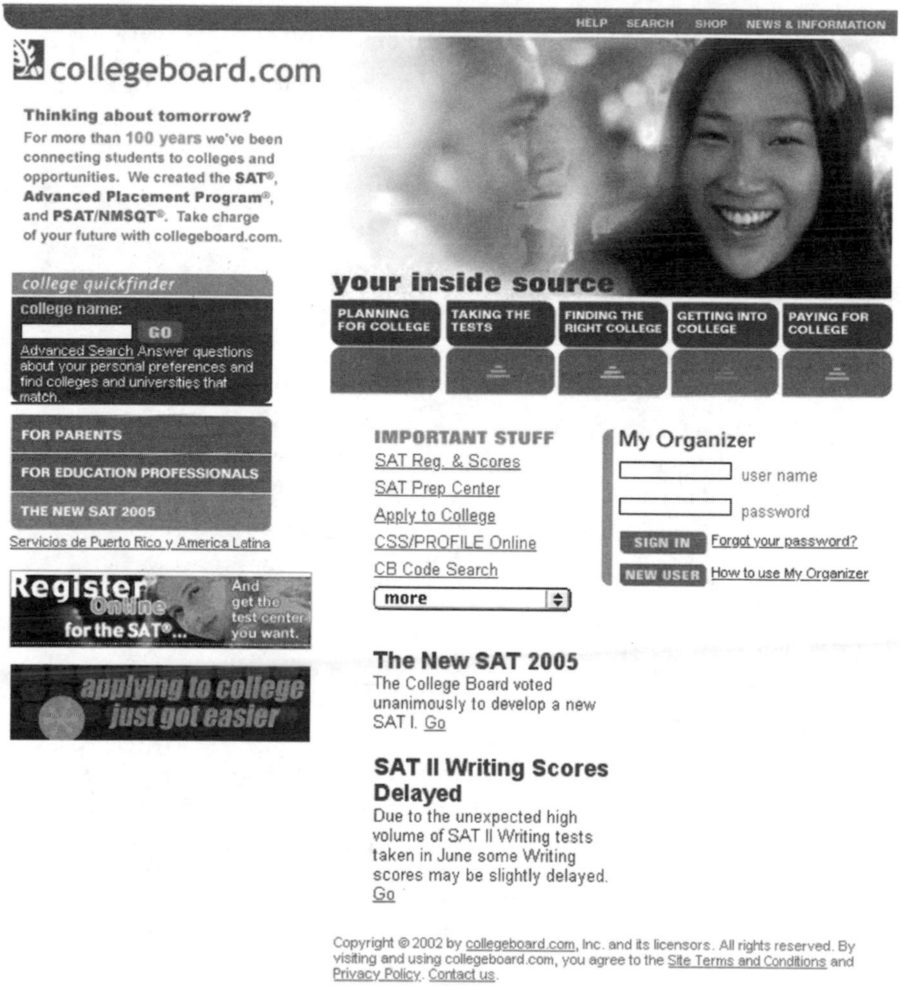

Source: Copyright © 2002 by collegeboard.com, Inc. Reprinted with permission. All rights reserved. www.collegeboard.com

Figure 4.7   College Costs and Savings Needs Worksheet

	Example (Assumes 7% Return)	Your Child
1. Current Annual College Costs	$10,000	$_____
2. Age of Your Child	6	_____
3. Future Cost of First Year of College (Multiply item 1, above, by number in column A next to your child's age, below.)	$22,520	$_____
4. Total Cost of Four Years of College (Amount needed at the beginning of college. Multiply item 3 by 3.624.)	$81,626	$_____
5. Amount You Must Save/Invest Each Year (Multiply item 4 by number in column B next to your child's age.)	$ 4,563	$_____
6. Amount You Must Save/Invest Each Month (Divide item 5 by 12.)	$ 380	$_____

Age of Child	A	B
Newborn	3.380	0.0294
1	3.159	0.0324
2	2.952	0.0359
3	2.759	0.0398
4	2.579	0.0443
5	2.410	0.0496
6	2.252	0.0559
7	2.105	0.0634
8	1.967	0.0724
9	1.838	0.0835
10	1.718	0.0975
11	1.606	0.1155
12	1.501	0.1398
13	1.403	0.1739
14	1.311	0.2252
15	1.225	0.3110
16	1.145	0.4831
17	1.070	1.0000

Figure 4.8   Money Accumulated by Investing $100 Per Month

# of Years until College	Rates of Return					
	5.5%	7%	8%	9%	10%	12%
1	$ 1,236	$ 1,246	$ 1,253	$ 1,260	$ 1,267	$ 1,281
2	2,542	2,583	2,611	2,638	2,667	2,724
3	3,922	4,016	4,081	4,146	4,213	4,351
4	5,380	5,553	5,673	5,795	5,921	6,183
5	6,920	7,201	7,397	7,599	7,808	8,249
6	8,546	8,968	9,264	9,572	9,893	10,576
7	10,265	10,863	11,286	11,730	12,196	13,198
8	12,080	12,895	13,476	14,091	14,740	16,153
9	13,998	15,073	15,848	16,672	17,550	19,482
10	16,024	17,409	18,417	19,497	20,655	23,234
11	18,164	19,914	21,198	22,586	24,085	27,461
12	20,425	22,602	24,211	25,964	27,874	32,225
13	22,814	25,481	27,474	29,660	32,060	37,593
14	25,537	28,569	31,008	33,703	36,684	43,642
15	28,002	31,881	34,835	38,124	41,792	50,458
16	30,818	35,432	38,979	42,961	47,436	58,138
17	33,793	39,240	43,468	48,251	53,670	66,792
18	36,936	48,323	48,329	54,037	60,557	76,544

market account on the day you write your first huge check to pay for college. When setting up a college fund, keep it in your name and pay tuition bills out of your pocket. If assets are titled in your child's name, when that child turns 18, he or she has full discretion on how to use the money. Plus, if the child applies for financial aid, colleges require a larger percentage of his or her assets be used to pay for tuition.

Here is a brief explanation of a few of the investment vehicles available.

Uniform Gift to Minors Act. Tax law limits the amount of income taxed at the child's rate to $1,500. For a child younger than age 14, the first $750 of income from interest and dividends is tax-free, and the second $750 is taxed at the child's tax rate, usually 15 percent. Anything above $1,500 is taxed at the parents' rate. Once the child turns 14, all earnings are again taxed at his or her rate. Therefore, you should fund a UGMA custodial account with investments that produce little, if any, taxable income and instead provide long-term capital growth.

Each parent also can give up to $11,000 a year to each child without incurring gift tax. (See additional tax information later in this section and in Chapter 6.)

Growth stocks or growth-stock mutual funds. Over the long term, you tend to earn the highest return from stocks with sharply rising earnings or from mutual funds that invest in growth companies.

Bonds or bond mutual funds. Fixed-income securities or the mutual funds that invest in them provide much more current income than stocks but much less growth potential. When bond yields are low, invest perhaps 30 percent of your portfolio in them while your child is young. By the time the child is nearing college age, you can put a higher percentage into bonds, which have less risk of falling sharply in value than do stocks.

Zero-coupon bonds. These bonds make no periodic interest payments but instead are sold at a deep discount. Zeros come in two principal varieties: Treasuries (usually called STRIPS, which stands for Separate Trading of Registered Interest and Principal of Securities) and municipals. Treasuries have no risk of default, because they are backed by the full faith and credit of the U.S. government, cannot be redeemed (or "called") by the government before maturity, and usually pay higher yields than the other variety of zeros, municipals. If you buy a zero issued by a municipality, the bond's interest compounds free of taxes.

Coverdell education savings accounts. These accounts allow you to put aside $2,000 a year into an account that grows tax-free as long as the money is used for education expenses. You can invest the money into any stocks, bonds, or mutual funds you choose.

Savings bonds. Series EE savings bonds (including Patriot Bonds), though they do not have the growth potential of growth mutual funds, can provide a solid base for funding at least part of your child's college education. The yield on savings bonds issued May 1, 1997, or later is based on 90 percent of the average yields of five-year Treasury securities for the previous six months. If your modified adjusted gross income falls between $57,600 and $72,600 for individuals and $86,400 and $116,400 for married couples filing jointly, all the interest you earn from savings bonds is totally tax-exempt if you use it for college tuition. For more information, see <www.savingsbonds.gov>.

Section 529 college savings plans. These state-sponsored education savings programs allow parents, relatives, and friends, no matter their income, to invest in a fund for a child's college education. As a parent, you set up an account for your child through a brokerage firm or mutual fund company. Each state designates a particular investment company to offer the plan to that state's residents, though you also can invest in plans from other states. The firm invests the money in the account for you.

Contributions to these plans are tax-deductible for the donor in some states, and distributions from state-sponsored qualified tuition programs are tax-free if used for qualified higher education expenses. Each state has a maximum amount you can contribute, with the largest state limits rising to $269,000.

Prepaid tuition plans. Some states allow you to prepay college tuition bills years in advance. For more information, check out Mapping Your Future at <www.mapping-your-future.org>.

Spend and save. Two firms, Upromise (888-434-9111; www.upromise .com) and BabyMint (888-427-1099; www.babymint.com), allow you to accumulate money for college expenses by registering and buying things from your everyday merchants and manufacturers of products you normally buy using your credit cards (similar to an airline frequent-flier program). This is a great example of microinvesting—investing very small amounts over a long period of time. It works quite simply: You sign up for free and register your credit cards with the services. As you spend on the cards and in the affiliated merchants, you get rebate dollars, which can either sit in an account or be transferred into a Section 529 plan to use for college expenses.

Winning at the Financial Aid Game

Many grants, loans, scholarships, and other programs also exist to help with your child's college education. Here are a few of them.

Grants. These cost you nothing and do not have to be repaid. There are federal programs like Pell Grants and Supplemental Educational Opportunity Grants, state grants, grants at individual colleges, and private grants. There is almost always money available to help with college costs if you know how and where to find it. A few good sources for your search: FinAID: The Financial Aid Information Page at <www.finaid.com>; FastWEB! (Financial Aid Search Through the Web) at <www.fastweb.com>; and a book by Alan Deutschman, *Peterson's Winning Money for College: The High School Student's Guide to Top College Scholarships* (Peterson's Guides, 2000 Lenox Drive, Trenton, NJ 08648; 800-338-3282; www.petersons.com). A note of caution, however: Beware of scholarship scams on the Internet. To find out more, check out the Federal Trade Commission's site at <www .ftc.gov/scholarshipscams>.

Working for cash. Cooperative education involves a full- or part-time job and a college career. For more information, contact the National Commission for Cooperative Education (360 Huntington Ave., 384CP, Boston, MA 02115; 617-373-3770; www.co-op.edu), or for federal co-op education opportunities, contact the employment divisions of federal agencies directly or Student Jobs.gov at <www.studentjobs.gov>.

Loans. There also are several types of local, federal, and private loans available for education, including Perkins loans (formerly National Direct Student Loans); Stafford loans (formerly Guaranteed Student Loans); Parents Loans to Undergraduate Students (PLUS); state loans; college loans, and commercial loans.

A few commercial lenders specializing in college lending include: College Credit (800-831-5626, www.collegeboard.com); ConSern Education (800-767-5626, www.consern.com); Key Education Resources (800-539-5363, www.key.com); Nellie Mae (800-367-8848, www.nelliemae.com), and Sallie Mae (800-239-4269, 800-891-1410, www.salliemae.com).

Applying for Financial Aid

Financial aid is designed to supplement, not replace, a family's contribution to college costs. Factors that determine how much financial aid a family qualifies for include the parents' and student's income and assets, the size of the family, and the number of children attending college. The more income and assets a family has, the more college costs it is expected to pay.

The financial aid forms you obtain from a college will help you go through the application process. Keep in mind that your child may qualify for more aid than normally is allowed, if unusual circumstances like a recent job loss or divorce can be documented. Be sure to mail your financial aid applications soon after January 1, even before a school accepts your child. For a more detailed look at how to save for college education, get grants and scholarships and play the financial aid game, see *Everyone's Money Book on College*.

Points to Remember

- A portfolio designed to fund college should be balanced among high-, medium-, and low-risk investments early on, and then switched to less risky products as the tuition bills draw closer.
- Even if you have another retirement plan, and if contributions are not deductible, open an IRA as a way to save where your earnings are tax-deferred or, even better, a Roth IRA where earnings grow tax-free.
- Your employee benefits—or lack of them—are crucial when it comes to putting together your personal financial plan.
- When you shop for disability insurance—a must if you are employed—read the fine print on how a policy defines disability, because it will affect the benefits you receive if injured.

- The Pension Benefit Guaranty Corp. is a guarantee fund, similar to the Federal Deposit Insurance Corporation (FDIC) for bank depositors, and guarantees basic pension benefits, including the monthly pension check, some early retirement and disability benefits, and some benefits for survivors of deceased beneficiaries.

RESOURCES: INSURANCE

Books/Publications

Annuity Shopper (United States Annuities, 8 Talmadge Dr., Monroe TWP, NJ 08831; 800-872-6684; www.annuityshopper.com). A newsletter that compares the current rates paid by most immediate annuities, as well as the returns on fixed annuities.

How to Get Your Money's Worth in Home and Auto Insurance, by Lynn Brenner and Barbara J. Taylor (McGraw-Hill, P.O. Box 543, Blacklick, OH 43004; 800-634-3961; www.mcgraw-hill.com). Shows readers how to figure out quickly and easily their personal insurance needs on homes and cars and answers vital questions.

Variable Annuity Research & Data Service Report (P.O. Box 1927, Roswell, GA 30077-1927; 770-998-5186). Tracks the investment performance of hundreds of variable annuities sold by insurance companies.

Organizations

American Insurance Association (1777 Church St., NW, Washington, DC 20036; 202-667-1798; www.aiadc.com). Property and casualty trade group that provides a forum for the discussion of problems. Promotes safety programs and lobbies on behalf of the insurance industry.

Society of Financial Service Professionals (270 S. Bryn Mawr Ave., Bryn Mawr, PA 19010-2195; 888-243-2258; www.financialpro.org). An association of insurance and financial services professionals who earn various credentials.

Health Insurance Association of America (1201 F. St., NW, Suite 500, Washington, DC 20004; 202-824-1600; www.hiaa.org). The lobbying group for health insurance companies. Also educates the public about health insurance.

Independent Insurance Agents of America (127 S. Peyton St., Alexandria, VA 22314; 800-221-7917; www.iiaa.org). Association of independent insurance agents who are not tied to selling any particular insurance company's products.

Insurance Education Foundation (P.O. Box 68700, Indianapolis, IN 46268; 317-876-6046; www.ins-ed-fdn.org). Organization dedicated to educating high school teachers and students about how the insurance industry works.

Life and Health Insurance Foundation for Education (2175 K St., Suite 250, NW, Washington, DC 20037; 202-464-5000, 888-543-3777; www.life-line.org). A not-for-profit education foundation committed to better educating the public about life, health, and disability insurance, and the value-added role of the agent.

National Committee for Quality Assurance (2000 L St., NW, Suite 500, Washington, DC 20036; 800-275-7585; www.ncqa.org). NCQA assesses and reports on the quality of managed care plans.

Quote Services

The following services quote insurance rates and help evaluate insurance policies:

AccuQuote (3180 McArthur Blvd., Northbrook, IL 60062; 800-442-9899; www.accuquote.com).

Best Quote (3700 Park East Dr., Beachwood, OH 44122; 888-521-7575; www.bestquote.com).

Insurance Quote Services (Building C, 3200 N. Dobson Rd., Chandler, AZ 85224; 480-345-7241, 800-972-1104; www.iquote.com).

QuickQuote (800-867-2404; www.quickquote.com).

SelectQuote (595 Market St., 6th Floor, San Francisco, CA 94105; 800-343-1985; www.selectquote.com).

Term4Sale (from Compulife, 108 Edgewood Plaza, Nicholasville, KY 40356; 800-798-3488; www.compulife.com).

TermQuote (6768 Loop Rd., Centerville, OH 45459; 937-434-8989, 800-444-8376; www.term-quote.com).

Ratings Services

A.M. Best & Co. (Ambest Rd., Oldwick, NJ 08858; 908-439-2200; www.ambest.com).

Moody's Investors Service (99 Church St., New York, NY 10007; 212-553-0377; www.moodys.com).

Standard & Poor's Insurance Ratings Services (55 Water St., New York, NY 10041; 212-438-2000; www.standardandpoor.com).

Weiss Ratings Inc. (4176 Burns Rd., Palm Beach Gardens, FL 33410; 800-289-9222; www.weissratings.com).

Federal Government Regulator

Centers for Medicare and Medicaid Services (formerly the Health Care Financing Administration; 7500 Security Blvd., Baltimore, MD 21244; 410-786-3000; www.hcfa.gov). This is the federal agency that oversees Medicare and Medicaid funding.

RESOURCES: EMPLOYEE BENEFITS

Books

The Complete Handbook of U.S. Government Benefits, by R.E. Neuman (United Research Publishing). Tells you how to collect Social Security, business loans, educational benefits, grants, pensions, and home and farm loans.

Employee Benefits, by Burton Beam, Jr., and John McFadden (Dearborn Trade, 155 N. Wacker Dr., Chicago, IL 60606; 800-245-2665; www.dearborntrade.com). Comprehensive explanation of employee benefits.

Maximize Your Benefits: A Guide for All Employees, by Neil Downing (Dearborn Trade, 155 N. Wacker Dr., Chicago, IL 60606; 800-245-2665; www.dearborntrade .com). Explains how company benefits fit into a household's overall financial plan; discusses issues related to pensions, vesting, and defined benefit plans and health plans.

Organizations

Employee Benefit Research Institute (2121 K St., NW, Suite 600, Washington, DC 20037; 202-659-0670; www.ebri.org). EBRI is a private, nonprofit, nonpartisan public policy research organization.

Employers Council on Flexible Compensation (927 15th St., NW, Suite 1000, Washington, DC 20005; 202-659-4300; www.ecfc.org). Studies and promotes use of flexible spending accounts, medical savings accounts, and other cafeteria-style employee benefit offerings.

International Foundation of Employee Benefit Plans, Inc. (P.O. Box 69, 18700 W. Bluemound Rd., Brookfield, WI 53008-0069; 262-786-6710, 888-334-3327; www.ifebp.org). An educational association for those in the employee benefits field.

Profit Sharing/401(k) Council of America (10 S. Riverside, Suite 1610, Chicago, IL 60606; 312-441-8550; www.psca.org). Devoted to explaining and promoting the use of profit-sharing and 401(k) plans.

Federal Government Regulators

Internal Revenue Service, Employee Plans (1111 Constitution Ave., NW, Washington, DC 20224; 800-829-1040; www.irs.ustreas.gov). Sets the complex rules on funding pension plans, vesting, and compliance with tax forms.

Labor Department, Pension and Welfare Benefits Administration (200 Constitution Ave., NW, Washington, DC 20210-0999; 866-4USA-DOL; www.dol.gov). Sets rules for and oversees all employee benefits programs. Can explain your rights under federal law.

Pension Benefit Guaranty Corporation (1200 K St., NW, Washington, DC 20005-4026; 202-326-4000, 800-400-7242; www.pbgc.gov). Insures corporate defined benefit pension plans to make certain that covered pensioners receive the money due them.

RESOURCES: COLLEGE FINANCING

Books

Don't Miss Out: The Ambitious Student's Guide to Financial Aid, by Robert and Anna Leider (Octameron Press, P.O. Box 2748, Alexandria, VA 22301; 703-836-5480; www.thinktuition.com). Lists many college loan programs offered by individual states.

Paying for College without Going Broke, by Kalman A. Chany and Geoff Martz (Princeton Review, 2315 Broadway, New York, NY 10024; 800-2-REVIEW). Helps the reader plan ahead to improve chances of getting financial aid.

The Scholarship Advisor, by Chris Vuturo (Random House/Princeton Review Books, 2315 Broadway, New York, NY 10024; 800-2-REVIEW.) A step-by-step how to hunt and locate a scholarship; includes information on more than 100,000 scholarships.

College Financial Aid for Dummies, by Herm Davis and Joyce Lain Kennedy (Hungry Minds, 919 E. Hillsdale Blvd., Suite 400, Foster City, CA 94404; 800-762-2974; www.dummies.com). Guides readers through the financial aid maze and identifies the key elements to make the financial aid system work for them.

The Scholarship Book, by Daniel J. Cassidy (Prentice-Hall Publishing, Englewood Cliffs, NJ 07632; 800-947-7700; www.phdirect.com). The ultimate listing of private-sector scholarships, loans, and grants assembled by the founder of the National Scholarship Research Service.

Organizations

College Savings Bank (5 Vaughn Dr., Princeton, NJ 08540; 800-888-2723; www.collegesavings.com). Sells the CollegeSure CD, designed to let parents prepay college education costs, either in a lump sum or in smaller amounts over time

CollegeNET (805 SW Broadway, Suite 1600, Portland, OR 97205; 503-973-5200; www.collegenet.com). Lets you search for and file applications at more than 1,500 colleges.

Federal Student Aid Information Center (800-4-FED-AID; www.ed.gov/offices/OSFAP/Students).

Federal Government Regulator

U.S. Department of Education (Information Resource Center; 400 Maryland Ave., SW, Washington, DC 20202; 800-872-5327; www.ed.gov). Everything you need to know about finding and financing college as well as loan consolidation and servicing.

CHAPTER 5

Retirement and Estate Planning

When it comes time for your supposedly "golden years," you don't want to get caught short on the money you will need to live comfortably because you failed to plan. The earlier you start to plan for retirement, the more you capitalize on your biggest ally: time. If you make the magic of compound interest work for you while you are in your 20s or 30s rather than your 40s or 50s, you will have a much better chance of amassing the capital you need to live on in retirement. Consider that if you earn $30,000 a year, save 6 percent ($150) from your salary every month starting at age 30, and earn a 10 percent average annual return, you will end up with $574,242 when you reach age 65. Starting at age 55, assuming all other variables remain constant, you will reap only $30,983 ten years later.

You also should think far in advance about how to dispose of your assets to your heirs. The scenes from old movies of the ailing patriarch signing over his assets to his children on his deathbed just don't apply to the real world anymore. In that situation today, the IRS would return all of those assets back into his estate, which in turn probably would have to pay estate tax at a rate of 37 percent or more.

Estate planning involves writing a will and setting up different kinds of trusts and giving gifts to several people over several years to reduce the size of your taxable estate. Estate planning also involves funeral and burial planning, which when done properly can make settling your affairs much easier for your survivors.

THE BASICS OF RETIREMENT PLANNING

The first step to assembling a realistic retirement plan is to calculate how much money you will likely need and to pinpoint potential sources of income you will rely on when retired. To some extent, how much money you need depends on the lifestyle you lead in retirement. Traditionally, financial planners have suggested that retirees plan on spending between 60 and 80 percent of the amount they spent during their working lives, though these days many retirees spend far more than that as they pursue new, and sometimes expensive, activities.

To estimate what percentage of your working-years expenses you might continue to pay in retirement, go back over the Cash Flow Analysis Worksheet in Chapter 1 (see Figure 1.9), adjusting your likely expenses for a retired lifestyle. Then calculate your retirement expenses as a percentage of your working-years expenses (the 60 to 80 percent).

For a rough idea of your expenses in retirement, use the simple worksheet in Figure 5.1. It is designed to adjust your working-years level of expenses for retirement and to factor in a long-term inflation rate of 4.5 percent. The savings called for in item 2 include all regular savings plus contributions to retirement plans such as 401(k)s and individual retirement accounts (IRAs). The worksheet's sample figures assume an annual income of $50,000, an annual savings of $5,000, a 70 percent level of retirement spending, and 20 years remaining before retirement. In completing this worksheet, refer to the numbers you used for income and savings in Figure 1.9.

Potential Income Sources

With this general idea of how much money you will need to live on each year in retirement, examine your potential sources of income. The three main income sources for retirees are Social Security, pensions, and private savings and investments. The Social Security Administration will estimate your benefit in current dollars, based on your earnings and years of service. Your company's employee benefits department can tell you in today's dollars what you should expect to receive from your pension based on your current age and salary level. Adjust both the pension and Social Security figures by the same 4.5 percent inflation factor. To calculate the amount of savings and investments you will need to make up the difference, subtract the adjusted pension and Social Security amounts from your projected annual living expenses.

Finally, to estimate the amount of capital you must amass to generate that level of annual investment income, assuming a 5 percent rate of return, multiply the number by 20. (For example, you need $20,000 in capital to produce $1,000 in interest if it earns 5 percent annually.) If you want to assume

Figure 5.1   Retirement Expenses Worksheet

		Example	Your Situation
1.	Present Gross Annual Income	$50,000	$ _____
2.	Present Annual Savings	$ 5,000	$ _____
3.	Current Spending (Subtract item 2 from item 1.)	$45,000	$ _____
4.	Retirement Spending Level (between 60% and 80%, depending on your assumptions of lifestyle)	70%	_____ %
5.	Annual Cost of Living (in present dollars) if You Retired Now (Multiply item 4 by item 3.)	$31,500	$ _____
6.	4.5% Inflation Factor (from table below)	2.4	_____
7.	Estimated Annual Cost of Living (in future dollars) at Retirement (Multiply item 6 by item 5.)	$75,600	$ _____

Years until Retirement	Inflation Factor
40	5.8
35	4.7
30	3.7
25	3.0
20	2.4
15	1.9
10	1.6
5	1.2

a higher rate of return than 5 percent, multiply by a smaller number. For example, multiply by 10 if you want to assume a 10 percent average annual return (because $10,000 will produce $1,000 in interest at 10 percent).

Using the assumptions in the Retirement Expenses Worksheet, you would therefore need to amass $312,000 over the next 20 years until retirement if you want to maintain a lifestyle similar to your current lifestyle (see the Capital Accumulation Worksheet in Figure 5.2).

The next step is to figure out how much money you must save each year before retirement to accumulate the needed capital. The amount of money calculated in item 8 in the Capital Accumulation Worksheet is not all the money you will need to fund your retirement. It is the amount needed to fund your *first year* of retirement. To keep pace with inflation, you must increase your savings by at least 5 percent a year until you reach retirement age. The Annual Savings Worksheet in Figure 5.3 will help you determine how much money you must save each year to meet this goal. The sample figures assume an after-tax rate of return of 7.5 percent on all investments and 20 years before retirement.

After running your numbers through these three worksheets, you should have a sense of how much money you need to save and invest each year to meet your retirement savings goal. If you would like to apply different rates of return and inflation rates and change other factors, various Web sites, books, and software mentioned in the "Resources" section at the end of this chapter offer calculators that can help. One example is mPower Café shown in Figure 5.4.

Social Security

An important aspect of the retirement income calculation is the amount that you will receive from Social Security. Don't believe the prophecies that the Social Security system will go broke, though it probably will make up a gradually smaller percentage of your retirement income in the years ahead.

To be eligible to receive Social Security, you must work and pay taxes into the system. As you work, you earn Social Security credits, up to four quarters of credit per year. Benefits are payable at full retirement age (with reduced benefits available as early as age 62). The full retirement age is 65 for those born before 1938. The age gradually rises until it reaches 67 for people born in 1960 or later. People who delay retirement beyond full retirement age get special credit for each month they don't receive a benefit until they reach age 70.

To get a current estimate of your Social Security benefit—you should get one every few years—write or call the Social Security Administration (6401

Figure 5.2   Capital Accumulation Worksheet

		Example	Your Situation
1.	Estimated Annual Cost of Living (in future dollars) at Retirement (item 7 from Retirement Expenses Worksheet)	$ 75,600	$ _____
2.	Annual Pension Income	10,000	_____
3.	Inflation-Adjusted Pension Income (Multiply item 2 by appropriate inflation factor on page 687.)	24,000	_____
4.	Annual Social Security Benefit	15,000	_____
5.	Inflation-Adjusted Social Security Benefit (Multiply item 4 by appropriate inflation factor.)	36,000	_____
6.	Inflation-Adjusted Pension and Social Security Income (Add items 3 and 5.)	60,000	_____
7.	Amount by which Expenses Exceed Pension and Social Security Income (Subtract item 6 from item 1.)	15,600	_____
8.	Needed Capital (Multiply item 7 by 20.)	$312,000	$ _____

Security Blvd., Baltimore, MD 21235; 800-772-1213). The agency's Web site <www.ssa.gov> also provides the estimate and various helpful calculators.

Defined Benefit Plans

A defined benefit plan provides a specified monthly benefit at retirement, often based on a combination of salary and years of service. Companies use several formulas to determine the size of your pension benefit. The best pension plan averages your salary for your final three or five years of work, when your income should be at its peak. To get a sense of what you might receive, contact your employee benefits department and ask for a personalized benefits statement.

Figure 5.3   Annual Savings Worksheet

		Example	Your Situation
1.	Capital Needed to Fund Retirement (item 8 from Capital Accumulation Worksheet)	$312,000	$ _____
2.	Current Investment Assets (value of stocks, bonds, mutual funds, etc.)	$ 30,000	$ _____
3.	7.5% Appreciation Factor (from table below)	4.2	_____
4.	Appreciation of Your Investment Assets until Retirement (Multiply item 2 by item 3.)	$126,000	$ _____
5.	Other Assets Required by Retirement Age (Subtract item 4 from item 1.)	$186,000	$ _____
6.	Savings Factor for Years until Retirement (from table below)	.0231	_____
7.	Savings Needed over the Next Year (Multiply item 5 by item 6.)	$ 4,296	$ _____

Years until Retirement	7.5% Appreciation Factor
40	18.0
35	12.6
30	8.8
25	6.1
20	4.2
15	3.0
10	2.1
5	1.4

Years until Retirement	Savings Factor
40	.0044
35	.0065
30	.0097
25	.0147
20	.0231
15	.0383
10	.0707
5	.1722

Figure 5.4 Web pages like this on mPower Café provide a wealth of information about your retirement options. <www.mpowercafe.com>

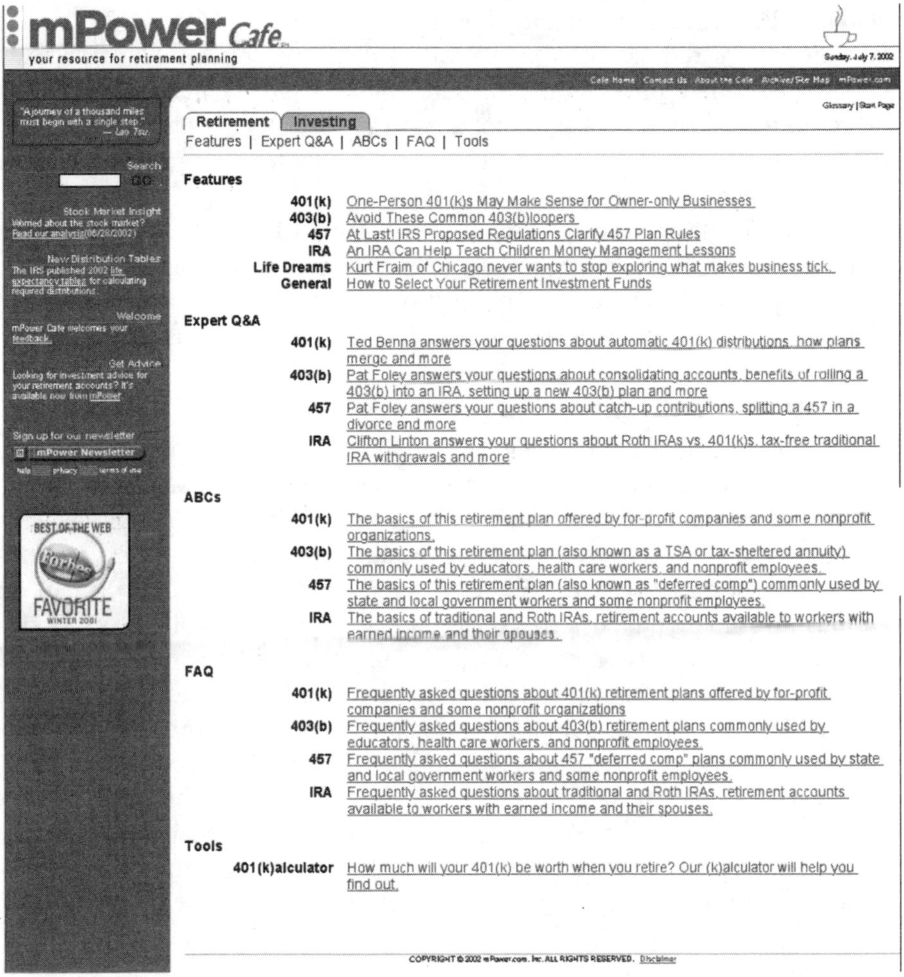

Defined benefit pension plans guarantee in advance the size of your monthly pension benefit up to a maximum amount. To qualify for a pension, you must work for your employer a certain number of years to become vested. If you are vested and die before retirement age, your spouse will receive a preretirement survivor's annuity. Your spouse can sign a document waiving the right to this annuity, boosting your pension benefit. But then if you die before retirement, your widow will not receive any pension. And buying a straight life annuity payout option—pension maximization—to make up the shortfall is usually not a good idea. Instead, opt for a joint and survivor pension payout option, so that payments to your spouse continue once you, the primary employee, die.

If you decide to leave an employer, a decision whether to take all of your pension money at once (known as a lump-sum distribution) is extremely complicated and has many tax implications, so consult a qualified financial planner before you grab what may look like a huge chunk of cash.

Defined Contribution Plans

A defined contribution plan gives you the opportunity to put aside money from your salary on a tax-deferred basis until you retire. Unlike a benefit plan, a contribution plan does not obligate your company to pay a certain pension benefit. Instead, you may set aside a certain contribution, which your employer may or may not match. Either way, however, you must choose among various investment options. This decision makes you responsible for the ultimate size of your pension benefit. Like income from all other pension plans, investment earnings from defined contribution plans grow tax-deferred.

To qualify for participation in a company's plan, you usually must work there at least one year. Any money that you contribute to a defined contribution plan is always vested, meaning that you can take it with you or roll it over into another firm's plan or a rollover IRA if you change employers. However, most firms make you wait three or four years before their contributions are fully vested.

Salary Reduction Plans

The most common type of defined contribution plan is a *salary reduction plan*. If you work for a private company, it is called a 401(k) plan after the obscure section of the IRS code that permits it. If you are employed by a tax-exempt organization, it is a 403(b) plan, and for state and local government workers it is a 457 plan (see Chapter 4 on employee benefits). Federal employees can sign up for the federal thrift savings fund. Though these plans have their differences, they work basically the same way.

In each of these plans, your employer deducts a percentage of your salary—usually between 2 and 10 percent, according to your wishes—and deposits the funds in your plan account. The money is deducted from your salary before being taxed at the federal, state, or local level. As a result, the earnings you report to the IRS and your state and local taxing authorities are lessened by the amount of your annual contribution. The money you set aside, whether or not it is matched by your employer, is invested in a range of stock, bond, and money-market options, and all investment earnings accumulate tax-deferred. You pay taxes only when you withdraw the money at retirement. The IRS limits how much you can contribute annually to your salary reduction plan; that amount is increased each year for inflation (see Chapter 6).

When deciding how to spread your money among investment options, assess your tolerance for risk and balance that against the length of time before you need the money. Also, look at how you have allocated your money outside the salary reduction plan. If you hold mostly conservative bonds and CDs in your regular taxable account, you may want to invest more pension plan money in aggressive options. On the other hand, if you have amassed a large portfolio of aggressive stocks and mutual funds outside the salary reduction plan, you might want to put more of your pension money in conservative assets. In general, the younger you are, the more money you should invest in aggressive growth options.

As a rule of thumb, invest between 60 and 80 percent of your defined contribution money in stock funds while you are in your 20s, 30s, and 40s. As you enter your late 40s and early 50s, cut that percentage to between 30 and 50 percent. From your late 50s into retirement, consider trimming stock investments to between 20 and 40 percent. If you invest in stocks, however, don't sink too much money (perhaps no more than 25 percent) in your own company's stock. If your company matches your contributions in company stock, you will surely benefit if the firm does well. However, the opposite can happen and leave you facing retirement with little or no savings.

Pension Plans for the Self-Employed

If you are self-employed, either full-time or part-time, you can contribute to either a Keogh plan or a Simplified Employee Pension (SEP) plan. Both allow you to make tax-deductible contributions, which you can invest in vehicles such as stocks, bonds, mutual funds, and CDs. Your funds' earnings compound tax-deferred inside all of these plans. (For more information on tax and retirement issues, see Chapter 6.) Here are some things to keep in mind:

- To avoid any penalties, invest only funds that you will not need for living expenses or emergencies before you retire.

- A Keogh must be established by December 31 of the year in which you will file for any tax deduction. Like regular IRAs, however, you can fund it any time up to April 15 (plus extensions) to claim the deduction for the previous year.
- A SEP can be opened and funded up to the April 15 tax-filing deadline.

THE IRA OPTION

An easy way to save is through traditional or Roth IRAs. Though the tax deductibility of a traditional IRA depends on a number of factors, including your employment status and income level, it is still a terrific tax-sheltered vehicle to save for retirement. Your compounded earnings grow tax-deferred, and you can contribute a maximum to $3,000 in 2002, climbing to $5,000 in 2008. Generally, the funds cannot be withdrawn without penalty until you are at least 59½, and you must start distributions by age 70½ according to an IRS minimum distribution table.

Even better than the traditional IRA is the Roth IRA. Though you do not receive a tax deduction for the initial contribution, the investment accumulates tax-free if you follow certain rules, and you can continue to contribute after age 70½ without having to start distributions at that age as you do with a traditional IRA. You can withdraw all the principal and earnings tax-free starting at age 59½ until you die, on whatever schedule you want, as long as the assets have remained in the IRA for more than five years after making the first contribution. Or, they can be withdrawn tax-free to buy a first home, pay college expenses, or cover the cost of a major disability. (For more details on your retirement investment options, see *Everyone's Money Book on Retirement Planning.*)

THE BASICS OF ESTATE PLANNING

Many people never plan their estates, because they are intimidated by the subject, think they have nothing of value to pass on, or are concerned about how much lawyers charge to draw up wills and other estate-planning documents. Only about one out of every three Americans has executed a will. The two-thirds of Americans who do no estate planning might be shocked to learn that when people die without wills (or, as lawyers put it, *intestate*), the probate court takes over and can dominate their survivors' lives for years. It is not a simple process.

What Estate Planning Entails

The following list is a quick look at some of the key areas covered by estate planning:

- Choosing who gets how much of your money and possessions that remain after subtracting the costs of settling the estate
- Preparing a strategy to give away assets as tax-free gifts while you are alive to minimize the assets socked by estate taxes when you die
- Selecting a guardian for your children if they are younger than age 18
- Selecting a trustee to administer any trusts you may establish
- Nominating an executor of your estate, who should be an independent person you trust, to carry out the provisions of your will faithfully
- Deciding what should be done with your body after you die, including opting for burial or cremation and determining where your remains will rest
- Appointing a successor custodian for the assets of a child or grandchild if you currently act as a custodian for a Uniform Gifts to Minors Act account
- Planning to make gifts of either money or property to your favorite charity, university, church, or synagogue. Without your specific written instructions, your estate's executor cannot authorize such gifts.
- Preparing for the time you are unable to care for yourself, including advance directives like living wills and health care powers of attorney

To help you, there are do-it-yourself books as well as easy-to-use computer programs like Quicken® Lawyer (Nolo Press, 950 Parker St., Berkeley, CA 94710; 800-955-4775; www.nolo.com).

Legal books, software, and clinics will take care of most common situations and are adequate if you have few assets and a limited number of people to whom you want those assets distributed. However, if you hold substantial assets or your wishes for giving away assets are complicated, you should think about assembling a team of financial experts to make sure that your will covers every contingency. Even if you take the do-it-yourself route, it is a good idea to have the will you produce with the software checked by an attorney.

Also, if you own or head a family business, don't overlook the importance of succession planning. Without it, your survivors could end up without the level of financial comfort that you worked a lifetime to build up for them. Organizations like Massachusetts Mutual Life Insurance Co. and its Family Business Network can help (1295 State Street, Springfield, MA 01111; 800-767-1000; www.massmutual.com). Their Web site has a wealth of information available on this topic.

WRITING AND EXECUTING A WILL

Writing a will is the key to estate planning. A will is a legal declaration that gives instructions on how to dispose of your assets when you die. The portion of your estate covered by the will includes both tangible assets, like homes, cars, boats, artwork, collectibles, and furniture, as well as intangible assets, like bank accounts, stocks, bonds, and mutual funds. To specify that certain people should inherit particular tangible assets, insert in your will a provision known as a tangible personal property memorandum (TPPM).

Other rights and benefits, like pension rights and life insurance proceeds, are normally handled outside of your will and are usually payable directly to beneficiaries. Property owned jointly, such as a home held with your spouse, is not affected by the will because by law it passes to that joint owner automatically when you die. Also, any property that you have placed in a *trust* passes to the beneficiary without going through your will or probate. Because trusts take assets out of your probate estate, they can save you a lot of money and your heirs a lot of hassle.

Another important aspect of your will is choosing an executor of your estate to carry out your wishes as set forth in the will as efficiently as possible. Once the will has been completed, keep the signed original and several unsigned copies. (If all the copies are signed, no one will know which is the actual, fully executed will.) Preserve the original in a secure place other than a safe-deposit box, which may be sealed at your death. Keep copies in several locations. You can even file a copy with the probate registrar at your county courthouse for a small fee. And review it generally every five years.

Living Will and Health Care Power of Attorney

A living will, which springs into action while you are alive, declares that you do not wish to be kept alive by extraordinary artificial life-support systems and authorizes doctors and named relatives to disconnect any equipment keeping you alive. It is activated when you become mentally or physically incapacitated and have no realistic hope of returning to your normal life. The easiest way to execute what is called an advance directive, which includes a living will and medical power of attorney, is to use one of the standardized forms available from most estate-planning lawyers or from Partnership for Caring (1620 Eye St., NW, Suite 202, Washington, DC 20006; 202-296-8071, 800-989-9455; www.partnershipforcaring.org).

Once you have executed a living will, keep a copy of it with your medical records and be sure your doctor has a copy. It is of little use in a safe-deposit box where no one is aware of it. Also, make sure that the people closest to you know of its location, so they can retrieve it in the appropriate situation, and that the executor of your estate has a copy. In conjunction with the living will, sign a health care power of attorney form, which gives someone you trust the power to make medical decisions for you if you cannot.

Probate Process

Probate court is unavoidable whether you die with or without a will. (Without a will, the process can be much more difficult.) The first step in the probate process is establishing that the will, if one exists, is valid as the last statement of the deceased, declaring the person's wishes for distributing his or her assets.

Next, the probate court appoints an executor to administer the estate, usually the person named in the will. If no will exists, the court assigns an administrator, then oversees the executor's work, which consists of identifying, or marshalling, all the assets; paying off all debts, taxes, and administrative costs; and finally, disposing of the remaining assets to the beneficiaries. If the surviving family needs money immediately to meet living expenses, the executor can distribute some income, or even principal, as needed while the probate process continues. The executor receives a fee paid by the estate.

If the will is clear with no one contesting it, the executor can distribute the assets. Once that is over and taxes paid, the executor closes the estate, which may require filing a form with the court. If the court and beneficiaries receive no challenges to the disposition of the estate, the matter is closed. The probate process can last from several months to several years. In some states, if you own less than $50,000 in assets, your estate may qualify for expedited treatment, which will save on legal and executor fees.

How to Avoid Probate

Avoiding a drawn-out probate process takes a great deal of planning and thorough comprehension of estate-planning rules. There are four main ways to avoid probating your estate.

Gifts. Current law allows you to give $11,000 a year in either cash or property to any number of people you want without incurring a gift tax. If you give gifts to relatives who are named in your will, add a provision that these gifts should not be considered advances on their inheritance.

Most large gifts must be transferred to recipients at least three years before your death to avoid having them added back to your estate, and thus possibly subject to estate taxes. You also may want to give assets that have appreciated sharply to a charity in return for an annuity—what is called a charitable gift annuity. The charity can sell the asset without paying capital gains tax, and you may take a charitable deduction. The annuity may be used to purchase insurance and establish a wealth replacement trust. For more on how these can work for you, contact the American Council on Gift Annuities (Suite 400, 233 McCrea Street, Indianapolis, IN 46225; 317-269-6271; www.acga-web.org).

Joint tenancy. By holding assets in joint tenancy with right of survivorship with your spouse or another when you die, everything you own automatically transfers to the survivor without going through probate court. While the approach sounds simple, it has its complications.

For couples, if both you and your spouse die simultaneously, your entire estate will be settled at once—and chances are the estate will have to pay enormous taxes. By holding assets jointly, however, you may lose one of the two lifetime exemptions you would receive if you held your assets separately. The lifetime estate tax exemption is $1 million per person in 2002, scheduled to rise to $3.5 million in 2009. For example, if in 2003 you and your spouse had an estate worth $2 million, all $2 million passes free of tax from one spouse to the other when one dies. If the surviving spouse wants the estate to escape estate taxes on his or her death, he or she must dispense $1 million before they die.

If you hold your assets in joint tenancy with a person who is not your spouse, the same estate tax consequences apply, except no marital deduction is allowed. Also, the assets will be valued in the deceased's estate for 100 percent of their value at death, unless the joint tenant can prove that he or she paid for some or all of the assets.

Contracts. You can avoid probate on some of your assets by using employee benefit plans and insurance contracts skillfully. Most retirement pension plans start paying benefits to your spouse as soon as you die, whether or not you are retired. Because these plans take effect so quickly after you die, they avoid probate altogether. If you die once you are retired and receiving pension checks, annuity payments to your spouse can continue until his or her death. Check with your employee benefits department to make sure that you have chosen the options that will protect your spouse when you die.

Life insurance contracts also provide proceeds directly to your beneficiaries without going through probate, if you choose to have them do so.

Trusts. The most common technique used to avoid probate is to set up a lifetime, or *inter vivos,* trust. A trust holds assets so that when you die those assets will not be considered part of your estate for probate and estate-tax purposes. A trust agreement permits you to set aside assets for the ultimate benefit of another person, called the beneficiary. In some cases, the beneficiary will receive income from the trust assets for life, while in other cases, he or she will receive principal from the trust.

A trust must be established with a formal, written, legal document. Though you may be able to write a trust with the help of do-it-yourself books or software, show the results to a qualified lawyer to make sure you have covered all your bases legally. If you establish a more complicated trust, consult an attorney who specializes in estate planning. Though it might cost several hundred or even a thousand dollars up front, seeking this expertise could save you and your family tens of thousands of dollars in the future. To find such an attorney near you, contact the American College of Trust and Estate Counsel (3415 South Sepulveda Blvd., Suite 330, Los Angeles, CA 90034; 310-398-1888; www.actec.org).

There are two basic kinds of trusts:

1. *Revocable trusts.* These can be changed or even canceled any time after they are established. For this reason, they do not remove assets from a grantor's taxable estate.
2. *Irrevocable trusts.* These cannot be altered or canceled once they are established. The assets placed into an irrevocable trust are permanently removed from your estate and transferred to the trust. The trust becomes a separate taxable entity that pays taxes on the income and capital gains it generates. Therefore, when you die, the appreciation of those assets is not considered part of your estate and thus avoids estate taxes.

Trusts also are useful if you want your assets held separately for your young children. On your death, the trustee must report expenditures annually to a judge. If the trustee and the guardian of your children differ, this requirement acts as a check against the guardian's running off with your children's inheritance.

FUNERAL AND BURIAL ARRANGEMENTS

Funerals and related items like burial plots can cost thousands of dollars and may, in fact, be one of the largest purchases your family will ever make after your home and children's education. The further in advance of your death you consider your options, the less chance you will waste money.

Some issues that you must consider are:

- What kind of final disposition do you want for your remains: burial in the ground or a mausoleum or cremation? All three require various details like grave or mausoleum markers, plaques, or burial urns.
- How should your funeral and burial be handled? However you choose to handle this, a good funeral director can be a great help and earns his or her fees by handling lots of the details.
- Your survivors will need at least ten death certificates for insurance companies, the probate court, Social Security offices, and other purposes.

One way to defray the high cost of funeral services is to join a local funeral consumer group. These organizations, which act as consumer advocates for funeral planning, are nonprofit, voluntary associations of people from all walks of life who support consumer choice for dignified, meaningful, affordable funerals. To find a nonprofit consumer group near you, call Funeral Consumers Alliance at 800-765-0107 or visit its Web site at <www.funerals.org>.

POINTS TO REMEMBER

- When deciding how to spread your money among investment options, assess your tolerance for risk and balance that against the length of time before you need the money.
- IRAs are a great tax-deferred (and tax-free for Roth IRAs) way to save for retirement, whether or not your initial contribution qualifies for a tax deduction.
- No matter how much Social Security you qualify for, it clearly may not be enough to maintain a comfortable standard of living in your retirement years, necessitating the need for you to save for the future.
- The four main tactics to avoid probate with your estate are giving your money away while you are alive, setting up trusts, skillful use of employee benefits plans and insurance contracts, and holding assets in the correct names to maximize your estate tax exemptions.

RESOURCES

Books

A Commonsense Guide to Your 401(k), by Mary Rowland (Bloomberg Press, 100 Business Park Dr., P.O. Box 888, Princeton, NJ 08542; www.bloomberg.com). Tells readers how to get the most out of a 401(k) and how to use it as the basis of a growing portfolio to reach retirement and preretirement goals.

Barron's Legal-Ease, Estate Planning—Step-By-Step, by Martin M. Shenkman (Barron's Educational Series, Inc., 250 Wireless Blvd., Hauppage, NY 11788; www .barronsedu.com). Takes you through the legal and practical details of planning your estate and coping with unforeseen contingencies; includes worksheets.

Beyond the Grave: The Right Way and the Wrong Way of Leaving Money to Your Children (and Others), by Gerald M. Condon and Jeffrey L. Condon (HarperBusiness, P.O. Box 588, Dunmore, PA 18512; 212-207-7000, 800-331-3761; www .harpercollins.com). A guide to estate planning, written by lawyers; explains how to provide fairly and equitably for family members, facilitate charitable bequests, and avoid probate.

8 Ways to Avoid Probate, by Mary Randolph (Nolo Press, 950 Parker St., Berkeley, CA 94710; 800-992-6656; www.nolo.com). Explanation of probate avoidance techniques, including setting up pay-on-death bank accounts, naming a beneficiary for retirement accounts, registering vehicles in transfer-on-death forms, holding property in joint ownership, and more.

Ernst & Young's Retirement Planning Guide (John Wiley & Sons, 1 Wiley Dr., Somerset, NJ 08875; 800-225-5945; www.wiley.com). This comprehensive guide has extensive sections on investment strategy, choosing financial advisors, and how to maximize 401(k)s, IRAs, and Keogh plans.

Estate Planning Made Easy, by David T. Phillips and Bill S. Wolfkiel (Dearborn Trade, 155 N. Wacker Dr., Chicago, IL 60606; 312-836-4400; 800-245-2665; www .dearborntrade.com). Offers the basics of estate planning and shows the advantages of early estate planning.

The New IRAs and How to Make Them Work for You, by Neil Downing (Dearborn Trade, 155 N. Wacker Dr., Chicago, IL 60606; 312-836-4400, 800-245-2665; www .dearborntrade.com). Explains how to maximize the use of the many types of IRAs.

Nolo's Simple Will Book, by Denis Clifford (Nolo Press, 950 Parker St., Berkeley, CA 94710; 800-992-6656; www.nolo.com). Explains why you need a will and shows you what the will must cover to be legally valid. Discusses guardianship, creating trusts, and avoiding probate. Also comes with a floppy disk with will forms on it.

Take Control with Your 401(k): An Employee's Guide to Maximizing Your Investments, by David L. Wray (Dearborn Trade, 155 N. Wacker Dr., Chicago, IL 60606; 312-836-4400, 800-245-2665; www.dearborntrade.com). Details the benefits and values of 401(k) plans in straightforward language.

Organizations

American Association of Retired Persons (AARP, 601 E Street, NW, Washington, DC 20049; 202-434-2277, 800-424-3410; www.aarp.org). The largest trade association for the preretired and retired, with loads of resources on every aspect of planning for and enjoying retirement.

Pension Benefit Guaranty Corporation (1200 K Street, NW, Washington, DC 20005-4026; 202-326-4000, 800-400-7242; www.pbgc.gov). Federal agency that insures defined benefit pension plan payments to pensioners in case the pension plans are unable to fulfill their obligations.

Pension Rights Center (1140 19th St., NW, Suite 602, Washington, DC 20036; 202-296-3776; www.pensionrights.org). A nonprofit organization that helps educate the public about pension issues. Offers a lawyer referral service for pension-related problems.

Web Sites

Aging with Dignity. Includes templates for several types of living wills and conforms to the law in 33 states and the District of Columbia. <www.agingwithdignity .org>

Estate Planning. Has a zip-code-based search engine for estate-planning attorneys, trust officers, and CPAs. <www.estateplanning.com>

Estate Plan for You. The site for the American Academy of Estate Planning Attorneys. A comprehensive introduction to a variety of trusts and other estate-planning tools for your use. <www.estateplanforyou.com>

Financial Engines. Gives you guidance on investing your 401(k) plan assets, depending on your assumptions for rates of return, inflation, how long you will be saving, and other factors. <www.financialengines.com>

mPower Café. Loaded with information on 401(k) and other retirement plans. <www.mpowercafe.com>

Senior.com. Categories include computing, health, money, news, shopping, and insurance. <www.senior.com>

Seniorresource.com. Subjects covered include housing, aging, finance, insurance, humor, and resources available by state. <www.seniorresource.com>

Third Age. For the over-45s; includes a section on finances that is heavily skewed toward retirement issues. <www.thirdage.com>

CHAPTER 6

Basic Tax Planning

T axes are probably the most unpleasant aspect of personal finance. Yet, a key part of financial planning is determining in advance the tax implications of all your other moves. This might involve bunching deductions into one year rather than the next, or selling your business in installments over several years instead of taking all the cash in one lump sum. To create more deductions, you also might opt to borrow against your home's equity as opposed to an unsecured line of credit, for which interest costs are nondeductible.

You need to understand basic tax strategies, how to file your taxes, and how to implement the best methods to cut your tax bill, including legal deductions, credits, and other tax-sheltered plans. Even if a tax preparation professional fills out your return, you need to act tax-smart all year long. There are plenty of helpful books, free pamphlets, and Web sites with a wealth of information. (The "Resources" section at the end of this chapter provides a sampling.) Banks, financial institutions, mortgage lenders, credit card companies, insurers, and investment advisors also generally have free tax-wise information for consumers.

The Internal Revenue Service has an extensive Web site <www.irs.gov> that provides information, tax forms, and advice. You also can call the IRS help lines: 800-829-1040 for answers to your questions; 800-829-3676 to order forms, instructions, and publications; or 800-829-4477 for Tele-Tax, prerecorded messages covering various tax topics. But don't rely solely on the IRS for advice. Many of its answers to questions are incorrect, and the IRS can still penalize you if you take the advice of one of their representatives and it turns out to be wrong. You can obtain tax forms at any IRS office or from most accountants or national tax preparation services. Lists of the forms you will need are available online at the IRS Web site at <www.irs.gov/forms_pubs/topic-index.html>. (For more on choosing a tax expert, see Chapter 7.)

HIGHLIGHTS OF RECENT TAX CHANGES

A number of changes in tax law were passed in the early 2000s that are being phased in over several years. For the latest in the changing tax laws, it's a good idea to check the IRS Web site or IRS brochures or contact a tax expert such as the Research Institute of America (395 Hudson Street, New York, NY 10014; 212-367-6300; www.riahome.com) or CCH Incorporated (2700 Lake Cook Rd., Riverwoods, IL 60015; 800-449-8114; www.cch.com).

Here are a few major changes now in the process of being implemented.

Revised Tax Rate Structure

In 2002, the top four tax brackets are 27 percent, 30 percent, 35 percent, and 38.6 percent. These rates are scheduled to fall gradually, so that they reach 25 percent, 28 percent, 33 percent, and 35 percent in 2006.

For the first time in 2002, the 10 percent tax bracket is being handled through normal rate schedules and withholding. Previously, the 10 percent bracket was handled as a tax credit. Also, the income range that applies to the tax brackets is adjusted for inflation, so that more income is taxed at lower rates. Many wage earners are benefiting, because the reduced income tax withholding is increasing their take-home pay.

Tax-Free Payouts from Qualified Tuition Programs

Qualified tuition programs (also called Section 529 plans) allow parents to save for their children's college expenses on a tax-favored basis. Distributions from state-sponsored qualified tuition programs are now tax-free if used for qualified higher education expenses.

Coverdell Education Savings Accounts

Coverdell education savings accounts (formerly known as Education IRAs) have been liberalized significantly. The annual contribution limit in 2002 and beyond is $2,000, and the money in these accounts may now be used for a wide array of education expenses, including elementary and secondary public, private, or religious school tuition and expenses, extended day programs, and computer purchases.

New Deduction for Higher-Education Expenses

Higher education expenses are now deductible, even if you claim the standard deduction. You can deduct up to $3,000, if you file as a married couple jointly with modified adjusted gross income (AGI) up to $130,000 and if you are single or a head of household with AGI up to $65,000.

Tax Credit for Low-Income Savers

Eligible lower-income taxpayers can claim a tax credit for contributions to qualified plans and IRAs (including Roth IRAs). The credit rate (50 percent, 20 percent, or 10 percent) that is applied against contributions of up to $2,000 per taxpayer depends on filing status and AGI.

Higher Elective Deferral Limits

The amount you can contribute to a 401(k) is $11,000, rising to $15,000 in 2006. If you are over age 50, you can make an extra catch-up contribution of $1,000, rising to $5,000 in 2006. These limits also apply generally to 403(b) annuities, SEPs, and 457 (governmental) plans. Additionally, the maximum amount you can contribute to a SIMPLE plan is $7,000 for 2002, which rises to $10,000 in 2005. If you are over age 50, you can make an extra catch-up contribution of $500 in 2002, rising to $2,500 in 2006.

Higher IRA/Roth IRA Contribution Limits

The maximum annual contribution to an IRA or Roth IRA is now $3,000 per person, rising to $5,000 in 2008. If you are age 50 or older, you can make an additional catch-up contribution of $500, rising to $1,000 in 2006.

Enhanced Portability for Tax-Sheltered Retirement Funds

Tax-free rollovers are permitted between more types of plans. For example, rollovers are now allowed between 403(b) plans and other types of eligible retirement plans, and after-tax qualified plan contributions may be rolled over to an IRA. And, more choices are available to surviving spouses who want to roll over a decedent's distributions.

Liberalized Estate and Gift Tax Rules

A number of important rules changed for individuals dying and for gifts made in 2002 and thereafter, including:

- The annual per-donee gift-tax exclusion is $11,000 and $22,000 for spouses who split gifts.

- The aggregate amount that can be transferred free of estate or gift tax during life or at death is $1 million, rising in stages to $3.5 million in 2009.
- The top estate and gift tax rate and the GST (generation-skipping transfer) tax rate is 50 percent, and it is scheduled to drop in stages to 45 percent in 2007. If you make a transfer to grandchildren, for example, the IRS imposes the GST tax to ensure you are not trying to avoid taxes.

Some other major tax changes include:

- The standard deduction for taxpayers who do not itemize on Schedule A of Form 1040 increased, for a single person to $4,700, for a head of household to $6,900, for a married couple filing jointly to $7,850, and for a married couple filing separately to $3,925. A person age 65 or older or blind can add as much as $1,150 to the standard deduction. People who are claimed as dependents by others receive a $750 standard deduction, unless they have earned income of more than $500.
- The exemption amount is $3,000 and increases annually, indexed for inflation, and phases out depending on your filing status: It begins at $99,725 for married persons filing separately, $132,950 for single individuals, $166,200 for heads of households, and $199,450 for married persons filing jointly.
- The standard mileage rate for the cost of operating your car, including a van, pickup, or panel truck, is 36.5 cents a mile.
- You can set up a medical savings account, which is a tax-exempt trust or custodial account, with a financial institution and you can save money for future medical expenses.
- The student loan interest deduction is $3,000, rising to $4,000 in 2005.
- The capital gain tax rates for "qualified five-year gains," which are long-term capital gains from the sale of property that you held for more than five years starting January 1, 2001, is 18 percent if you are in the top four tax brackets. If you are in the lower 10 or 15 percent tax bracket, your long-term capital gain rate is 8 percent.
- The self-employment tax rate on net earnings is 15.3 percent, with the maximum amount subject to the Social Security withholding at $84,900.

FILING A TAX RETURN

The first rule of taxes is that you must file a return if your gross income meets certain minimums. Over the years, millions of people have not filed for many reasons, but whatever the excuse, it won't work with the IRS.

Who Should File?

You must file a federal return if your gross income exceeds the following amounts, which are adjusted annually. For the 2002 tax year:

- Single: Younger than age 65, $7,700; age 65 or older, $8,850.
- Married, filing jointly: Both spouses younger than age 65, $13,850; one spouse age 65 or older, $14,750; both spouses age 65 or older, $15,650. (A married couple will almost always pay less tax if they file jointly.)
- Married, filling separately: All ages, $6,925; over age 65, $8,075. (A couple might file separately if they like to keep their financial affairs distinct.)
- Head of household: Younger than age 65, $9,900; age 65 or older, $11,050. You can claim to be the head of a household if you are single and pay for at least half the cost of keeping an unmarried child or grandchild in your home. You can also file as the head of a household if you support and claim as a dependent your married children or grandchildren, your parents, or another close relative.
- Widow or widower supporting a dependent child: Younger than age 65, $10,850; age 65 or older, $11,750.

Even if you do not earn a gross income high enough to qualify under any of these income categories, you must file a return if you meet any of the following conditions:

- You have self-employment earnings of $400 or more.
- You are due a refund from withheld wages because (1) you qualify for the earned income credit for low-income working families or (2) you received an earned income credit payment from your employer.
- You owe tax or paid a penalty for withdrawing money from an individual retirement account (IRA) or other qualified retirement plan before age 59½.
- You owe Social Security taxes on income earned from tips (for example, if you are a waiter).
- You are a nonresident alien with an American business, or you owe taxes that have not been covered by withholding.

Electronic Filing

Electronic filing of tax returns—now known as e-File—has become increasingly popular, particularly with those taxpayers to whom the IRS owes a refund. Many accountants offer the e-File service for a fee of about $18 to $50, or you can file electronically through a national tax service like H&R Block at <www.hrblock.com> or CompleteTax (see Figure 6.1) at <www.completetax.com> from CCH Incorporated ProSystem fx (21250 Hawthorne Blvd., Torrance,

CA 90503; 800-PFX-9998). (A list of some of those firms that partner with the IRS on e-File is available online at <www.irs.gov/elec_svs/partners.html>.

If you owe the IRS, your payment options in addition to writing a check may include direct debit from your checking or savings account—check with your financial institution to be sure it is allowed and to get the correct routing and account numbers. You also can pay by credit card through some tax software packages and tax professionals. You can authorize a tax payment by credit card by contacting either Official Payments Corporation (800-272-9829, 877-754-4413; www.officialpayments.com), or PhoneCharge Inc. (888-255-8299, 877-851-9964; www.about1888alltaxx.com). Fees vary.

If You Don't File

If you legally must file but don't and the IRS catches you, not only will you pay hefty fines, you also may end up in prison. The harshest penalties are imposed for fraudulently failing to file. In this case, you may pay up to a 75 percent penalty plus what you owe. If fraud is not an issue and you file late, there is an additional 5 percent penalty for each month you are tardy—up to 25 percent of the taxes you owe—on top of interest and late-payment penalties, which vary depending on current interest rates. If you file but don't remit the taxes due, you must pay 0.5 percent per month up to 25 percent of what you owe.

Therefore, you should file your return even if you don't have the money to pay your taxes, because the penalties for not paying are lighter than the fines for not filing at all. If you can't file your return by the April 15 deadline, you can get an automatic extension until August 15 by filing Form 4868 electronically by phone or online. If you file the form electronically, you can make a tax payment by authorizing an automatic withdrawal from your checking or savings account (see IRS Form 4868 for instructions). You must pay based on your best estimate of what you will owe.

TAX RATES

Depending on your filing status (single, married, etc.), different levels of income are taxed at different rates (see Figure 6.2). The United States has a marginal tax rate system, which means that all income up to a certain limit is taxed at one rate. Income over that limit and under the next limit is taxed at a higher rate, and so on. Over the years, there have been many marginal rates and brackets as the government has expanded and contracted these numbers to generate more income. Adding to the confusion, each year the income that qualifies in each bracket is adjusted upward slightly for inflation, plus current law provides that tax rates continue to decrease throughout the first decade of the 2000s. Stay tuned and pay attention to what happens in Congress.

Figure 6.1   CompleteTax at <www.completetax.com> is one of the many Web sites that help you do your taxes online and file them through the IRS e-File service.

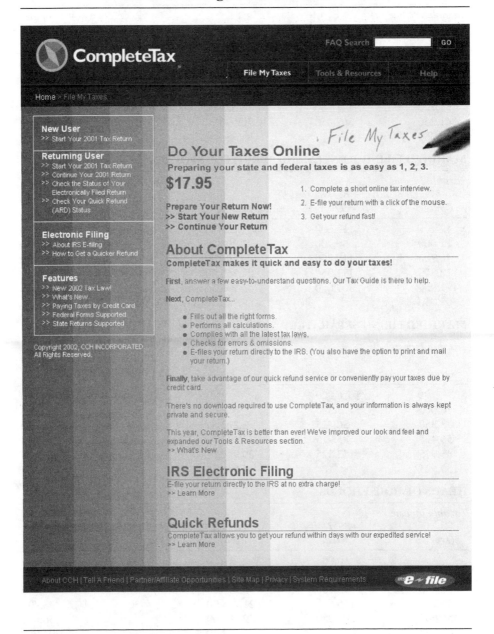

Source: Reprinted with permission of CCH Incorporated.

Figure 6.2   2002 Tax Rates and Brackets

SINGLE

Taxable Income					of the
Over	But Not Over	Pay	+	% on Excess	amount over
$ 0	$ 6,000	$ 0		10%	$ 0
6,000-	27,950	600.00		15	6,000
27,950	67,700	3,892.00		27	27,950
67,700-	141,250	14,625.00		30	67,700
141,250-	307,050	36,690.00		35	141,250
307,050-		94,720.00		38.6	307,050

MARRIED FILING JOINTLY AND SURVIVING SPOUSES

Taxable Income					of the
Over	But Not Over	Pay	+	% on Excess	amount over
$ 0	$ 12,000	$ 0		10%	$ 0
12,000-	46,700	1,200.00		15	12,000
46,700-	112,850	6,405.00		27	46,700
112,850-	171,950	24,265.50		30	112,850
171,950-	307,050	41,995.50		35	171,950
307,050-		89,280.50		38.6	307,050

MARRIED FILING SEPARATELY

Taxable Income					of the
Over	But Not Over	Pay	+	% on Excess	amount over
$ 0	$ 6,000	$ 0		10%	$ 0
6,000-	23,350	600.00		15	6,000
23,350-	56,425	3,202.50		27	23,350
56,425-	85,975	12,132.75		30	56,425
85,975-	153,525	20,997.75		35	85,975
153,525-		44,640.25		38.6	153,525

HEADS OF HOUSEHOLDS

Taxable Income					of the
Over	But Not Over	Pay	+	% on Excess	amount over
$ 0	$ 10,000	$ 0		10%	$ 0
10,000-	37,450	1,000.00		15	10,000
37,450-	96,700	5,117.50		27	37,450
96,700-	156,600	21,115.00		30	96,700
156,600-	307,050	39,085.00		35	156,600
307,050-		91,742.50		38.6	307,050

Source: Reprinted with permission of CCH Incorporated.

Defining Your Income

When you determine how much you must pay on your income, examine what constitutes income under the tax rules. Three broad categories of income exist: gross, adjusted gross, and taxable.

Gross income. This is the income you receive on which taxes are due before you take any deductions, credits, or exemptions. Excluded are: interest from tax-exempt municipal bonds and bond mutual funds that hold such bonds; insurance settlements from personal injuries or death benefits; and reimbursement of health insurance claims.

Adjusted gross income (AGI). Your *AGI* is your total gross income minus any allowable losses generated from the operation of a business, the sale of a capital asset, any deductible passive-activity losses (perhaps a real estate venture or limited partnership), and certain partnership and shareholder interest. Deductible contributions to qualified retirement plans such as IRAs and Keoghs also are used in computing your AGI as well as a number of other things.

Taxable income. You calculate your taxable income by subtracting all your exemptions and deductions from your adjusted gross income. You can also take the standard deduction in calculating taxable income.

LEGAL DEDUCTIONS

To lower your taxable income, you should take steps to qualify for as many deductions as possible. Each year, everyone qualifies for the standard deduction, which is a part of your income on which you do not pay taxes. If your individual deductions total more than your standard deduction, it makes sense to itemize those individual deductions. However, if your income is too high (according to IRS standards), you do not get the full benefit of your deductions. If your adjusted gross income is more than $132,950 for single or $199,450 for a married couple filing jointly, some of your itemized deductions are disallowed. To figure out how much, you should first total up your itemized deductions under the regular rules. Then subtract deductions generated by medical and dental expenses; investment interest; and casualty, theft, and gambling losses. The remaining deductions are reduced by 3 percent of the amount of your AGI over the $132,950 or $199,450 threshold. The higher your income, the less the deductions are worth. In effect, this reduction in the value of your deductions increases the taxes you pay on each extra dollar of income you earn. The phase-out of these itemized deductions is scheduled to be repealed in stages starting in 2006, meaning that higher-income people will get more value out of their deductions as the law is phased in.

With these limitations in mind, the following are some of the most common deductions that you can take under current federal tax law:

- *Casualty and theft losses.* Major property losses due to damage or theft that are not reimbursed by an insurance policy.
- *Charitable contributions.* Those made to qualified charities in cash, securities, real estate, or physical property (a written receipt required for $250 or more in contributions).
- *Interest expenses.* On home mortgage interest, mortgage points, interest on business loans, investment interest, and interest on student loans.
- *Points.* The up-front interest charges levied by lenders when you take on or refinance a mortgage. Usually deductible over the term of the loan, but may also be deductible in a lump sum the year you paid them.
- *Interest on business loans.* Considered an expense of doing business.
- *Investment interest paid on margin accounts to brokerage firms.* Deductible up to the amount of net investment income you earn that year.
- *Student loan interest.* Deductions of up to $2,500 from gross income.
- *Medical expenses.* Unreimbursed medical expenses that exceed 7.5 percent of your AGI.
- *State and local income taxes and property taxes.* Any local income taxes or property taxes are deductible on your federal return.
- *Miscellaneous expense deductions.* If they exceed 2 percent of your adjusted gross income.

Personal and Family Exemptions

You can claim at least one exemption for everyone in your household. Each exemption equals a deduction of $3,000 (an amount adjusted slightly for inflation each year). If you are married with dependent children, you can claim an exemption for yourself, your spouse, and each of your children. You can also claim an exemption for a dependent parent living with you. (The parent is a dependent if you provided at least 50 percent of his or her support in the past year.)

For certain high-income taxpayers, exemptions are phased out at various levels of AGI. For example, for a married couple filing jointly, you start to lose your exemption if your AGI totals $199,450 ($99,725 for a married couple filing separately). If you are single, the value of your exemption diminishes when you report an AGI of $132,950, and for heads of households at $166,200. You reduce the dollar value of your exemptions by 2 percent for each $2,500 that your AGI exceeds the threshold. For married couples filing jointly, the exemption disappears completely if the reported AGI is over $321,950. For married couples filing separately, the exemption is gone if AGI is over $160,975. This phase-out of personal exemptions is scheduled to be repealed in stages starting in 2006.

TAX CREDITS

The best tax-saving device is a tax credit, which lowers your tax bill by one dollar for every dollar of credit you receive. Therefore, if you receive a $1,000 credit, you can take $1,000 off your tax bill.

The earned income tax credit either reduces your taxes or can result in a refund if you earn too little to owe taxes. In 2002, if you have one child, you can claim the credit if your earned income, such as wages, or your adjusted gross income is less than $29,201 (except joint filers, $30,201). If you had two or more children, you qualify for the credit if your income is less than $33,178 (except joint filers, $34,178). You don't have to have children to claim the credit. If you are childless and earn under $11,060 (except joint filers, $12,060), you still qualify. The more you earn, the less credit you receive. The maximum credit for a one-child family is $2,506, while the top credit for a two-child family is $4,140 and $376. To find out what credit you may qualify for, look at the IRS Earned Income Credit (EIC) tables, which are updated annually.

Here, with the help of CCH experts, is a brief look at some of the credits.

Adoption credit. You can earn a credit up to $10,000 if you adopt a child under age 18 or if the child is mentally or physically handicapped. That credit is phased out if your adjusted gross income is between $150,000 and $190,000.

Child tax credit. You can claim a tax credit of $600 for each child you support under age 17, but the credit is phased out if your modified adjusted gross income is more than $110,000 for a married couple filing jointly, $55,000 for a married couple filing separately, and $75,000 for single parents. This credit is scheduled to rise in stages to $1,000 in 2010.

Education tax credits. The Hope Scholarship Credit is available for expenses of at least $2,000 incurred in the first two years of postsecondary education, up to a maximum of $1,500 per student per year. The Lifetime Learning Credit applies to tuition costs for undergraduates, graduates, and those improving their job skills through a training program and is worth up to 20 percent of up to $5,000 of qualified expenses, or $1,000.

Elderly and disabled credit. You may qualify if you are at least age 65 and earn a low income or you have a permanent disability preventing you from working. The tax credit you can get is 15 percent of the base amount provided under the law. If you are single, the head of a household, or a widow or widower, or you file a joint return and only one spouse is eligible for the credit, the base amount is $5,000. If you file a joint return and both spouses are eligible, the base amount is $7,500. If you are married and file separately, the base amount is $3,750. For those with permanent disabilities who are under age 65, the base amount is the base amount listed above or last year's disability income, whichever is less.

CAPITAL GAINS AND LOSSES

If you sell an asset like a stock, bond, or mutual fund for a profit, you must pay capital gains tax on that profit. Under current law, you are taxed at a maximum rate of 20 percent on the gain if you have held the asset for more than 12 months, and if you are in the regular top tax brackets of 27 percent or higher. For those in the 10 and 15 percent tax bracket, the long-term capital gains rate is 10 percent.

If you held the asset you sold for more than 12 months, report the profit as a long-term capital gain. If you owned it for 12 months or less, report the profit as a short-term capital gain. Long-term gains are assessed at the maximum 20 percent tax rate. Short-term gains are assessed at regular income tax rates.

If, instead of choosing a winning stock, you select a loser, you can get a tax benefit out of the capital loss. Taxpayers can deduct up to $3,000 in such losses if the losses exceed the gains ($1,500 for married couples filing separately), thereby reducing capital gains taxes. If you have no gains to offset your losses, you still can deduct up to $3,000 ($1,500 for married couples filing separately) from your ordinary income. If you still have losses left over, you can carry them indefinitely into future years to offset capital gains or $3,000 in losses per year to offset ordinary income if you have no capital gains.

ALTERNATIVE MINIMUM TAX

The government wants everyone to pay his or her fair share of taxes, so it has instituted the alternative minimum tax (AMT). Calculate your tax with both the regular tax tables and the AMT tables, which charge 26 percent on minimum taxable income up to and including $175,000 for a married couple filing jointly ($87,500 for a married couple filing separately) and 28 percent on minimum taxable income over $175,000 for a married couple filing jointly ($87,500 if filing separately).

To determine whether you will be hit by the AMT, add up your preference item deductions, including accelerated depreciation, percentage depletion and intangible drilling costs for oil and gas drilling, and other tax shelter deductions. Even if you don't have such elaborate preference items, you might have to pay the AMT if you have huge itemized deductions from state and local income taxes, interest expenses, interest on AMT municipal bonds issued after August 7, 1986, or other miscellaneous deductions.

To calculate what you owe under the AMT (and probably only your accountant with a good computer program can actually figure it out), add all your tax preference items to your taxable income and take one big exemption—$49,000 if you are married filing jointly; $35,750 if you are single or the head of a household; $24,500 if you are married filing separately; and $22,500 for estates and trusts. Just to make the AMT more complicated, Congress mandated that these exemptions be phased out when your AMT income exceeds $150,000 if you file jointly, $112,500 if you file singly or as the head of a household, or $75,000 if you file separately while married.

STRATEGIES TO CUT YOUR TAXES

The two basic tax-saving techniques are to delay paying taxes using tax-deferral strategies and to sidestep taxes altogether. Here is a brief look at a few of the strategies:

- *Charitable contributions.* That includes donating cash, property, or assets to qualified charities and unreimbursed expenses from volunteer work.
- *Children.* Available tax breaks include the child tax credit, adoption tax credit (if applicable), dependent care credit, Hope Scholarship, higher education and student loan expense deductions, and more.
- *Employee benefits.* You can shelter investment capital from taxes until you retire—when you probably will be in a lower tax bracket—by contributing to Keogh plans, 401(k) or 403(b) salary reduction plans, simplified employee pension (SEP) plans, SIMPLEs, IRAs, and profit-sharing plans.
- *Growth stocks.* Because you control when you sell them, the growth in the value of the stock is, in effect, a tax shelter.
- *Income shifting.* By transferring a tax burden from someone in a high tax bracket to someone in a lower tax bracket—like your child—you can reduce the total amount of taxes your family pays.
- *Individual retirement accounts.* You can save a significant amount of taxes in the long run by maximizing all the different kinds of IRA accounts available to you.
- *Insurance.* The tax-deferred buildup of cash value in an insurance policy provides a major long-term tax benefit.
- *Municipal bonds.* The interest on tax-free municipal bonds is not taxed by the federal government and usually is not taxed by the state government for its residents if the bonds are issued in the state.

- *Real estate.* Interest is deductible on a qualified residence mortgage up to $1 million ($500,000 if married filing separately), and on a home equity credit line up to $100,000. Local property taxes also are deductible. When you sell your primary residence, you do not have to pay capital gains taxes if your profit is $500,000 or less for a married couple filing jointly, or $250,000 or less for a single (if you have lived there for at least two of the past five years).
- *Treasury bonds.* Interest on bonds, bills, and notes issued by the U.S. government is not taxable at the state or local level.
- *Trusts.* By establishing various kinds of trusts, you can sidestep estate taxes.

IF YOU'RE AUDITED

If you have a dispute with the IRS, you may be able to get help through the agency's Problem Resolution Program (800-829-1040). Also, good reading is *Stand Up to the IRS,* by Frederick W. Daily (Nolo Press, 950 Parker St., Berkeley, CA 94710; 800-955-4775; www.nolo.com).

POINTS TO REMEMBER

- Don't overlook the IRS Web site <www.irs.gov> for information, forms, and more when it comes to understanding your taxes.
- Even if you don't have the money to pay your taxes, file your return because the penalties for not paying are lighter than the fines for not filing.
- The best tax-saving device is a tax credit, which lowers your tax bill by one dollar for every dollar of credit you receive.
- Some tax breaks are phased out at various levels of adjusted gross income.
- You can file your tax return online through the IRS e-File service. Many accountants and tax services offer the option for a reasonable fee. For more information, see the IRS Web site.

RESOURCES

Books

Ernst & Young Tax Guide (John Wiley & Sons, 1 Wiley Dr., Somerset, NJ 08875; 800-225-5945; www.wiley.com). Annual guide that explains the tax code and provides all the forms you need to file your taxes.

How to Pay Zero Taxes, by Jeff A. Schnepper (McGraw-Hill, P.O. Box 543, Blacklick, OH 43004; 800-634-3961; www.mcgraw-hill.com). It is organized around deductions, shelters, credits, and exemptions.

J.K. Lasser's™ *Your Income Tax* (J.K. Lasser Institute, John Wiley & Sons, 1 Wiley Dr., Somerset, NJ 08875; 800-225-5945; www.wiley.com or www.jklasser .com). Everything you need to know to fill out your tax return.

U.S. Master Tax Guide (CCH Incorporated, 2700 Lake Cook Road, Riverwoods, IL 60015; 800-449-8114; www.cch.com). A complete guide to the tax code, aimed mostly at and used by professional tax preparers.

Software

Kiplinger TaxCut (Block Financial Corporation, 4435 Main St., Kansas City, MO 64111; 800-235-4060; www.taxcut.com). A comprehensive tax planning and preparation software package. It comes in downloadable software and CD-ROM versions, with TaxCut Deluxe Multimedia offering a CD-ROM with two hours of explanatory videos.

TurboTax and *TurboTax Deluxe* (Intuit, 2698 Marine Way, Mountain View, CA 94043; 800-446-8848; www.turbotax.com). Takes you through a tax preparation exercise using a series of questions and answers; available in both software and CD-ROM versions, as well as on the TurboTax online Web site.

Web Sites

CompleteTax (CCH Tax Compliance, 21250 Hawthorne Blvd., Torrance, CA 90503; 900-225-4TAX - $1.95/minute; www.completetax.com). Low-cost online tax preparation and filing service with solutions for simple 1040s to more complex returns common for small business owners or individuals with special tax situations.

Tax Sites. This site has a list of tax and accounting sites throughout the United States. <www.taxsites.com>

Federal Government Regulators

Internal Revenue Service (1111 Constitution Ave., NW, Washington, DC 20224; 800-829-1040; www.irs.ustreas.gov). The main tax collection organization for the government. Some contacts at the IRS:

- Problem Resolution Program: 800-829-1040
- Hearing impaired: 800-829-4059
- Tele-Tax: 800-829-4477
- Free publications: 800-829-3676
- Download publications and tax forms: www.irs.ustreas.gov or direct dial via modem 703-321-8020

U.S. Tax Court (400 2nd St., NW, Washington, DC 20217; 202-606-8754). Hears cases involving disputes between taxpayers and the IRS.

CHAPTER 7

Getting Financial Advice

The world of personal finance is complex and can be confusing, so do not expect to be an expert in every aspect of this subject. There are some things you can do yourself, like drawing up a budget or even researching and buying stocks online from a discount broker. There are plenty of sources online and in print to help you. (This book is loaded with some of them.) But for many other tasks, it makes sense to hire an expert whose job it is to know the details of his or her financial field. If you find a qualified financial advisor, fees or commissions can pay for themselves many times over if the advisor's recommendations are wise. An insurance plan assembled by a top-rate agent, for example, can protect you from some taxes and your heirs from financial turmoil when you die.

Following is a look at some factors to consider when seeking out financial professionals, such as accountants/tax preparers, bankers, lawyers, financial planners, insurance agents, money managers, or stockbrokers.

WHO CAN YOU TRUST?

Plenty of sharks will take your money if you are not wary, but the fear of being cheated so paralyzes some people that they trust no one—and therefore never take advantage of the many trustworthy financial experts. There are a number of things you can do to help separate the knowledgeable advisors from the charlatans, including asking questions that apply to most varieties of advisors.

Some Generalities

First, here are a few general tips that can help no matter the financial arena.

Think about the experts you need. Your financial situation must be complicated enough or you must have enough money at stake to make an advisor's fees worthwhile. Determine what you already know and what you need to know, then hire someone to help only in your areas of uncertainty.

Qualified advice. Listen to someone because he or she is a true expert in a particular field, not because the person happens to have an opinion, well founded or not.

Interview candidates. Arrange meetings with at least three advisors before you settle on one. Factors to consider: Do you get along with the advisor temperamentally? Will you work with the advisor or an assistant? Does the advisor have a network of other experts to tap if necessary? A good advisor will ask about your financial needs and goals.

References. Ask for references from friends, relatives, and business colleagues. Also ask any potential advisor for clients and contact them. Ask if the advisor ever did anything that displeased them.

Professional affiliations. Check out your potential advisor with the local professional group with which he or she should be affiliated, or call your state attorney general's office. If you learn that several complaints or lawsuits have been filed against an advisor, look for another.

Face-to-face meetings. Choose someone you can meet face to face. It is reassuring if you can meet your advisor in person at least occasionally.

Credentials. Ask the advisor what professional degrees or credentials he or she has earned. Some credentials may sound impressive but have little meaning. For example, all it takes to become a Registered Investment Advisor (RIA) with the Securities and Exchange Commission (SEC) is to file a certain form and pay a fee. The SEC imposes no education or competency requirements.

No friends or relatives. Do not hire friends or relatives as your financial advisors. It can be dangerous to entangle your interpersonal relationships with your business dealings.

Understanding fees. The method of compensation is important, because it can sway an advisor to recommend a course of action that earns him or her larger fees by collecting commissions on products that may not be in your best interest.

Stay involved. Even after you've hired an advisor, stay involved in your financial affairs. You ask for trouble if you disengage yourself completely.

Avoiding Problems

The following qualities should tip you off to potential trouble with an advisor:

- The advisor brags about how well he or she does and ostentatiously displays fancy clothing, jewelry, and cars.
- Your advisor rushes you into decisions without making sure that you understand the details.
- Your advisor promises high returns at no or low risk. Usually, promises of high returns mean guarantees of lavish fees for the advisor and low yields—and possible loss of capital—for you.
- Your advisor pressures you to act quickly, telling you that he or she offers a limited-time opportunity that will never come your way again.

The best way to work with a financial advisor once you have chosen one is to develop written guidelines and expectations. With these general principles in mind, following is a closer look at more ways to help you identify the right specialized financial professionals.

FINDING AN ACCOUNTANT AND TAX PREPARER

When it comes to preparing tax returns, many people opt to do it themselves; others hire experts. Many professional organizations can help you locate competent preparers near you. Whichever option you choose, remember that ultimately you are responsible for your tax return.

Levels of Advice

The level of tax advice that is appropriate for you depends on the money you earn and the amount of deductions and credits you claim. Here is a rundown of the various sources of advice, starting with the simplest and ending with the most specialized.

Internal Revenue Service (IRS). The IRS offers free advice in person, via telephone, or on the Internet (see Chapter 6). Unfortunately, it does not hold its agents responsible for inaccurate information, so take the tax return you completed with IRS help to a professional preparer to see whether he or she can spot any glaring mistakes.

Local tax preparers. Be especially wary if someone guarantees a tax refund. They usually deliver on this promise by taking aggressive tax preparation risks that may trigger an audit and penalties. Interview such a tax preparer carefully and ask to see written testimonials or other references.

National tax preparation chains. Large companies with offices across the country, like H&R Block, offer convenience and often a bargain price if your taxes are relatively simple. (Check their Web sites to find the nearest office.) If your situation is more complex, consider using the national chains' higher level services.

Accredited Tax Preparers[SM] **(ATP) or Accredited Tax Advisors**[SM] **(ATA).** These professionals are qualified to prepare tax returns, based on their successful completion of the College for Financial Planning's Accredited Tax Preparer Program. Both preparers and advisors who have earned these designations have passed an exam administered by the Accreditation Council for Accountancy and Taxation (ACAT, 1010 N. Fairfax St., Alexandria, VA 22314; 888-289-7763; www.acatcredentials.org).

Enrolled agents. These are tax experts who worked for the IRS at least five years as auditors or who have passed a strenuous test of federal tax law and complete continuing education courses. For more information, contact the National Association of Enrolled Agents (200 Orchard Ridge Dr., Suite 302, Gaithersburg, MD 20878; 301-212-9608, 800-424-4339; www.naea.org).

Certified public accountants (CPAs). To be licensed and accredited, CPAs must have earned at least a bachelor's degree and have passed a stringent uniform national examination that is administered on a state level. For more information, contact the American Institute of Certified Public Accountants (1211 Avenue of the Americas, New York, NY 10036-8775; 212-596-6200, 888-777-7077; www.aicpa.org).

Tax attorneys. Lawyers who specialize in taxes offer advice to your CPA or enrolled agent on tricky or controversial areas of tax law. Their services can be worthwhile if you become embroiled in a serious dispute with the IRS that may have to be resolved in tax court.

THE RIGHT BANKER

Most larger banking institutions offer not only traditional banking services but also a full family of name-brand mutual funds, discount brokerage operations to buy and sell individual stocks, annuities from major life insurance companies, and rudimentary financial planning services as well. To offer a mutual fund or an annuity, these bank employees must pass certain tests and be licensed to sell securities. Some banks pay their investment consultants by the commissions they generate, as do regular full-service brokers. Other banks pay these specialists a flat salary.

Convenience Factor

Banks with all these services offer the convenience of conducting all your financial transactions through one institution with one comprehensive monthly statement. Many also have an automated telephone system or online home banking connection that can give you the latest account information with a few clicks of a mouse or by pushing a few numbers on the telephone. As with any other financial advisor, interview those at the bank to find out their background and whether they plan to stay at the bank. You don't want to develop a relationship with someone who isn't planning to be there long.

The Trust Department Alternative

Bank trust departments offer a higher level of service that includes financial and estate planning, insurance advice, and investment expertise. They typically cater to wealthier customers with assets of at least $100,000, but usually to those who have $300,000 or more. Clients also tend to pay lower interest rates on loans, earn higher yields on CDs and money-market accounts, and are not nicked for the per-check fees on accounts.

Most banks employ a chief investment officer to invest bank-sponsored pools of money similar to mutual funds collected from trust customers. Before you commit to a particular bank, interview their advisors and ask how their funds' returns compare to other bank pools with the same investment objective over the last year, three years, and five years. Trust departments tend to base fees on the total dollar value of your account; for example, they might charge between 1 and 2 percent of the value of your assets each year.

GETTING RELIABLE LEGAL ADVICE

When you run into legal trouble or need legal advice for some other reason, determine whether you can handle the problem yourself or whether you need someone with special training. Some questions to ask yourself:

- Is the issue simple enough to be settled outside of court, possibly by alternative dispute resolution (ADR), or is it likely to end up in court?
- Does it involve a sufficient amount of money, property, or time to warrant a lawyer's attention?
- Analyze whether complex papers must be prepared and filed to defend your rights or whether such papers are superfluous.

Alternatives to an Attorney

Even if it looks like your problem is serious enough to hire a lawyer, there are several less expensive alternatives you may want to check out first.

Online dispute resolution. This option is growing in popularity. A few of the organizations that offer this service include Click N' Settle <www .clicknsettle.com>; SquareTrade <www.squaretrade.com>; CyberSettle <www.cybersettle.com>; and Online Resolution <www.onlineresolution .com>. The American Bar Association's Web site <www.abanet.org> also has links to online ADR organizations.

Small claims court. You can resolve claims from a few hundred dollars up to thousands of dollars by representing yourself at minimal cost and at informal proceedings. Almost every local community has some kind of small claims court.

Arbitration. This is far quicker and less expensive than a court proceeding. An impartial arbitrator resolves your dispute with a binding decision. For more information, contact the American Arbitration Association (335 Madison Ave., 10th Floor, New York, NY 10017; 800-778-7879; www.adr.org), or see "Resources" at the end of this chapter.

Mediation. This involves a neutral third party that tries to help resolve the dispute. The mediator may offer suggestions to help the process along, but ultimately, you and your opposition must agree on the terms of the settlement. Like arbitration, mediation is quick, private, informal, inexpensive, and often successful. Contact the American Arbitration Association for more information.

Consumer protection agencies. Federal, state, or local consumer protection agencies may be able to help you resolve the problem at little or no cost, if they think your concern presents a danger to many citizens who need to be protected. Your state attorney general is a good place to start. (The National Association of Attorneys General at 202-326-6000 has a list of attorneys general by state online <www.naag.org/about/aglist.cfm>).

Do-it-yourself legal guidebooks, software, and Web sites. Check out the American Bar Association (800-285-2221; www.abanet.org). Other sources include HALT, an Organization of Americans for Legal Reform (1612 K St., NW, Suite 510, Washington, DC 20006; 888-367-4258; www.halt.org) and Nolo Press (950 Parker St., Berkeley, CA 94710; 510-549-1976, 800-992-6656; www.nolo.com). As a backup, you may want to have an attorney look over your proposed settlement.

Private counselors. Various independent advisors, such as a marriage counselor, credit counselor, or clergy, may be able to resolve the dispute.

Media hotlines. These consumer hotlines may be able to draw attention to the problem if it makes a good story, but they publicize only a small number of cases that the public brings them.

Where to Look

If your problem cannot be solved by any of these means or is too complex for all these alternatives, it's time to shop for a lawyer, many of whom specialize in one area. Some sources to help you find a law firm include:

- Ask friends, relatives, and business associates for recommendations.
- Bar associations may offer free lawyer referral services listed by legal specialty. See the ABA's Web site at <www.abanet.org> for contact information.

Figure 7.1   Lawyers.com, from Martindale-Hubbell, publishers of the *Martindale-Hubbell Law Directory* and a division of Reed-Elsevier Inc., can help you determine whether you need a lawyer and where to find one.

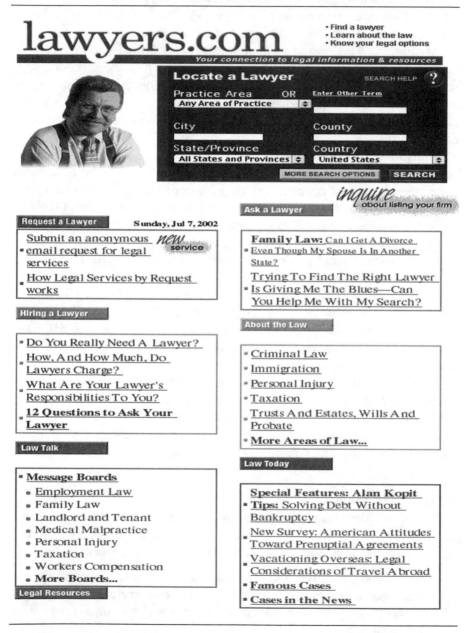

- The *Martindale-Hubbell Law Directory* (Martindale-Hubbell, 121 Chanlon Rd., New Providence, NJ 07974; 908-464-6800, 800-526-4902; www.martindale.com), has a complete listing of U.S. and international lawyers by state and specialty and is available in most public libraries. Or, check out their affiliate Web site <www.lawyers.com> (see Figure 7.1).
- You can subscribe to a prepaid legal services plan, or your employer may make such a plan available to you.

The Interview

Once you have found a lawyer who is qualified and willing to help with your legal issues, set up an initial consultation, which might be free or may require a small fee. Before the meeting, write down the points you want to make and questions you want answered, and make sure to bring copies of any important documents.

Some things to consider and questions to ask the attorney:

- What are the potential outcomes of my case? No good lawyer should guarantee that you would win.
- Make sure that your lawyer will consult you regarding all decisions that affect your case and will explain everything in terms you can understand.
- Agree in advance how to negotiate a resolution of any dispute that you have with the lawyer.
- Determine in advance the method of compensation.

How Lawyers Get Paid

The most common methods of paying lawyers follow:

- Flat fees for a straightforward task that is predictable in the skills and amount of time it will require.
- Hourly fees ($25 to $500 or more), if it is not clear in advance how many hours your lawyer must spend on the case, plus out-of-pocket expenses.
- Retainer or fixed amount paid on a regular basis to ensure the lawyer will be available whenever you need him or her.
- Referral fees if your lawyer refers your case to another lawyer who is more of an expert in your problem.
- Percentage fees based on the management or disposition of assets.
- Contingency fees paid to a lawyer if he or she wins your case.

Smart Strategies

Once you have chosen a lawyer and have agreed on a payment method, get an agreement in writing that includes what the lawyer has agreed to do, how he or she will charge, how expenses will be covered, what kind of itemized bills you will receive, and how any disputes will be settled. Also, try to obtain a written estimate of how much the lawyer thinks your case will cost. If you finally find a lawyer you like and trust but cannot pay his or her fees in a lump sum, ask whether the lawyer offers a payment plan or takes credit cards.

FINANCIAL PLANNERS

In the best of all worlds, your financial planner should be a jack-of-all-financial-trades and maintain objectivity, so as not to recommend an investment just because he or she gets a commission on it. Do such paragons of virtue exist? Indeed they do, but to find one, you must weed out the incompetent and self-serving neophytes from the experienced professionals who can help you obtain your financial goals. The first step is to assess whether you truly need a financial planner. If you just need one financial service, like tax return preparation, it is probably not cost effective to pay the fees that a planner charges.

Several associations and organizations grant credentials that signify a planner's level of education. Some of the most commonly recognized designations include:

- *Certified Financial Planner (CFP)*. From the Certified Financial Planner Board of Standards (1700 Broadway, Suite 2100, Denver, CO 80290; 303-830-7500, 888-237-6275; www.cfp-board.org).
- *Chartered Financial Analyst (CFA)*. From the Association for Investment Management and Research (560 Ray C. Hunt Dr., Charlottesville, VA 22903-0668; 804-951-5499, 800-247-8132; www.aimr.org).
- *Chartered Financial Consultant (ChFC)*. From the American College (270 S. Bryn Mawr Ave., Bryn Mawr, PA 19010-2196; 610-526-1490; www.amercoll.edu).
- *Personal Financial Specialist (PFS)*. For CPAs who offer financial planning services from the American Institute of Certified Public Accountants (1211 Avenue of the Americas, New York, NY 10036-8775; 212-596-6200, 888-777-7077; www.aicpa.org).

The Interview

As with any financial professional you consider hiring, arrange a face-to-face interview, where you can get a sense of the planner's personality and areas of expertise. The Financial Planner Disclosure Form in Figure 7.2 will help you gather and evaluate information about the planners that you interview.

Some other questions to ask prospective financial planners:

- Specifically, what services do you provide?
- Can you show me a sample financial plan that you have done recently?

Figure 7.2   Financial Planner Disclosure Form

PLANNERSEARCH

FINANCIAL PLANNER DISCLOSURE FORM

FPA
THE FINANCIAL
PLANNING
ASSOCIATION

Consumers who contact the Financial Planning Association for a CFP practitioner will receive the information that you provide on and with this form.

1.   GENERAL INFORMATION

Name _____ Phone: ____-____-____, ext. _____ Email _____

Title _____ Fax: ____-____-____

Company _____

Address _____

City, State, Zip _____

2.   GENERAL OVERVIEW OF YOUR BUSINESS

On a separate sheet, please provide us with information (limit: approximately 200 words) you would like to share about yourself and your practice. This includes, but is not limited to; your financial philosophy, specialty areas, and other personal information. Any information that you feel will accurately represent you and your practice can be included. This section should be typed.

3.   EXPERIENCE

I have been offering financial advice to clients since 19_____. Other relevant experience includes:
(Limited to 50 words.) This section must be typed – you may attach a separate sheet if you wish.

4.   FINANCIAL SERVICES PROVIDED (CHECK ALL THAT APPLY)

- ❑ Comprehensive financial planning
- ❑ Investment & asset management
- ❑ Tax preparation
- ❑ Insurance
- ❑ Charitable giving
- ❑ Elder and long-term care planning
- ❑ Education funding
- ❑ Work with owners of closely-held businesses

- ❑ Retirement planning
- ❑ Banking and/or trust management
- ❑ Cash management and budgeting
- ❑ Stock and bond brokerage
- ❑ Employee benefits and qualified retirement planning for businesses
- ❑ Estate planning
- ❑ Other _____

5.   INVESTMENT ADVISER REGISTRATION

At my last reporting to regulators, I personally had assets under management in the amount of $_____ .
Check the most appropriate description of your status:
- ❑ I am or my firm is registered with the SEC as an investment adviser.
- ❑ I am or my firm is a state registered investment adviser.
- ❑ I am exempt from registering as an investment adviser with the SEC or any state because:
  - ❑ providing investment advice is incidental to my practice as a teacher, engineer, accountant, or lawyer.
  - ❑ I am employed by a bank.
  - ❑ providing investment advice is incidental to my business as a broker-dealer.
  - ❑ Other

6.   LICENSES, CERTIFICATIONS, EDUCATION, AND AFFILIATIONS

A. Securities Licenses
- ❑ Stocks and bonds
- ❑ Mutual funds
- ❑ Limited partnerships

B. Broker-Dealer Affiliation (include home office name/address/phone):
_____
_____
_____

C. Insurance Licenses
- ❑ Life insurance
- ❑ Health/disability insurance
- ❑ Property/casualty
- ❑ Fixed annuities
- ❑ Variable annuities

D. Education **Area of Study** **University** **Year Received**

Bachelors _____

Masters _____

Doctorate _____

Please return this form to: FPA, Suite B-300, 5775 Glenridge Dr., NE, Atlanta, GA 30328-5364 or fax to: 404.845.3660.

Source: Reprinted with permission of the Financial Planning Association.

Figure 7.2   Financial Planner Disclosure Form (continued)

6. LICENSES, CERTIFICATIONS, EDUCATION, AND AFFILIATIONS (CONTINUED)

E. Other Licenses and Designations Year Received   Year Received

- ❑ Certified Financial Planner Licensee (CFP) _____
- ❑ Certified Public Accountant (CPA) _____
- ❑ Certified Trust & Financial Advisor (CTFA) _____
- ❑ Chartered Financial Analyst (CFA) _____
- ❑ Chartered Financial Consultant (ChFC) _____
- ❑ Chartered Life Underwriter (CLU) _____
- ❑ Enrolled Agent (EA) _____
- ❑ Personal Financial Specialist (PFS) _____
- ❑ Admitted to Bar – State(s): _____ _____
- ❑ Other _____ _____

7. CHARGES TO CLIENTS FOR SERVICES (CHECK ALL THAT MAY APPLY)

Adviser Controlled Charges

- ❑ Fee for financial planning (initial, hourly, and/or retainer)
- ❑ Fee based on percentage of assets managed:
  percentage ranges:
  (_____% to _____%)
- ❑ Other _____

Charges Not Set By Adviser

- ❑ Commissions and/or loads for investment products purchased
- ❑ Trail fees on mutual funds or insurance products
- ❑ Redemption fees on mutual funds or insurance products
- ❑ Commissions on insurance products purchased
- ❑ Account fees (such as those for IRA accounts)
- ❑ Other _____

8. COMPENSATION (CHECK ALL THAT APPLY)

- ❑ My clients' interests come first. I will recommend products based on what is in their best interest and not based on which one would give me more earnings.
- ❑ When appropriate, I may refer my clients to other related professionals for services they are better able to provide than I am.
  - ❑ I sometimes receive referrals or other fees from these professionals.
  - ❑ I do not receive referrals or other fees from these professionals.
- ❑ I work on a fee-only basis.
- ❑ When requested, I will work with clients on a fee-only basis.
- ❑ When requested, I will inform clients of the dollar amount of fees, including commissions or loads, they will pay on the purchase of any product.
- ❑ My firm does not, nor does any affiliate or member of my firm, act as general partner, participate in or receive compensation as a general partner from the investments that I recommend.

9. CLIENT MINIMUMS

In order to ensure that consumers are matched with appropriate planners, during the opt-in process you must tell us the manner in which you prefer to be listed:

❑ **A) I have no minimum financial requirements for new clients.**

By selecting "A", you are indicating that:
- Your practice is open and you still accept new clients.
- You find value in working with consumers that are dedicated to saving and investing but might be in the beginning stages of accumulating assets.
- You do not have asset or income minimums that would exclude lower to middle income consumers.
- You are willing to speak with every consumer that calls you via FPA's PlannerSearch even if it is only to offer them a next step such as:
  — Giving them the name of another CFP professional in your area that would be interested in serving the consumer
  — Suggesting that the consumer contact an entity that can better serve the needs of their particular situation

❑ **B) My minimums for new clients are 1) assets to invest of at least: _____ and/or 2) income of at least: _____**

By selecting "B", you are indicating that you wish to serve clients whose assets to invest and/or annual income meet your specified minimum. You must specify the minimum during the opt-in process.

10. MISCELLANEOUS (CHECK ALL THAT APPLY)

- ❑ To maintain my licenses and/or designation, I am required to earn _____ continuing education credits every _____ (period).
- ❑ I will provide prospective clients with references.
- ❑ I have been cited by a professional or regulatory governing body for disciplinary reasons. (If this box is checked, please attach more information.)
- ❑ I will provide a free initial consultation to prospective clients so that we may determine if their needs and my practice are well-matched.

- What type of clientele do you serve? (If you are nearing retirement, do not hire a planner whose clients are mostly young entrepreneurs.)
- Will your advice include specific product recommendations or only generic product categories?
- How will you follow up to ensure that the plan is implemented?
- Will you have direct access to my money? (Be careful about giving a planner discretionary control over your money. If you do, make sure that the planner is bonded.)
- Are you registered as an investment advisor with the Securities and Exchange Commission or the state? (All planners who provide investment advice should be registered with either the SEC or your state. The North American Securities Administrators Association [NASAA] can provide you with more information about these requirements at 888-846-2722 or <www.nasaa.org>.)
- Have you ever been cited by a professional or governmental organization for disciplinary reasons? (Even if the planner says "no," double-check with the state attorney general's office, the state securities office, and the state societies of financial planning organizations.)

Methods of Payment

Planners are compensated in four basic ways:

Commission only. These planners offer free consultation and get paid only when you buy a product, so be aware of his or her incentives as you consider the advice. There may also be ongoing fees with the investment that you should be aware of before buying any product.

Fee only. Some planners assess your financial situation for a fee, which is set in advance. To locate a fee-only planner, contact the National Association of Personal Financial Advisors (888-FEE-ONLY; www.napfa.org) or the Financial Planning Association Adviser Referral Program (800-322-4237; www.fpanet.org).

Fee and commission. Many financial planners charge a fee for providing a basic plan and make most of their income from commissions on the products they recommend. When considering their advice, you may want to try to determine a way to accomplish the same goals with lower-priced products.

A variation on this form of compensation is called fee offset, meaning that any commission revenue from selling products to you reduces the advisor's planning fee.

Salary. Many financial organizations provide financial planning services through a salaried planner. These planners do not have as strong an incentive to sell products to you, but they still steer you toward products offered by their financial institution on which the institution earns a sales fee.

The Best Option

From these descriptions, a fee-only planner probably sounds best. However, this alternative also has several drawbacks. First, not many fee-only planners exist. Second, because these planners make their living only from fees, you typically need enough cash and assets to justify their fees. Depending on the planner, you may have to invest as much as $100,000 or more. Third, you must take the initiative to follow up on a fee-only planner's advice, which means contacting other financial service companies, such as insurance or mutual fund firms, to implement the advice.

Therefore, don't dismiss commission-only, fee and commission, and salaried planners. Many of them are truly helpful professionals, and the commissions or salaries they earn by selling products may help keep the cost of their services within your reach. Just remember, when such a planner makes recommendations, be as fully informed as possible about his or her background and incentives as you decide how much of the advice to take.

CHOOSING AN INSURANCE AGENT

The idea of seeking out a life insurance agent might sound ironic, because so many people spend time avoiding life insurance solicitations. But taking the initiative to find a reliable agent with a good reputation makes more sense than waiting for a phone call from someone "dialing for dollars" off a phone list.

Finding an Agent

Start by calling the local office of an insurance company with a good reputation, or ask friends, relatives, and business associates for names of agents with whom they have had good experiences.

Ask the agent that you are interested in how long he or she has been in the business and about his or her qualifications. Does the agent sell policies for only one company—an exclusive or a captive agent—or are they an independent who can sell for multiple companies? Either one may offer you the best deal, depending on your situation and the products available.

The Interview

A qualified agent first should help you assess your need for insurance. Therefore, if an agent starts your meeting with an intense sales pitch, move on to your next candidate. A policy's returns and price are incidental to the main purpose of insurance, which is to protect your family from losing its main source of income if you die.

Once the agent has evaluated your needs, he or she should propose several insurance programs tailored to your budget and desire for protection.

When the agent explains these alternatives, he or she usually will use policy illustrations, which are columns of numbers that project what your life insurance cash value and death benefit could be worth in 5, 10, 20, and 30 years, under certain conditions. Be skeptical of these illustrations, because the underlying assumptions may not hold true. For example, a policy might project how dramatically your cash value will grow if you earn 10 percent a year for the life of the policy. But if interest rates drop, you may not earn anywhere near 10 percent. The agent also should point out the column illustrating the guaranteed minimum return.

Qualifications

Each state requires that agents pass standard tests and take continuing education courses to obtain a license to sell insurance. Beyond this bare minimum, however, several professional designations indicate a higher level of professional and ethical standards. Following are the credentials you are likely to encounter:

- *Certified Financial Planner (CFP).* From the Certified Financial Planner Board of Standards (CFP Board) in Denver.
- *Chartered Financial Consultant (ChFC).* From the American College in Bryn Mawr, Pennsylvania.
- *Chartered Life Underwriter (CLU).* Also awarded by the American College.

In addition to watching for these designations, you can ask your agent whether he or she is a member of the National Association of Insurance and Financial Advisors (877-866-2432; www.naifa.org), formerly the National Association of Life Underwriters, which is the umbrella group for agents.

SETTLING ON A REAL ESTATE ADVISOR

Before you hire a real estate agent to sell your home, you might try saving commission costs by selling it on your own—at least for a month or so. If you are selling in a hot market, you could save thousands of dollars in commissions. However, if your home languishes on the market for more than a month, it is probably time to call in a real estate agent or broker.

Agents have earned a state real estate license allowing them to sell real estate. Brokers are also licensed, but they may own a real estate company and are responsible for the actions of the agents working for them. For brevity's sake, this section of the book uses the terms *agent* and *broker* interchangeably.

Brokers and agents size up your property, estimate what price it might bring, pre-qualify buyers to make sure that they can afford your home, handle negotiations between seller and buyer, and advise the seller on strategies to obtain the highest price possible. The agent also can arrange to bring in-spectors or appraisers, direct buyers to sources of mortgage financing, and make sure the sale closes on schedule.

The Interview

Ask friends, relatives, and business associates for recommendations on a possible agent, then interview several. Notice which agencies have the most For Sale signs in your neighborhood and also which homes sell the fastest. Attend a few open houses sponsored by different agencies to see how well they are run. Request the names of satisfied clients from any broker you are considering; call to ask those clients whether they would sell their home through that agent again.

Once you narrow your search to a few agents, give each a tour of your home and ask him or her for a competitive market analysis, which is a frank appraisal of what price your home might bring in the current market. Each broker will then make a listing presentation. This is basically a sales pitch for the agency. The broker should tell you how many similar homes the agency currently lists, and how many sales it has completed in the last two or three months. Also, ask how many listings expired or were canceled recently be-cause the agency was unable to locate a buyer.

Other questions you should ask each potential broker:

- How long have you worked in this neighborhood?
- Are you licensed to sell real estate in this state? (Ask to see the agent's license, which proves he or she passed the state real estate examination.)
- Are you a member of the National Association of REALTORS®?
- What is your marketing plan to sell my home? (A good agent should be able to tell you specifically what he or she will do and how long it should take to attract qualified buyers.)
- What services does your company offer, such as computerized multi-ple listing services (MLS)?

Also, consider whether the broker works for a small local agency or for a large national company like Century 21 or Coldwell Banker. A local com-pany may have more connections and expertise in selling homes in your neighborhood. However, a national firm may have tie-ins to relocation ser-vices, which provide names of potential buyers moving to your town, or mortgage financing options.

The Listing Agreement

Next, carefully examine the listing agreement. The contract specifies the asking price of the home, what personal property—such as appliances—are included in the asking price, what services the broker will provide, how much you will pay the broker if the home sells, and when the contract expires. Most contracts last for 90 or 180 days, though you should retain the right to cancel the contract at any time (with some notice), if your broker does little to sell your home.

Once you agree with a buyer on a price, have a real estate attorney draw up a sales contract. Your agent can help make sure that the contract lists all necessary details.

Commissions

In return for advising you on a strategy to sell your home, finding a buyer, and bringing the deal to completion, most real estate agents receive a commission of 5 to 7 percent of the sales price. They do not receive one dime until title to your home is transferred to the buyer at a closing, however, so they have a strong incentive to get the job done. Commission percentages are negotiable and may be less if the home is expensive or competition among agents is fierce.

Buyer's Broker Alternative

For the most part, real estate agents represent sellers of homes. Nevertheless, they can help you identify properties and serve as intermediaries during negotiations over sales contracts. If you are dissatisfied with one broker for whatever reason, take your business to another. As a buyer, you are under no obligation to any particular broker.

Another alternative is to hire a broker who works only for you, the buyer. The buyer's broker can make sure that you receive full disclosure from a seller regarding any problems in a home before you purchase it and help negotiate the lowest price. Buyer's brokers usually share in the commission once the home is sold, get paid on an hourly fee basis, or earn a set fee if they locate a home that you end up purchasing. Make sure, however, that the broker works only for you. To find a qualified buyer's broker, contact the Home Referral Network Buyer's Homefinding Network (800-500-3569; www.finderhome.com).

FINDING MONEY MANAGERS AND BROKERS

If you don't have the time or knowledge to invest your capital, you might need a personal money manager. When you buy shares in a mutual fund, you in effect hire a money manager. Retaining your own money manager differs from opening a mutual fund account in several other ways:

- Individual money managers offer more personal service and record-keeping.

- Money manager fees are generally more than mutual fund fees.
- The required minimum initial investment imposed by money managers is much higher than it is for mutual funds—$50,000 to $1 million.

Because money managers charge higher fees and impose larger minimums, why would you want to hire one? Usually, the answer is performance. Many money managers provide far better long-term results to clients than do mutual funds. In addition, you often can meet with your money manager to discuss how he or she allocates your assets.

Ensure Your Money's Safety

To protect you against the possibility that a money manager will run off with your money, your assets should be held by a separate custodian, such as a bank or brokerage firm, not by the money manager directly. You do not have to restrict yourself to a money manager in or near your hometown. The manager should agree to send you regular statements, usually quarterly, explaining where your money is invested and what returns you are earning.

Check Track Records

Before you commit to any money manager, check into his or her background and track record. Keep in mind that many of them take higher risks and provide lower returns than advertised. Every legitimate fund manager must register as an investment advisor with the SEC. Ask to see a copy of the advisor's ADV form, which he or she files with the SEC. Part II of this form describes the manager's education, experience, fee structure, and investment style and results. The form should also reveal any trouble the manager has had with the SEC or any other government agency.

Ask the advisor for the names of three or four satisfied clients, then contact them and ask whether they have earned the returns the manager claims. Look closely at the manager's performance record. Most compare their returns to the S&P 500 performance. Do not expect your manager to outperform the S&P 500 or any other index every year, because few manage that feat.

Nevertheless, hire a manager only if he or she can beat the index over a longer period of time, preferably at least five years. Ideally, settle on a stock fund manager who has provided at least a 10 to 15 percent long-term gain or a bond manager who has achieved an 8 to 10 percent average annual return. Most managers who quote their returns to clients should include the effect of all fees and brokerage commissions.

It is probably best if you hire a manager who has been in business at least five years, and preferably ten, so he or she has had experience in both bull and bear markets. The money manager also should have accumulated a significant pool of assets—at least $10 million and probably more than $50 million—to show that he or she has kept many clients satisfied.

Evaluate the Fees

Usually, a manager will levy a fee based on an annual percentage of your account's value. The fee may range from 1 to 2 percent of your account balance. As your account grows, so does the amount of money the manager earns for himself; therefore, he or she has a strong incentive to provide superior returns. Most managers will give you a discount on fees if you invest far more than the minimum they require.

Most money manager fees include brokerage commissions, but certain money management firms will nick you with another round of fees, commonly called reporting or administrative charges.

Many brokerage and other financial firms offer what are known as wrap accounts as a way for investors to have access to top money managers. The total fee on a wrap account, which includes money management services and brokerage commissions, should never exceed 3 percent of the value of your portfolio. Currently, most managers charge between 1.5 and 2 percent. Wrap accounts usually have lower minimums than direct accounts with money managers—sometimes as little as $25,000 or $50,000.

Once you are satisfied that the manager is honest, possesses a good record, and charges reasonable fees, examine his or her style of investment and see if it is compatible with yours. But remember, the greater the risks a manager takes, the higher your returns should be in the long term.

Investment Management Consultants

If the whole process of choosing a money manager seems difficult and time consuming, another option is to hire an investment management consultant. He or she hires money managers to select stocks and bonds and evaluate the managers' performance based on the client's guidelines.

The consultant constantly monitors many money managers possessing different investment styles and may recommend that you transfer assets from one manager to another if the manager's performance slips. The consultant, often associated with a brokerage firm, also performs all necessary record-keeping and sends you quarterly statements. If the money manager fails to perform as expected, the consultant will switch your money from that firm to another money manager with more promise to perform better. The consultant continues to earn annual consulting fees no matter which manager handles your money, as long as they keep your account.

A good investment management consultant will help you determine what kind of money manager best suits your needs, explain different money management styles, and recommend several money managers who have superior records in each style. Finally, the consultant should design a portfolio using several managers, so if one performs badly, your portfolio will not suffer too large a loss.

Consultants usually work under a wrap-fee arrangement. If they charge a 3 percent annual fee, for instance, the consultant might get 1 percent of it and the money manager, 2 percent. You can locate a qualified investment management consultant through most major brokerage firms. To locate a Certified Investment Management Analyst, contact the Investment Management Consultants Association (IMCA, 9101 E. Kenyon Ave., Suite 3000, Denver, CO 80237; 303-770-3377, 800-599-9462; www.imca.org).

CHOOSING A STOCKBROKER

The key to selecting a stockbroker is to separate the truly helpful professional from the out-to-make-a-buck salesperson. Because the key benefit of working with a full-service broker is the advice he or she gives, investigate carefully any broker you consider hiring. As with other professionals, the best way to locate a qualified broker is to ask friends, relatives, or business associates for referrals. If that method doesn't uncover a satisfactory professional, visit the branch office of a nearby brokerage house and ask to see the branch manager. Explain your situation and investing needs and describe approximately how much money you have to invest. If the branch manager values you as a customer, he or she will refer you to a broker whose experience matches your situation.

The Process

Interview at least three brokers and look for one that has dealt with clients in situations similar to yours. Then ask for their names and contact them to see what they say about the broker. Also, ask the broker how long he or she has been in the business, and whether the broker specializes in one investment type. The broker you choose should offer a specialty that matches your level of experience and the amount of money you have to invest.

Most of all, however, you should feel that he or she genuinely understands your concerns, that the broker is trustworthy, and that he or she will not push you into products that you might not understand or that are not appropriate for your situation.

Finally, check the broker's record with your state securities department. You can locate it through the North American Securities Administrators Association (10 G St., NE, Suite 710, Washington, DC 20002; 202-737-0900, 888-846-2722; www.naasa.org).

National versus regional firms. National firms, such as Merrill Lynch, Salomon Smith Barney, Morgan Stanley, Prudential Securities, and Bear Stearns, are commonly known as wirehouses. These firms sell products and create their own mutual funds or unit investment trusts.

The other type of full-service brokerage firm, called a regional firm, specializes in a region of the country, and its analysts tend to focus on stocks in that region. Regional brokers may therefore discover local companies with good long-term potential long before the national firms hear about them. The best broker, whether he or she works for a wirehouse or a regional firm, often does his or her own research in addition to screening the research performed by the firm's analysts.

Brokers' Services

Both national and regional full-service firms offer asset management accounts, where your stocks, bonds, and mutual funds are held. All dividends and interest received are automatically swept into a money-market mutual fund until you decide where to reinvest the money. Your broker will hold all your securities in *street name*—the name of the brokerage firm—making it easy for the brokerage to transfer ownership when you decide to sell. In case the brokerage goes bankrupt, the federal Securities Investor Protection Corporation (SIPC) insures your brokerage account for up to $500,000 in securities and $100,000 in cash.

Commissions and Fees

In return for advice and service, you must pay retail commissions to national or regional full-service brokers. The lower your volume of trading, the higher your commissions per share. If you buy just a few shares of a low-priced stock, for example, you might pay a commission of up to $.40 or $.50 a share, or as much as 5 percent of the money you invest. On the other hand, if you buy several hundred shares of a high-priced stock, you may pay as little as $.10 a share, or less than 1 percent of the purchase price. If you become a regular customer, you can demand and will receive discounts.

Brokers also charge commissions on mutual funds, although you may not have to pay it up front. The traditional commission, or load, is about 5 percent off the top. So, for every $100 you invest, $95 goes to the fund. Some brokers, instead of charging up front, take a back-end load—a fee you must pay if you sell the fund within the first few years of owning it.

For individual bonds, brokers usually do not charge an explicit commission. Instead, they buy the bond at one price and sell it to you at a higher price. The difference between the brokers' price and yours is known as the spread, and it acts as the commission. As with stocks, the size of the spread is determined by the amount of money you invest. The more bonds you buy, the smaller the spread. Other products, such as unit investment trusts, limited partnerships, annuities, life insurance, options, and new stock and bond issues, all charge different commissions. Usually, the broker keeps between 35 and 45 percent of the fee, with the rest going to the brokerage firm.

Brokers also receive ongoing fees as a cut of management fees to mutual funds, partnerships, or annuity companies. In the end, be aware of all these commissions and fees before you buy anything from a broker. Remember, transactions generate fees. In the most blatant cases, brokers will *churn* clients' accounts, meaning that they trade excessively just to generate commissions.

The Discount Broker Alternative

One sure way to cut your commission expenses is to work with a discount broker. Discounters generally do not offer advice but execute orders at much lower fees than full-service firms. Three kinds of discount brokers exist: full-service, deep-discount, and electronic. The three largest full-service discounters—Charles Schwab based in San Francisco, Fidelity Investments in Boston, and Quick & Reilly in New York City—offer almost every service that you can get from a national full-service firm like Merrill Lynch, except for explicit buy-and-sell recommendations by their brokers. Yet the commissions they charge can be anywhere from 20 to 60 percent lower than a national full-service brokerage house charges, depending on the size of your trades.

Deep-discount firms charge even less but offer fewer services and do almost all of their business with customers over the phone or online. Generally, they are designed for active investors who know what they're doing.

The third kind of discount broker is electronic. These brokers operate through their Web sites and because they have much lower expenses can pass the savings on to their customers in the form of even lower commissions. You can open an account online. All of these online brokers offer real-time price quotes, account information, research links, and technical support. A few of the major electronic brokers: Credit Suisse First Boston Direct (800-825-5723; www.CSFBdirect.com), E*Trade Securities (800-387-2331; www .etrade.com), National Discount Brokers NOW Ameritrade Plus (800-888-3999; www.Ameritradeplus.com), and Wall Streete (888-925-5783; www .wallstreete.com).

When seeking the lowest commissions, call several firms to determine what you will pay to execute a particular trade. The most comprehensive survey of discount and full-service brokers' fees and a rating of their services is compiled by Gomez, Inc., the Internet quality measurement firm (610 Lincoln St., Waltham, MA 02451; 781-768-2100; www.gomez.com).

For more on the advantages and disadvantages of the various kinds of brokers, see *Everyone's Money Book on Stocks, Bonds, and Mutual Funds.*

POINTS TO REMEMBER

- Friends, relatives, and business associates are a good starting point to suggest potential candidates for your various financial advisors.
- Before hiring advisors, figure out what you already know and what you need to know, then hire someone to help only in your areas of uncertainty.
- Take your time selecting an advisor and make sure you ask for references, credentials, and how the advisor will be compensated.
- When it comes to legal advice, don't overlook often cost-saving alternative dispute resolution options like mediation or arbitration.
- When selecting a stockbroker, look for someone whose expertise matches your needs and interview at least three before settling on one.
- A personal money manager may be an option if you don't have the time or knowledge to invest your capital.
- One option that cuts broker commission expenses is to work with a discount broker.

RESOURCES

Books

E-Investing: How to Choose and Use a Discount Broker, by Rob Carrick and Guy Anderson (John Wiley & Sons, 1 Wiley Dr., Somerset, NJ 08875; 212-850-6000, 800-225-5945; www.wiley.com). Coverage of brokers includes how they work, how to choose one, detailed cost and service comparisons, and who should maintain an account at a discount broker versus a full-service brokerage.

The Online Broker and Trading Directory, by Larry Chambers and Karen Johnson (McGraw-Hill, P.O. Box 543, Blacklick, OH 43004; 800-634-3961; www .mcgraw-hill.com). Profiles top brokerages; explains online trading and Wall Street terms and examines the services offered by online trading companies.

The Right Way to Hire Financial Help: A Complete Guide to Choosing and Managing Brokers, Financial Planners, Insurance Agents, Lawyers, and Tax Preparers, by Charles A. Jaffe (The MIT Press, 292 Main St., Cambridge, MA 02142; 800-356-0343; http://mitpress.mit.edu). Takes readers through the basics of hiring and managing brokers, financial planners, insurance agents, lawyers, tax preparers, bankers, and real estate agents.

Using a Lawyer . . . What to Do If Things Go Wrong, by Kay Ostberg (HALT, 1612 K St., NW, Suite 510, Washington, DC 20006; 888-367-4258; www.halt.org). A complete guide to shopping for and working with a lawyer. Provides sample fee agreements and a state-by-state list of lawyer grievance committees.

Financial Planning/Investing Organizations

Society of Financial Service Professionals (270 S. Bryn Mawr Ave., Bryn Mawr, PA 19010-2195; 888-243-2258; www.financialpro.org). An association of insurance and financial services professionals that offers many qualifying credentials.

Consumer Federation of America (1424 16th St., NW, Suite 604, Washington, DC 20036; 202-387-6121; www.consumerfed.org). Consumer-oriented group has done several studies on the financial advice industry.

Invest Counsel Association of America (1050 17th St., Suite 725, Washington, DC 20036; 202-293-4222; www.icaa.org). Professional organization of independent investment counsel firms that manage the assets of individuals, pension plans, trusts, and nonprofit institutions, such as foundations.

National Association of Insurance and Financial Advisors (2901 Telestar Ct., Falls Church, VA 22042-1205; 703-770-8100; www.naifa.org). Educates the public about insurance and how to work with insurance agents and brokers.

Insurance Organizations

Chartered Property Casualty Underwriters Society (720 Providence Rd., Malvern, PA 19355; 610-644-2100, 800-932-2728; www.cpcusociety.org). Professional association for agents and other insurance professionals selling property and casualty insurance and risk management services.

Life and Health Insurance Foundation for Education (2175 K St., Suite 250, NW, Washington, DC 20037; 202-464-5000, 888-543-3777; www.life-line.org). A not-for-profit education foundation committed to better educating the public about life, health, and disability insurance, and the value-added role of the agent.

Real Estate Organizations

National Association of REALTORS® (430 N. Michigan Ave., Chicago, IL 60611; 312-329-8200, 800-874-6500; www.realtor.org). The trade group for real estate agents. Can help find a qualified real estate broker or agent in your area.

Legal Organizations

Association for Conflict Resolution (formerly Society of Professionals in Dispute Resolution; 1527 New Hampshire Ave., NW, Washington, DC 20036; 202-667-9700; www.acresolution.org). A group of people interested in alternative dispute resolution techniques, such as mediation and arbitration, which avoid expensive lawsuits.

National Senior Citizens Law Center (1101 14th St., NW, Suite 400, Washington, DC 20005; 202-289-6976; www.nsclc.org). Specializes in litigation, research, lobbying, and training lawyers on issues of concern to retired people.

Tax Preparer/Accountant Organizations

American Institute of Certified Public Accountants (1211 Avenue of the Americas, New York, NY 10036-8775; 212-596-6200, 888-777-7077; www.aicpa.org). Represents and maintains standards for CPAs; also licenses Personal Financial Specialists (PFS), who are accountants concentrating on financial planning. For a list of PFS members nationally, call 888-999-9256.

National Association of Enrolled Agents (200 Orchard Ridge Dr., Suite 302, Gaithersburg, MD 20878; 301-212-9608, 800-424-4339; www.naea.org). A group of enrolled agents (former IRS employees) who offer tax advice and preparation services. Will send names of four enrolled agents in your area.

National Society of Accountants (1010 N. Fairfax St., Alexandria, VA 22314; 703-549-6400, 800-966-6679; www.nsacct.org). Accredits specialists in accounting and taxation who serve the financial needs of individuals and small businesses.

General Organization

Council of Better Business Bureaus (4200 Wilson Blvd., Suite 800, Arlington, VA 22203-1838; 703-276-0100; www.bbb.org). An excellent source of information about many consumer matters, including choosing a financial advisor.

Federal Government Regulators

Federal Trade Commission (6th St. and Pennsylvania Ave., NW, Washington, DC 20580; 202-326-2222, 877-FTC-HELP; www.ftc.gov). Offers many helpful brochures, including "Facts about Financial Planners" and "How to Talk to and Select Lawyers, Financial Planners, Tax Preparers and Real Estate Brokers."

North American Securities Administrators Association (10 G St., NE, Suite 710, Washington, DC 20002; 202-737-0900, 888-846-2722; www.nasaa.org). Represents state securities enforcement agencies. Responsible for investor protection.

CHAPTER 8

Smart Money Strategies for Every Age and Situation

The first seven chapters of this book introduced you to what you need to know about personal finances. Only one element remains: how to apply all this advice to your current situation. This chapter offers some guidelines to help you tailor the book's general principles of personal finance to your specific situation (see Figure 8.1). Following are some rules of thumb appropriate for every age and situation that you can take and apply to account for your unique circumstances.

YOUR 20S AND 30S—ESTABLISHING YOUR FINANCIAL FOUNDATION

The transition from school to the workforce can be both exhilarating and frustrating. You may feel the thrill of financial independence, yet your starting salary may be far too low to purchase your first home or even rent your own apartment. In addition, you may have debts accumulated from paying for college. As you progress through your 30s, your career should become more firmly established, and your income and assets should grow. But even in your early 20s, you can do plenty to establish good financial habits.

Giving Yourself a Financial Checkup

As you work through the exercises in Chapter 1, don't feel discouraged if you haven't yet built up much in income or assets or if your expenses seem out of control. Don't expect substantial income until you have several years

Figure 8.1   Kiplinger's Personal Finance Web site
<www.kiplinger.com> from the Kiplinger Washington
Editors is one of scores of solid financial information
sources no matter your age or personal situation.

of job experience, perhaps by your late 20s or early 30s. Asset accumulation will follow.

In the meantime, establish solid financial habits. Set up an efficient recordkeeping system, track your cash flow carefully, and create a budget you can follow. Even if you still rely on your parents for financial help, balance your income and expenses without regard to parental support. Prioritize short-, medium-, and long-term goals. In assessing your risk tolerance, realize that while you may not yet have a great deal of money, you do have a great deal of time for your investments to grow. Take more risk in hopes of higher long-term returns.

Investing. Start to assemble a portfolio of stocks, bonds, and mutual funds as early as you can afford to save. Aim to set aside as much as 10 percent of your after-tax income. If you don't have much capital, mutual funds probably make the most sense. An easy way to invest in funds is to enroll in an automatic investment program in which a mutual fund company deducts a set amount from your checking account. Several fund groups even waive their minimum initial investments if you commit to an automatic investing plan, allowing you to start for as little as $100 a month.

Favor stock funds over bond funds, because they have much more growth potential over the long haul than bond funds. You might allocate 70 to 80 percent of your savings to equity funds, with a high proportion of that money in aggressive growth, growth, and international funds, which will probably provide the highest long-term returns. Unless you have a great deal of extra money and time to learn, avoid speculating in futures, options, gold, and collectibles while in your 20s and 30s. Also, establish a good relationship with a bank. And don't forget to have an emergency reserve fund—at least three months' living expenses—in a bank money fund or money-market mutual fund.

Real estate. If your dream is to buy a home instead of renting forever, it will take a disciplined savings program to assemble the down payment of 5 to 10 percent of a home's value plus closing costs. If you cannot afford a home, spend as little as possible on rent and invest any excess earnings in a savings or mutual fund account to build up capital.

Credit. Get off to a good start by establishing credit with several lenders and paying your loans punctually. If necessary, have your parents cosign a loan or credit card application so you qualify. Then, as soon as possible, take over the payments until you qualify for the loan on your own record. One easy way to save money is to apply for the credit cards with the lowest interest rates and annual fees.

If you have outstanding education loans with a high interest rate, look into consolidating them into one lower rate loan (Sallie Mae Inc.; 800-448-

3533; www.salliemae.com). Expect some debt as you get established, but don't take on so much that you let it overwhelm you.

Cars. Depending on whether you are single or married, with or without children, buy a less expensive car while you are young. Because your car needs will probably change if you get married, have children, or move, it might be worth leasing and trading in the car several years from now for a model that suits your new circumstances.

Insurance. You will need all five types of insurance: auto, disability, health, homeowners (or renter's), and life. Your auto insurance rates will probably be higher than they will be in later years. But if you have no accidents, your rates should fall by the time you reach your 30s. Disability insurance is vital when you are in your 20s and 30s in case you are seriously injured and suffer several decades of lost wages.

Health insurance is also important. If you are no longer on your parents' policy, consider taking out a short-term one until an employer's plan covers you. Scrutinize any potential employer's plan to learn how much both you and the company pay. Also, ask whether the health plan offers alternatives such as health maintenance organizations (HMOs) or preferred provider organizations (PPOs). As you move into your 30s, you might switch your insurance coverage from a traditional policy to an HMO if you must cover a spouse and children. If your employer provides no health insurance or you are self-employed, look into obtaining coverage through some group that you already belong to or may be able to join.

Homeowners insurance is a must if you own a home; make sure that you have enough. Update the policy as the value of your home and belongings increases over the years. If you rent, look into renter's insurance and decide if its cost is worthwhile. Life insurance is not necessary if you are young and no one else depends on your income, though if you anticipate having a family some day, you can buy some coverage and lock in much cheaper rates while you are still young and healthy.

Retirement and estate planning. Though it may seem eons into the future, the earlier you start saving, the more you will accumulate by retirement. For example, if you make $25,000 annually and begin saving $125 a month when you are age 25, and if you earn an average 8 percent rate of return, you will amass $288,647 by age 60. If everything in this example remains the same except that you begin your retirement savings at age 35, you will end up with $119,671. And if you procrastinate until age 45, you will build up only $43,543.

It also is a good idea to have a will so that your assets can be distributed according to your wishes when you die. If you have children, estate planning establishes guardianship and often sets up trusts to pass assets to the children over time.

Employee benefits. By participating in all your employer's benefits programs as soon as you start your job or qualify for the programs, you can get off to a solid start in laying your financial foundation. Enroll in every available retirement savings program and allocate most of your money to growth vehicles such as stocks. Also, you can borrow against your retirement savings at reasonable interest rates if necessary, so don't consider the money totally out of reach until retirement.

If you are self-employed or work for a small company with no retirement plan, fund a traditional or Roth individual retirement account (IRA), a Keogh, or another qualified plan. Within these plans, invest most of your assets in growth stocks or mutual funds, which offer maximum growth potential.

YOUR 40S AND 50S—THE PEAK EARNING YEARS OF MIDDLE AGE

At this age, you may join what many call the sandwich generation— supporting your kids, yourself, and your parents. Many middle-agers short- change themselves by spending their money on their children and parents. The only solution to this dilemma is careful planning and tracking your personal fi- nances, so you can set targets and monitor your progress toward them.

Giving Yourself a Financial Checkup

By the time you reach your 40s and 50s, your income should be sub- stantially higher than it was in your 20s and 30s, reflected in a sizable net worth. Working through the cash flow and budgeting exercises in Chapter 1 is as important as ever, because you should have more sources of income as well as more expenses. If you have built up a substantial pool of assets, you may be more interested in preserving that capital than in making it grow. On the other hand, if you have not invested much, you will have to take more risks to earn the high returns you need to finance a comfortable retirement.

Investing. If you have already established a substantial portfolio of stocks and equity mutual funds, you might begin to scale back the risk level of your holdings as you move through your 40s and 50s. If 70 percent of your portfolio consisted of aggressive growth or growth stocks when you were in your 20s and 30s, 40 to 50 percent is more appropriate now. You can allocate the rest of your capital to more conservative growth and income investments, such as equity-income, balanced, and convertible mutual funds. Also, in- crease your bond holdings to about 50 to 70 percent of your portfolio over time, and reinvest the dividends if you don't need the income the bonds generate to live on. If you are in the top tax bracket, consider investing your money in municipal bonds rather than taxable Treasuries or corporates.

If you have not saved or invested over the years, start doing so immediately. Aim to set aside at least 10 percent of your after-tax income—as much as 15 percent, if possible. If your employer offers a salary reduction plan and you have not yet enrolled, do so to the maximum extent possible. Once you are over age 50, tax law allows you to make additional "catch-up" contributions to your 401(k) or IRA plans.

Real estate. Owning real estate is often appealing to those in their 40s and 50s, because the deductions from mortgage interest and property taxes produce significant tax savings. If you rent, use any cash that would normally be applied to home ownership costs to build up your stock, bond, and mutual fund portfolio. If you already own a home, you may be in a position to invest in rental real estate, which—if it generates positive cash flow—can provide a regular source of income in retirement.

Credit. If you have paid your bills on time over the last few years, you should have established a solid credit record that allows you to borrow as much as you need. But, you should borrow less as you near retirement. Instead of taking on a loan to buy a new car, consider leasing. If you run into a cash squeeze, you might need to borrow against your employee benefits plans or life insurance policies. As you move into your late 50s, aim to pay off most or all your debt—except, perhaps, your mortgage—by the time you retire. If you remain heavily in debt, reexamine your budget and cut back on spending to bring expenses in line with income.

Insurance. You will need all five types of insurance: auto, disability, health, homeowners, and life. Be sure your auto coverage is appropriate for the value of the vehicle you have. Disability insurance also is important, because you could lose years of income if you are injured or become sick on the job. If the premiums, deductibles, and copayments on adequate health insurance become too expensive, look into a health maintenance organization (HMO) or a preferred provider organization (PPO) as a way of capping your out-of-pocket health care costs. If you own your home and have homeowners insurance, make sure that your policy is up-to-date and you have replacement coverage.

If someone else depends on your income, such as your spouse and children, life insurance coverage is worthwhile. But if you start a cash-value policy in your mid- to late 50s, you probably will not have enough time to accumulate significant cash values, because such policies are loaded with front-end costs. You might also look into annuities as tax-deferred savings vehicles funded by regular contributions. Or, you may want to use a lump sum from your employer's benefits plans to buy an immediate annuity, which will establish an income stream starting at age 59½.

Taxes. Maximize all the legal tax reduction strategies discussed in Chapter 6 on tax planning, including those benefits available from your employer. If you are self-employed, fund a Keogh or SEP account with as much money as you can afford. Invest in tax-sheltered vehicles such as municipal bonds and municipal bond funds, annuities, and life insurance. If your calculations show that it is advantageous, buy a home and use the mortgage to generate interest deductions. If you already own a home and have built up a substantial amount of equity, convert your nondeductible consumer loans to deductible home-equity debt. If you want to downsize to a smaller home or apartment, you may want to rent and invest the proceeds of your home sale in income-producing stocks, bonds, and mutual funds. Maximize deductions by bunching them in one year. And, finally, set up trusts to pass on your assets to your children with a minimal amount of estate taxes.

Retirement. You still have time to plan for and fund your retirement. Put aside as much as possible over the years. Contact the Social Security Administration to make sure that it has correctly recorded your earnings. Review the retirement plans your employer offers, so you understand what benefits they provide. If you have access to a defined contribution plan like a 401(k), maximize your contributions. Once you've reached age 50, tax law allows you to make an additional "catch-up" contribution each year. As you move through your 50s, be prepared for an unexpected early-retirement offer from your employer, so that you know your alternatives ahead of time if it happens.

Estate planning. The more assets you accumulate through your 40s and 50s, the more important estate planning becomes. Once your family's assets exceed $1 million (rising to $3.5 million in 2009), you might need to transfer the ownership of some assets to your spouse, so you can both take advantage of the unified tax credit. If your assets exceed $2 million for a married couple filing jointly, you might need to set up a trust for your children and other beneficiaries. Also, make sure that you have a valid will and update it regularly.

YOUR 60S AND UP—THE RETIREMENT YEARS

If you have planned for retirement most of your working life, the transition into retirement starting in your 60s should be relatively smooth. Ideally, you will have accumulated enough capital through a combination of employee benefits plans and personal investments to produce enough income to live comfortably. However, don't think of retirement as lasting a few short years before you die, as earlier generations did. Today, the average life expectancy for someone in good health who retires in his or her early 60s is at least 20 years, and many retirees live into their 90s or even 100s.

Giving Yourself a Financial Checkup

As you make the transition from the working years into retirement, complete the worksheets in Chapter 1 to assess your current net worth and cash flow. Once you retire, you should receive income from Social Security, your company's defined benefit and/or defined contribution pension plan, your investments, and your annuities. On the other hand, if your living expenses exceed your income, use the budgeting exercise in Chapter 1 to find ways to reduce your expenses as well as increase your income.

Be sure to complete the Recordkeeping Worksheet, so your family knows the location of all records and can locate all financial advisors when you die. As you move through your 60s into your 70s and 80s, give yourself a complete financial checkup every few years.

Investing. Do not convert your investment portfolio from a broad mix of stocks, bonds, and cash instruments to solely income-oriented bonds. If you lock yourself into current yields by buying only bonds, your capital will not grow as it most likely would if you own stocks. The best investing strategy is to assemble a conservative mix of stocks, bonds, and cash vehicles that produces enough income to live on but also grows in value over time. This might mean keeping about 80 percent of your assets in cash instruments, like money-market funds, and fixed-income assets, such as Treasury, high-quality corporate, junk, and municipal bonds, mortgage-backed securities, and the mutual funds that hold these assets. In assessing which bond fund is best, scrutinize expense ratios—the greater a fund's expenses, the lower your yield. Also, consider closed-end bond funds, which can offer very attractive yields, particularly if they sell at a discount of their net asset value. Depending on whether yields make it worthwhile, some of this fixed-income money could be invested in CDs. You can shop for the highest-yielding FDIC-insured CD anywhere in the country by looking at Web sites such as <www.bankrate .com>.

Invest the remaining 20 percent of your money in stocks or stock mutual funds, which provide an inflation hedge. Most of these stocks and funds should pay a dividend, so they give you current income as well as growth. To find safe, high-yielding stocks, search such industries as electric, gas, water, and telephone utilities; banking; oil; and insurance. For a more diversified portfolio, buy mutual funds holding mostly high-yielding stocks. Types of funds you might want in your portfolio that offer growth potential and current income include total return, balanced, flexible, equity-income, growth and income, and convertible funds. As the value of your portfolio changes over time, keep a proper mix of income and growth components.

Real estate. If you sell your home, reinvest the proceeds in income-producing stocks and bonds. Remember, you can avoid all capital gains taxes on the sale of your home as long as your profit is less than $500,000 for a married couple filing jointly or $250,000 for a single, and as long as it has been your primary residence for two of the past five years. If you remain in your home, pay off your mortgage. You might want to take out a reverse mortgage, in which the bank sends you a monthly check until you die while you get to live in the home.

Also, consider various forms of real estate as income producers. Rental real estate—as long as the rent is higher than your operating costs—can be attractive, though you may not want the headaches of being a landlord. You can also earn significant income without management hassles by buying into real estate investment trusts (REITs are companies that manage a portfolio of real estate investments), real estate mutual funds, or income-oriented real estate limited partnerships.

Credit. Try to minimize debt and use it for the convenience of arranging large purchases, such as a new car or extensive travel. Before you take on such an obligation, however, make sure that you have the income to pay off the debt quickly.

Cars. As long as you can drive safely, keep your car. Leasing may be a less costly option—especially if you only plan to keep your car three to five years—because it doesn't take a big down payment and allows you to keep more of your capital invested in income-producing stocks, bonds, and mutual funds. If you plan to hold onto the car for many years, however, purchasing it probably makes more sense.

Insurance. Your needs for the five types of insurance—auto, disability, health, homeowners, and life—differ significantly in retirement from your insurance needs during your working years.

Auto insurance is mandatory in most states. Many insurers offer mature driver discounts of 10 percent off your premium if you have a good driving record. Depending on the condition of your car, you may be able to lower your premium by reducing the amount of collision damage coverage you carry.

Disability insurance is not necessary once you retire, and a life-extension rider on disability insurance that pays benefits for the rest of your life is expensive and usually not worthwhile.

With health insurance, the best coverage is probably that provided by the company from which you retired, even though you must pay the full premiums. You might find a good preferred provider organization (PPO) that provides good care and controls your health costs. In addition, sign up for Part

A and Part B of Medicare and get a good Medigap policy. If your income is low enough, you can also qualify for Medicaid. If you are a veteran, you may be able to obtain medical care through the Department of Veterans Affairs (VA). If you anticipate needing a nursing home or medical care in your own residence, look into the many long-term-care policies offered by insurance companies. A good independent source for finding the best coverage is Long-Term Care Quote at 800-587-3279 or <www.searchltc.com>.

Homeowners insurance continues to be necessary if you still own your home. Life insurance can be very useful for retirees. If you have funded a cash-value policy for many years, you probably have built up considerable cash value. One way to tap that asset is to convert it into an annuity that pays monthly income. If you have term insurance, the premiums are now probably so high that it makes little sense to continue coverage.

Taxes. To minimize the tax bite, receive your retirement income in a way that will stretch out your tax liability for as many years as possible. For example, unless you absolutely need the capital to live on, do not take distributions from your IRA or Keogh until you reach age 70½. Or you may consider converting your traditional IRA assets into a Roth IRA that will allow you to draw the money out tax-free at whatever pace you want. If you withdraw funds from an insurance contract, first take out your original principal that is not taxable, then receive distributions from investment earnings, which are subject to taxation. If you are in the top tax bracket, you may want to sell investments producing taxable income, such as Treasury or corporate bonds, and buy municipal bonds paying tax-free income. If you live in a high-tax state, buy bonds issued by that state to sidestep both federal and state taxes.

Estate planning. If you have accumulated assets worth more than $1 million (rising to $3.5 million in 2009), you need to execute a detailed estate plan, which may involve establishing trusts. To guard against the possibility that you may become mentally or physically incapacitated, execute a living will, durable power of attorney, or health care power of attorney, which allows your spouse, children, doctor, or close friend to make vital medical decisions if you are incapable of doing so.

Employee benefits. Determine when it is most advantageous to retire. The later you stop working, the greater your monthly Social Security and defined benefit pension checks. Your benefits counselor can calculate your monthly pension check at different retirement ages. If you receive an early retirement offer, your company may add a few years to your actual years of service to allow you to qualify for a more generous pension. You will be offered several options for the payout of the accumulated value in your defined contribution plan. That includes a lump sum to roll into your IRA or buy an annuity; or leave the money with the company and withdraw cash regularly.

Consult an employee benefits counselor or a financial planner when making such decisions.

WHEN YOU'RE SINGLE

If you are single, either you have chosen to remain single because you like the lifestyle and never plan to marry (a committed single) or you are currently single but hope to marry someday (a temporary single). Couples who live together represent a compromise between the lifestyles: both people are legally single, but their financial lives are closely intertwined. The best financial strategies for you depend heavily on which kind of single you are.

If you live with your partner, avoid mingling your investment assets or your credit lives and be careful of buying or leasing a car jointly. Also if you purchase real estate with someone you have been living with outside of marriage, have a lawyer draw up a cohabitation agreement that specifies who is responsible for how much of the mortgage and maintenance payments, and who gets what if you break up or if one of you wants to sell his or her share of the property.

Financial Checkup

No matter what your age or family situation, you need to work through the exercises in Chapter 1 to evaluate where you stand financially, where you want to go, and how you plan to get there.

Investing. Singles can handle a bit more risk in search of higher returns than investors financially responsible for others can. But before you invest, be sure you have an emergency reserve fund of at least three months' salary. Then enroll in every investment program your employer offers. In your younger years, invest aggressively for capital growth, but as you approach retirement, allocate your assets more conservatively to preserve enough capital to produce the income you need for the rest of your life. Set up an investment account separate from your employer's in which you accumulate stocks, bonds, mutual funds, and cash instruments.

Insurance. Your highest insurance priority should be disability coverage, because you will need to replace your income if you are injured on the job. Look into a supplemental policy that will pay 60 to 70 percent of your salary if you become incapacitated. (A major provider is AFLAC–American Family Life Assurance Company of Columbus, Ga., 800-992-3522; www.aflac.com.) Adequate health insurance is extremely important, because with only one income you are more vulnerable to a severe financial reversal if you suffer an expensive medical treatment that is not reimbursed by your insurer.

For singles living together outside of marriage, life insurance might make sense, because the surviving partners may depend on the income generated by their mate. You must make sure to designate your mate as the beneficiary of the policy. For a tax-deferred retirement savings vehicle, consider an annuity. You can buy either a fixed annuity, which pays a specified rate of interest each year, or a variable annuity, which gives you far more growth potential, because it offers the ability to move your assets between stock, bond, and money-market funds within a tax-deferred insurance contract. By the time you retire, you might have amassed a large amount of assets, which you can then convert into a monthly stream of income.

Retirement. Take advantage of the fact that you have no one else to support financially and stash away cash in your retirement plans as soon as you can afford to do so. If you are not eligible for any pension plan, open a traditional or Roth individual retirement account (IRA) and make tax-deductible contributions every year. If you run your own business or produce self-employment income through freelance activities, you can also fund a Keogh and deduct your contributions. Your money grows tax-deferred inside both an IRA and a Keogh.

Estate planning. If you live with someone outside of marriage, both you and your partner should write wills distributing all your possessions to each other. To avoid problems with relatives contesting your will, have it drawn up by a qualified estate-planning lawyer and witnessed properly. You may also want to place assets in a living trust, so that when you die they pass immediately from you to your housemate outside of probate court.

WHEN YOU'RE MARRIED

Three types of married couples exist: those with children, those currently without children but hoping to have them someday, and those who anticipate never having children. The state of marriage itself affects many financial decisions; when you add children, even more financial planning is necessary.

Financial Checkup

It is vital that each married couple assess and then discuss their financial situation, whether they are newlyweds or have celebrated their golden anniversary. Quite frequently, a husband who has taken care of the family finances by himself for decades dies suddenly, leaving his widow without a clue about their investments, insurance, estate plans, and every other financial matter, causing considerable trauma for the widow.

If you have children, involve them in your family's finances as much as possible as they grow older. You also might tap into the tremendous number of resources on the Internet to teach your children about money. Some child-oriented financial sites include: Young Investor <www.younginvestor .com>; Kids' Money <www.kidsmoney.org>; KidsBank.com <www.kidsbank .com>; and Young Americans Bank and Education Foundation <www .theyoungamericans.org>.

Another site, sponsored by the Mutual Fund Education Alliance and called Inve$ting for Kid$ & College <www.mfea.com/InvestmentStrategies /KidsCollege>, links you to the sites of "kid-friendly" mutual funds.

A few general guidelines for talking about money with your children:

- From the time they speak coherently to the time they enter preschool, explain what money is and how it works. When you shop, have them hand the cashier the money so they grasp the concept of receiving goods in exchange for cash.
- From preschool to first grade, give your children a weekly allowance in exchange for behaving well or doing certain chores. However, make it clear that such behavior is expected and need not be compensated.
- From second grade through junior high school, boost your children's weekly allowance in return for additional and more responsible chores and encourage them to save. As incentive, match their deposit dollar for dollar.
- From high school through college, encourage them to participate in important financial discussions and give them a family credit card so they learn to use credit responsibly.

Investing. Begin and maximize a regular investment program with the defined contribution, salary reduction, or profit-sharing plan offered by your and your spouse's employers. Also, deposit a certain amount of your earnings in a joint savings and investment account aside from the one your employer offers. Start by building your emergency cash reserve to at least three months' salary.

If you do not have kids, try to save 10 to 20 percent of your gross income. While you are young, invest most of it in growth-oriented vehicles, such as growth stocks or aggressive growth and international stock mutual funds. You can also enroll in one of the approximately 1,000 dividend reinvestment plans (DRIPs). Or you can set up an automatic investment program with almost any mutual fund that regularly will debit your bank account for whatever amount you specify.

Credit. Discuss your attitudes about debt with your spouse and come to an agreement about how much debt is appropriate for your income and lifestyle. Though a couple's finances may be intertwined, each spouse's credit records are maintained separately by credit reporting bureaus. Therefore, it is important that both husband and wife take out credit cards and other loans in their own names and repay these loans responsibly. Set a limit on the total amount of your income devoted to debt service. While you are young, this may be up to 20 percent; over time, try to reduce it to 10 percent or less.

Insurance. Married couples need all five types of insurance—auto, disability, health, homeowners, and life—whether they have children or not; however, the amount of coverage often depends on whether or not you have children.

With auto insurance, make sure that you have adequate comprehensive and liability protection to defend your family's assets against a lawsuit. Retain enough collision coverage to pay for the complete repair of your car in case of an accident. Disability insurance is critical. Your employer may offer some disability coverage but look into buying a supplemental policy that would generate between 60 and 70 percent of your salary. If both spouses work, each should have adequate disability protection.

If your employer offers the option with health insurance, look into health maintenance organizations (HMOs) or preferred provider organizations (PPOs) in your area. And if your company offers flexible spending accounts (FSAs) for health and dependent care, take advantage of them. With life insurance, if your spouse produces income, you need insurance policies for both of you to replace the lost income stream if either of you dies. You might also consider an annuity as a tax-deferred retirement savings vehicle.

Taxes. Most couples save money if they file a joint return. However, it could be more profitable to file separately, if both spouses earn significant taxable income and generate substantial deductions. The IRS says that you must file separately if you and your spouse have different tax-reporting fiscal years, if one spouse is a nonresident alien, or if either spouse is claimed as a dependent on someone else's return. The "marriage penalty" in the current tax law is in the process of being phased out, starting in 2005, so that by 2009 you should end up paying the same amount of taxes whether you are married or single, all other factors being equal.

Estate planning. Married couples should plan their estates whether or not they have children. If a couple has no will, many state laws say that all the assets of one spouse automatically transfer to the surviving spouse when the first one dies. In other states, they do not.

Under federal estate law, however, there is an unlimited marital deduction, so no estate taxes are due when assets pass from one spouse to the other. However, the estate of the surviving spouse will be taxed heavily when he or she dies, if none of the assets has been gifted away or no estate planning has been done and the assets exceed the estate tax exemption amount. If you have children, one of various kinds of trusts may be appropriate. You also need a will to designate a guardian to raise your underage children, if both you and your spouse die unexpectedly.

Employee benefits. Coordinate your employee benefits with those of your spouse. Many companies offer cafeteria-style plans that allow you to mix and match benefits according to your needs. If both you and your spouse have such flexibility, you may be able to create a combined set of benefits far superior to those you could obtain on your own. Discuss your benefits package with your spouse, so he or she understands the main provisions of the plans in case you die unexpectedly.

WHEN YOU'RE DIVORCED OR WIDOWED

The emotional trauma of losing a spouse through either death or divorce can be life shattering. But, the financial consequences might be even more devastating.

Financial Checkup

Whether your spouse dies or you go through a divorce, it dramatically changes your net worth statement as well as your cash flow and budgeting worksheets from Chapters 1 and 2. Also, prioritize your financial goals and reassess your risk tolerance.

Investing

Widowed. Depending on your age and the assets you inherit, you probably will want to invest conservatively and stress income over growth of capital. Some income-producing securities include utility stocks; Treasury, municipal, or corporate bonds; or mutual funds holding such stocks and bonds. Stock mutual funds that are conservative and produce a steady stream of income include equity-income, growth and income, convertible, balanced, and flexible funds. All bond funds (except zero-coupon funds) pay regular income, though you will probably want to concentrate on government, corporate, municipal, and international bond funds.

Nevertheless, do not invest all of your inherited capital in income-oriented funds. Assuming that you will live a long time, you should have some percentage—perhaps as much as 25 percent—of your portfolio in growth-oriented stocks and stock mutual funds. You still will need an emergency cash reserve to pay bills and meet unexpected expenses. This might amount to 5 to 10 percent of the value of your portfolio.

Divorced. If you are a divorcee who ends up with few assets, establish a disciplined savings program to get you back on your feet. Each month, set aside a regular amount of money in a bank account or mutual fund, so you can build a capital base. If you are a divorcee who ends up with some assets, also establish a regular savings program, though you might be able to create a larger and more diversified portfolio. If you are young, invest more aggressively in a growth-oriented stock or mutual fund. If you are elderly, keep the money in income-producing vehicles, such as bonds, bond funds, or certificates of deposit (CDs). For more information, read Chapter 2 on cash instruments and various investment vehicles.

Real Estate

Widowed. If cash is tight, one way to remain in your home and still receive income from the property is to take out a reverse mortgage. (See Chapter 3 for more information.) If possible, while your spouse is still alive, determine whether you would have enough income to stay in your residence if he or she died. If you decide that you would have to move, buy a life insurance policy on your spouse that would provide enough capital to let you stay.

Credit

One of the biggest problems facing widows, widowers, and divorcees is that they often do not have their own credit histories or earnings records, both used by lenders to assess their ability to repay debts. If you have trouble finding a bank that will grant you an open-end line of credit, consider assuming a secured line of credit to build your creditworthiness (see Chapter 3).

Insurance

Widowed. Disability insurance may be very important. The Social Security Administration has established many complex rules regarding the amount of disability benefits that widows and widowers receive, depending on their situation and age. For more details, contact the Social Security Administration (800-772-1213; www.ssa.gov).

Divorced. If you receive the car as part of a divorce settlement, make sure that the auto insurance policy is in your name. Divorcees generally do not have access to their ex-spouses' health insurance programs, but they do have rights to receive health insurance coverage under COBRA for 36 months. Try to line up health insurance through your own employer or through any group of which you are a member, such as a trade association. Better still, when negotiating the divorce settlement, try to obtain some provision from your former spouse to pay for health insurance, at least for a transitional period of a year or two.

Taxes

Widowed. For tax purposes, a widow or widower is considered unmarried and therefore usually must file his or her return as a single person. If you were widowed in the last two years, however, you may submit a return using the married-filing-jointly status (usually more advantageous than single status), if you meet the following four conditions:

1. You continue to maintain a primary home for a dependent child, and you provide at least half of the living costs of that child.
2. You are entitled to claim that child as a dependent.
3. You could have filed a joint return in the year your spouse died.
4. You have not remarried by January 1 of the following tax year. For example, in filing your 2003 tax return, you can use married status if you do not remarry before January 1, 2004.

As the surviving spouse of a marriage that filed jointly, you inherit all the tax liabilities of your marriage. If you find it to your advantage, file as head of household. To do so, you must support a dependent child with at least half of his or her living expenses. Your spouse must have died in a year prior to the current tax year. And you must have filed jointly in the year your spouse died. Widows or widowers younger than age 65 who support children on an income of $10,850 or less need not file a tax return. Widows or widowers age 65 and older who support children need not file a return if their income is $11,750 or less.

Divorced. Some of the most important issues to be resolved in a divorce include who will pay alimony and child support and in what amounts, how property will be distributed, who will receive the exemptions for dependent children, and how assets from qualified retirement plans such as pensions, 401(k)s, and Keoghs will be distributed. Certain IRS rules apply specifically to divorce. For example, transfers of property between a divorcing couple are considered tax-free exchanges as long as they take place within one year of the final divorce decree. If your divorce decree becomes final in the current tax year, you cannot file your tax return jointly with your ex-spouse.

Retirement

Widowed. Calculate what you might receive from Social Security in the future, counting both retirement and survivor's benefits. You can obtain these numbers from the Social Security Administration (800-772-1213; www .ssa.gov). Next, set up your savings regimen using an automatic investment program. If possible, contribute to employer-sponsored tax-deferred retirement plans. Also, establish a Keogh account if you produce self-employment income, or fund a traditional or Roth individual retirement account (IRA) whether or not your contribution is deductible.

If you are widowed while already retired, and you receive regular income from an annuity, those payments will continue until you die, as long as you and your spouse chose the joint and survivor payout option. Depending on your age, your spouse's earnings record, and whether you have children, you might be eligible for Social Security benefits. You will receive survivor's benefits if you are younger than age 60 and support children younger than 16 years old. However, if you are younger than 60 years old but have no children, you will not. Nevertheless, register your spouse's death with the Social Security Administration by supplying a copy of your marriage certificate and the death certificate. You then may be eligible for a small death benefit payment of $255.

Widows and widowers between age 60 and 65 are eligible for survivor's benefits from Social Security. However, your monthly check will be less than if you begin receiving benefits at age 65. If your spouse was married to someone else for at least ten years and then divorced, the former spouse is also entitled to receive Social Security benefits on your spouse's earnings record, as long as the ex-spouse did not remarry.

Divorced. If you divorce at a young age, take the same steps as a young widow. Often retirement plan benefits are considered a marital asset and are divided as part of a divorce settlement. You will receive no Social Security benefits based on your former spouse's work record unless you meet several conditions:

- Your marriage must have lasted at least ten years.
- You must be at least 62 years old and unmarried.
- Your ex-spouse must also be at least 62 years old. However, if you have been divorced for at least two years, you can receive benefits even if your ex-spouse is not retired.

To find out how much you deserve in divorcee Social Security benefits, call the Social Security Administration (800-772-1213; www.ssa.gov).

Estate Planning

Widowed. If your spouse is terminally ill, you still have time to set up trusts and write a will that spells out who is to inherit which assets and who will serve as executor of your estate. Working with a financial planner or estate-planning lawyer, divide your assets between yourself and your spouse to minimize estate taxes. Each person can pass up to $1 million (rising to $3.5 million in 2009) worth of assets to beneficiaries free of estate tax. Therefore, balance the ownership of your assets, so that both you and your spouse have roughly the maximum that passes estate-tax-free. If your assets exceed the maximum, use your will to establish trusts to pass assets to your children or other people you care about, and to appoint a guardian for your children if they are minors. Also, have a power of attorney and, if desired, a living will and keep them up-to-date.

If you planned your estate while your mate was alive, you may inherit some assets at his or her death. However, if your assets are significant enough, they might be funneled into a trust, which will pay you income for the rest of your life.

Divorced. Once your divorce is final, you are likely to be cut out of your ex-spouse's will. Make sure that this will is invalidated and destroyed, so you can write a new one for yourself. All the assets that you receive from your divorce settlement should be taken out of joint name and placed in yours alone. If those assets total more than $1 million (rising to $3.5 million in 2009), you may want to set up trusts through your will to avoid estate taxes. You also need a will to tell a probate court how you want your assets distributed. (For more details, consult Chapter 5.)

Employee Benefits

Widowed. If the employee benefits department has not yet been notified of your spouse's demise, write a letter informing the department of his or her date of death and Social Security number. Request information about the benefits you should expect to receive and what steps you must take to begin the payments. As the surviving spouse, some of the benefits you may be entitled to include: term life insurance, accidental death payout if your spouse died while traveling on company business, or some type of survivor income.

Depending on the employer's benefits plan, you may be eligible to receive pension benefits based on defined benefit and defined contribution plans, if your spouse was vested at the time of his or her death. Your spouse may have worked at several companies and become vested in many pension plans during his or her working life, so contact all past employers as well as the current employer.

If you feel able to invest the money wisely, take the pension plan in a lump sum and invest in a diversified portfolio of stocks, bonds, and mutual funds that will provide steady income as well as growth potential. However, if you have little confidence in your investing ability, opt for the annuity, which will relieve you of the responsibility of investing the money and will ensure stable income for life.

You and your family also are eligible to continue coverage under your spouse's health insurance plan for three years at the same price the employer would have paid, plus a small administrative fee, according to the federal Congressional Omnibus Budget Reconciliation Act (COBRA).

Divorced. Do not expect many perks from your ex-spouse's employee benefits package. However, you may try to claim part of your ex-spouse's defined contribution plan assets as part of your divorce settlement. You might receive title to some of those assets.

As long as you notify you ex-spouse's employer within 60 days after formal termination, COBRA guarantees the right to continue health insurance under your ex-spouse's policy for up to three years. Furthermore, your dependent children must continue to be covered under your ex-spouse's health insurance policy, and the premiums must be paid under the same terms as before the divorce.

If you are divorced and still working, maximize whatever benefits options your employer provides. This means you should participate in retirement savings plans, health and disability insurance plans, and educational scholarship programs.

CONCLUSION

The lessons in *Everyone's Money Book on Financial Planning* can be applied to your particular circumstances, no matter what your age or family situation. I have given you the information you need to take charge of every aspect of your personal finances, both in the eight chapters of this book and in the "Resources" section at the end of each chapter. Now is your chance to put all of this information into action!

RESOURCES

Books

Divorce & Money: How to Make the Best Financial Decisions During Divorce, by Violet Woodhouse (Nolo Press, 950 Parker St., Berkeley, CA 94710; 800-992-6656; www.nolo.com). This is a practical guide to evaluating assets during divorce.

The Dollars and Sense of Divorce, by Judith Briles, Edwin Schilling, and Carol Ann Wilson (Dearborn Trade, 155 N. Wacker Dr., Chicago, IL 60606; 312-836-4400, 800-245-2665; www.dearborntrade.com). Explains what you need to know if you are contemplating divorce.

Get a Financial Life, by Beth Kobliner (Fireside Books, 1230 Avenue of the Americas, New York, NY 10020; 212-698-7000; www.simonsays.com). Written specifically for people in their 20s and 30s, this book shows anyone how to manage money and make it grow. It teaches how to refinance high-rate credit cards and student loans.

Investing from Scratch: A Handbook for the Young Investor, by James Lowell (Penguin Putnam, 405 Murray Hill Pkwy., East Rutherford, NJ 07073; 800-788-6262; www.penguinputnam.com). Author speaks to readers ages 25 to 35 about current economic issues and offers advice about how to reduce the risks associated with investing while achieving a decent return on their money.

Love, Marriage & Money: Understanding and Achieving Financial Compatibility Before—and After—You Say "I Do," by Gail Liberman and Alan Lavine (Dearborn Trade, 155 N. Wacker Dr., Chicago, IL 60606; 312-836-4400, 800-245-2665; www.dearborntrade.com). Explains how to integrate financial considerations into a successful marriage.

On Your Own: A Widow's Passage to Emotional and Financial Well-Being, by Alexandra Armstrong and Mary R. Donahue (Dearborn Trade, 155 N. Wacker Dr., Chicago, IL 60606; 312-836-4400, 800-245-2665; www.dearborntrade.com). Covers the financial and emotional needs of widows.

Your Wealth Building Years: Financial Planning for 18 to 38 Year Olds, by Adriane G. Berg (Newmarket Press, 18 E. 48th St., New York, NY 10017; 212-832-3575, 800-233-4830; www.newmarketpress.com). A basic financial primer for 18- to 38-year-olds.

Web Sites

BuckInvestor.com. A good site for young investors to learn the basics of investment. <www.buckinvestor.com>

DivorceSource.com. This site discusses financial issues resulting from a divorce. This is a women's financial site that offers online banking and is an online broker for buying and selling stocks. <www.financialmuse.com>

Fleet Kids. This site educates children about money and managing through the use of educational and entertaining games. <www.fleetkids.com>

ka-Ching. An Oprah Winfrey site targeted to women and their financial lives. <www.ka-ching.com>

MsMoney.com. A women's financial services site, full of helpful information about personal finances, investment, and purchasing a car or house. Also operates as an online brokerage and online bank and has links to lenders and insurance companies. <www.msmoney.com>

Salomon Smith Barney. This site offers a good overview of investing principles for children. <www.smithbarney.com/yin/intro.html>

United States Treasury Historical Archives. U.S. Treasury site for children. <www.treas.gov>

Women's Financial Network. Offers financial advice targeted to women; gives them access to the financial information they need. Also offers bill-paying and other financial services. Also offers brokerage services for women. <www.wfn.com>

Index

A

Accountant, 146–47, 167
Accredited tax advisor, 147
Accredited tax preparer, 147
Adjustable-rate mortgage (ARM), 63
Adjusted gross income (AGI), 137
Adoption assistance, 99
Adoption credit, 139
Advance directive, 121, 122
Alimony, 4, 25, 27
All-risk insurance, 91
Alternative dispute resolution (ADR), 148
Alternative minimum tax (AMT), 140–41
American Society of Appraisers, 4
American Society of Home Inspectors, 61, 62
AMEX Composite Index, 46
Annual budget, 31–32, 33
Annual fees, 70
Annual percentage rate (APR), 69, 70
Annuity
    asset category, 3
    40s and 50s age bracket, 173
    income source, 25
    pension options, 96–97

single person, 179
types, 93
widowed person, 184–85
Appraisal, 61
Appraisal Institute, 61
APR. *See* Annual percentage rate
Arbitration, 149
ARM. *See* Adjustable-rate mortgage
Asset
    allocation, 98
    classes of, 2–4
    management accounts, 40–41
    worksheet, 5–7
Attorney
    agreement with, 151–52
    alternatives to, 148–49
    fees, 151
    interview, 151
    sources for, 149–51
Auto broker, 68
Automatic investment program, 180
Automatic rate cut (ARC), 63
Automatic savings plan, 27
Automobile
    buyer's service, 68
    dealer's cost, 68
    expense, 27

financing worksheet, 67
insurance, 83–86, 176, 181, 183
lease option, 69–70
leasing costs worksheet, 66
loan rates, 69
purchase, 67–68
resources, 80–81
service contract, 68
trade-in allowances, 68
transportation needs, 66–67
20s and 30s age bracket, 171
Average daily balance, 70

B

Back-end load, 163
Balloon mortgage, 63
Bank
    accounts, 2
    fees, 28
    investment strategy, 40
    products, 26
    rust department, 148
Banker, 147–48
Bankruptcy, 77
Beneficiary, 124
Billing problems, 76
Bodily injury, 84
Bond mutual funds, 104

Bonds
    college financing, 104
    income from, 26
    investment strategy,
      44–45
    repayment risk, 49
    types of, 44–45
Bonus, 25
Bottom line, 30
Budget
    annual, 31–32, 33
    monthly, 32, 34
    purpose of, 30–31
Burial arrangements, 125–26
Business
    loan interest, 138
    travel, 29
Buy-down mortgage, 63
Buyer's broker, 61, 159
Buyer's Home Finding
    Network, 62

C

Cafeteria plans, 94, 182
Capacity, 73
Capital, 73
Capital gains, 4, 132, 140
Career-average formula plan,
    96
Cash flow
    analysis, 15–17
    bottom line, 30
    expenses, 26–29
    income, 17, 25–26
    worksheet, 18–24
Cash instruments, 39
Cash out, 98
Cash-value policies, 93
Casualty and theft loss, 138
Catastrophic policies, 89
Catch-up contributions, 173,
    174
Certificate of deposit (CD), 42,
    45
Certified public accountant
    (CPA), 147
Chapter 13 bankruptcy, 77
Chapter 7 bankruptcy, 77
Character, 73
Charitable contribution, 28,
    138, 141
Charitable gift annuity, 123
Checking account, 39–40

Children
    dependent care benefits,
      99
    expense, 28
    finances, 180
    tax credit, 139
    tax strategies, 141
Child support, 4, 25, 27
Closed-end credit, 71
Closed-end lease, 69
Closing costs, 59
Clothing expense, 28
COBRA. *See* Congressional
    Omnibus Budget
    Reconciliation Act
CODA (cash-or-deferred
    arrangement), 97
Collateral, 71
Collection agencies, 77
College financing
    cooperative education,
      105–6
    cost estimates, 100
    cost and savings needs
      worksheet, 102
    financial aid application,
      106
    grants, 105
    investments, 100, 103–5,
      106
    loans, 106
    resources, 101, 110
    tax laws and, 100
Collision, 84
Commission
    financial planner, 155
    real estate advisor, 159
    stockbroker, 163–64
Company-sponsored insurance
    programs, 99
Compound interest, 111
Comprehensive coverage, 84
Condominium insurance, 91
Congressional Omnibus
    Budget Reconciliation Act
    (COBRA)
    benefits, 90
    divorced person, 183, 187
    widowed person, 186
Consumer protection agencies,
    149
Contracts, 124
Convertible mortgage, 63

Cooperative education, 105–6
Coverdell education savings
    account, 104, 130
CPA. *See* Certified public
    accountant
Credentials
    advisors, 145
    financial planner, 152
    insurance agent, 157
Credit bureau, 75
Credit card, 5, 72, 76
Credit life insurance, 69
Credit management
    bankruptcy, 77
    billing problems, 76
    closed-end credit, 71
    credit building, 73–75
    credit score, 75
    debt percentage, 76–77
    divorced person, 183
    40s and 50s age bracket,
      173
    loan types, 72–73
    married person, 180–81
    open-end credit, 70–71
    resources, 78
    risk, 49
    secured credit, 71–72
    60s+ age bracket, 176
    Truth-in-Lending Act, 72
    20s and 30s age bracket,
      170–71
    unsecured credit, 71–72
    widowed person, 183
Credit unions, 40
Currency risk, 47–48
Current assets, 2
Current liabilities, 4
Custodian, 121

D

Death benefit, 92, 185
Debit card, 72
Debt collection, 77
Debt planning
    bankruptcy, 77
    billing problems, 76
    closed-end credit, 71
    credit building, 73–75
    debt percentage, 76–77
    loan types, 72–73
    open-end credit, 70–71
    secured credit, 71–72

Truth-in-Lending Act, 72
unsecured credit, 71–72
Deductions, 137–38
Deep-discount broker, 164
Deferred annuities, 93
Deferred compensation, 25
Defined benefit plan, 95–97, 115, 118
Defined contribution plan, 95, 97–98, 118
Deflation risk, 48
Dependent care, 99
Disability insurance
basics, 84, 87, 106
40s and 50s age bracket, 173
income worksheet, 88
60s+ age bracket, 176
single person, 178
20s and 30s age bracket, 171
widowed person, 183
Disabled credit, 139–40
Discount broker, 164–65
Discretionary spending, 26
Dividend reinvestment plan (DRIP), 180
Divorced person, 182–87
Do-it-yourself legal, 149
Dow Jones Composite Average, 46
Dow Jones Industrial Average, 46
Dow Jones Transportation Average, 46
Dow Jones Utilities Average, 46
Down payment, 59–61, 69
DRIP. See Dividend reinvestment plan
Dues, 28

E

Earned income, 25
Earned income tax credit, 139
Education. See College financing
assistance, 99
expense, 28, 131
IRA. See Coverdell education savings account
tax credit, 139

Elderly credit, 139–40
Electronic broker, 164
Electronic filing, 133–34
Emergency cash reserve, 170, 180, 182
Employee assistance program, 99
Employee benefits
cafeteria plans, 94, 182
divorced person, 186–87
estate planning, 124
health insurance options, 94
health/wellness, 99
married person, 182
pension, 95–98
resources, 109
retirement savings programs, 93–94, 95–98
60s+ age bracket, 177–78
tax strategies, 141
20s and 30s age bracket, 172
widowed person, 186
Employee stock ownership plan, 97
Enrolled agents, 147
Entertainment expense, 29
Equifax, 75, 74
Equipment expense, 28
Equities, 42
Estate planning
coverage areas, 120–21
divorced person, 186
40s and 50s age bracket, 174
funeral/burial arrangements, 125–26
gift tax rules, 131–32
married person, 181–82
purpose of, 111
resources, 126–28
single person, 179
60s+ age bracket, 177
20s and 30s age bracket, 171–72
widowed person, 185–86
will, 121–25
Estate tax
exemption, 124
rate, 111
rules, 131–32

Excess major medical policies, 89
Executor, 121, 122, 123
Exemption, 132
Expense
fixed, 26–28
flexible, 28–29
Experian, 75
Experts, 145

F

Fair Debt Collection Practices Act, 77
Family
exemptions, 138
expenses, 27
income, 25
Family and Medical Leave Act (FMLA), 99
Fee-for-service indemnity policy, 87
Fees
advisor, 145
attorney, 151
financial planner, 155–56
investment management consultant, 162
money managers, 161
real estate advisor, 159
stockbroker, 163–64
trust department, 148
Final-pay formula plan, 96
Finance charge, 70
Financial checkup
divorced person, 182–87
40s and 50s age bracket, 172–74
married person, 179–82
single person, 178–79
60s+ age bracket, 175–78
20s and 30s age bracket, 168–72
widowed person, 182–87
Financial goals
categories, 12
monthly savings, 17
setting, 11–15
tracking, 12–15, 16
Financial institutions, 40
Financial planner
credentials, 152
disclosure form, 153–54
interview, 152, 155

Financial planner *continued*
  payment methods, 154–55
  resources, 166
Financial professionals
  accountant, 146–47
  avoiding problems,
    145–46
  banker, 147–48
  insurance agent, 156–57
  legal advice, 148–52
  money managers, 159–62
  real estate advisor, 157–59
  stockbroker, 162–65
  tax preparer, 146–47
  tips, 144–45
Financial services expense,
  28
First-person loss, 83
Fixed annuities, 93
Fixed expense, 26–28
Fixed-rate mortgage, 63
Flat-benefit formula plan, 96
Flexible expense, 28–29
Flexible spending account
  (FSA), 94, 181
Flextime, 99
Floater, 91
FMLA. *See* Family and
  Medical Leave Act
Food expense, 29
Foreign index, 47
401(k) plan
  basics, 27, 97, 118–19
  catch-up contributions,
    173, 174
  expense category, 27
  investment strategy, 119
  loan against, 5
403(b) plan
  basics, 27, 97, 118–19
  investment strategy, 119
  rollovers, 131
457 plan
  basics, 27, 97, 118–19
  investment strategy,
    119
Front-end load, 163
FSA. *See* Flexible spending
  account
Full-service discount broker,
  164
Funeral arrangements,
  125–26

G
GEM. *See* Growing equity
  mortgage
Generation-skipping transfer
  (GST) tax, 132
Gifts, 121, 123
Gift tax rules, 131–32
Gold, 45
Government income, 25
Government regulators
  automobile, 80
  college financing, 110
  employee benefits, 109
  financial advice, 167
  insurance, 108
  real estate, 80
  tax planning, 143
Grace period, 70
Grants, 105
Gross income, 137
Growing equity mortgage
  (GEM), 63
Growth stock, 141
Growth-stock mutual funds,
  104
GST. *See* Generation-skipping
  transfer tax
Guardian, 121

H
Head of household, 133, 136
Health care power of attorney,
  122
Health insurance
  divorced person, 183, 187
  married person, 181
  options, 87, 89–90
  out-of-pocket expense, 29
  single person, 178
  60s+ age bracket, 176–77
  20s and 30s age bracket,
    171
  widowed person, 186
Health maintenance
  organization (HMO), 89, 171
Higher-education expenses,
  131
Home equity loans, 72
Home ownership
  advantages, 57–58
  appraisal, 61
  down payment, 59–61
  first-time buyers, 61

  maintenance expense, 29
  mortgage, 59, 61–63
  property inspection, 61
  selling tips, 65
  tips, 59–60
Homeowners insurance, 90–92,
  171, 177
Home-related expense, 27
Hope Scholarship Credit, 139
Housing needs, 57–65

I
Immediate annuity, 93, 173
Income, 17, 141
Income tax
  expense, 4, 27
  categories, 137
  state/local, 138
Individual retirement account
  (IRA)
  basics, 25
  catch-up contributions,
    173, 174
  contribution limits, 131
  conversion, 177
  options, 120
  retirement planning, 99,
    106
  tax strategies, 141
  withdrawal penalty, 133
Inflation risk, 48
Installment debt, 4
Installment loans, 72
Insurance
  advisor, 83
  agent, 156–57
  auto, 83–86
  basics, 83
  company ratings, 82
  company-sponsored
    programs, 99
  disability, 84, 87, 88, 106
  divorced person, 183
  estate planning, 124
  expense, 27
  40s and 50s age bracket,
    173
  health, 87, 89–90
  homeowners, 90–92
  life, 93–94
  married person, 181
  organizations, 107–8, 166
  quote services, 108

ratings services, 108
resources, 107–8
single person, 178–79
60s+ age bracket, 176–77
tax strategies, 141
20s and 30s age bracket, 171
widowed person, 183
Interest expense, 138
Interest rate
bonds, 44
CDs, 42
closed-end credit, 71
MMDA, 41
mortgage, 60
open-end credit, 70
savings/checking accounts, 39
risk, 48
Internal Revenue Service (IRS)
advice, 129–30, 146
audit, 142
electronic filing, 133–34
estate tax, 111
exchanges, 184
failure to file, 134
filing status, 181
guidelines, 133
rollover rules, 73
tax refund, 2
Interview
attorney, 151
financial planner, 152, 155
insurance agent, 156–57
money manager, 160
real estate advisor, 158
stockbroker, 162
tips, 145
Inter vivos trust, 124–25
Intestate, 120
Inventory, 91–92
Investment
divorced person, 182–83
fixed expense, 27
flexible expense, 29
40s and 50s age bracket, 172–73
income, 26
interest, 138
management consultants, 161–62
married person, 180
real estate, 65

resources, 166
risk pyramid, 50–51
risk tolerance, 47–54
salary reduction plans, 119
single person, 178
60s+ age bracket, 175–76
strategy, setting up, 39–45
tracking, 45–47
20s and 30s age bracket, 170
widowed person, 182
IRA. *See* Individual retirement account
Irrevocable trust, 125
IRS. *See* Internal Revenue Service

J–K
Joint and survivor annuity, 96, 118
Joint tenancy, 124
Keogh plan, 25, 99, 119–20

L
Lack of diversification risk, 48
Lack of liquidity risk, 49
Late fees, 70
Legal advice, 148–52, 166
Legal services, 99
Liability
categories, 4
coverage, 92
insurance, 91
worksheet, 8–9
Life annuity with ten-year certain, 96
Life insurance
cash value, 3
coverage types, 92–93
40s and 50s age bracket, 173
loans, 73
married person, 181
single person, 179
20s and 30s age bracket, 171
Lifetime Learning Credit, 139
Lifetime trust, 124–25
Limited partnerships, 26
Liquidity, 2
Listing agreement, 158–59
Living will, 122

Load fund, 44
Loan, 72–73
Local income tax, 138
Long-term assets, 3
Long-term care policies, 90
Long-term goals, 12, 15
Low-income savers, 131
Lump-sum distribution, 118
Lump-sum payout, 96–97

M
Management fee, 41, 44
Margin accounts, 138
Marginal tax rate system, 134, 136
Margin loans, 73
Married person
financial checkup, 179–82
marriage penalty, 181
tax status, 133, 136
Media hotlines, 149
Mediation, 149
Medical care repricing policies, 90
Medical expense, 29, 138
Medical power of attorney, 122
Medical savings account (MSA), 99, 132
Medicare, 89, 177
Medigap plan, 90
Medium-term goals, 12, 14
MedSup plan, 90
Merrill Lynch Mortgage 100 program, 60
Microinvesting, 105
Mileage rate, 132
Minimum payment, 70
Miscellaneous expense, 29
MMDA. *See* Money-market deposit account
Money managers, 159–62
Money strategies
divorced person, 182–87
40s and 50s age bracket, 172–74
married person, 179–82
single person, 178–79
60s+ age bracket, 174–78
20s and 30s age bracket, 168–72
widowed person, 182–87
Money-market deposit account (MMDA), 41

Money-market mutual funds, 2, 41
Money-purchase pension plan, 97
Monthly budget, 32, 34
Mortgage
  interest rates, 60
  lenders, 61–62
  loans, 73
  refinance, 64
  subsidy, 63
  types, 63–64
Mortgage-backed securities, 49
MSA. *See* Medical savings account
Municipal bonds, 104, 141
Mutual fund
  automatic investment program, 170, 180
  college financing, 104
  investment strategy, 44
Mystery cash, 29

N

Named-peril insurance, 91
Nasdaq Composite Index, 46
National Association of Master Appraisers, 62
National Center for Home Equity Conversion, 64
National tax preparation chains, 146
Negative cash flow, 30
Net worth
  assets, 2–4, 5–7
  comparisons, 10
  determination of, 1–10
  liabilities, 4, 7–10
No-load fund, 44
Nonresident alien, 133
NOW (negotiable order of withdrawal) account, 39
NYSE Composite Index, 46

O

Online dispute resolution, 148
Open-end credit, 70–71
Open-end lease, 69
Organizations
  accountant, 167
  college financing, 110
  employee benefits, 109

estate planning, 127
financial planning, 166
insurance, 107–8, 166
investment, 166
legal, 166–67
real estate, 166
retirement planning, 127
tax preparer, 167

P

Passbook savings accounts, 39
Payout option, 96, 98
PBGC. *See* Pension Benefit Guaranty Corporation
Pension
  assets, 3
  benefits, 112
  defined benefit plan, 95–97
  defined contribution plan, 95, 97–98
Pension Benefit Guaranty Corporation (PBGC), 97, 107
Personal exemptions, 138
Personal injury protection (PIP), 84
Personal property, 3–4
Playing-it-too-safe risk, 49
PMI. *See* Private mortgage insurance
Points, 138
Point of service (POS), 89
Political risk, 49
Positive cash flow, 30
Postage, 29
Power of attorney, 122
Precious metals, 45
Preferred provider organization (PPO), 89
Premium, 83
Prenatal leave, 99
Prepaid tuition plans, 105
Preretirement survivor's annuity, 118
Private counselors, 149
Private mortgage insurance (PMI), 60
Probate, 123–25, 126
Professional affiliation, 145
Professional services expense, 28
Profit-sharing plan, 3, 97

Property
  damage, 84, 90–91
  inspection, 61
  tax, 4, 27

Q

Qualified five-year gains, 132
Qualified joint and survivor annuity (QJSA), 96
Qualified tuition programs, 130
Quote services, 108

R

RAM. *See* Reverse annuity mortgage
Rapid payoff loan, 63
Ratings services, 108
Real estate
  advisor, 157–59
  current worth, 2–3
  debt, 4
  40s and 50s age bracket, 173
  investment, 65
  limited partnerships, 2–3
  resources, 78–80, 166
  60s+ age bracket, 176
  tax strategies, 142
  20s and 30s age bracket, 170
  widowed person, 183
Recordkeeping system, 10–11
Recreation expense, 29
References, 145
Rent, 58–59
Renter's insurance, 91
Repayment risk, 49
Replacement cost coverage, 90–91
Residual value, 69–70
Resources
  accountant organizations, 167
  automobiles, 80–81
  college financing, 110
  credit, 78
  employee benefits, 109
  estate planning, 126–28
  financial advice, 165–67
  financial checkup, 35–36
  financial planning, 166
  insurance, 107–8, 166

investment organizations,
166
investment strategy, 55–56
legal organizations,
166–67
money strategies, 187–88
real estate, 78–80, 166
retirement planning,
126–28
tax planning, 142–43
tax preparer organizations,
167
Retirement plan loans, 73
Retirement planning
annual savings worksheet,
114, 116
capital accumulation
worksheet, 114, 115
compound interest, 111
defined benefit plans, 115,
118, 95–97
defined contribution plans,
95, 97–98, 118
divorced person, 185
expense worksheet, 112,
113
40s and 50s age bracket,
174
fund portability, 131
income sources, 25, 112,
114
IRA, 120
options, 117
resources, 126–28
salary reduction plans,
118–19
savings programs, 93–94
self-employed, 98, 119–20
single person, 179
20s and 30s, 171
widowed person, 184–85
Reverse annuity mortgage
(RAM), 64
Reverse mortgage, 64
Revocable trust, 125
Revolving credit, 70–71
Rider, 91
Risk
tolerance quiz, 52, 53–54
20s and 30s age bracket,
170
types of, 47–50
Risk pool coverage, 89

Rollovers, 73, 131
Roth IRA
contribution limits, 131
conversion, 177
options, 120
retirement planning, 99,
106

S

Salary, 25, 155
Salary reduction plan
basics, 97, 118–19
investment strategy, 119
tax savings, 95
SAM. *See* Shared appreciation
mortgage
Savings
accounts, 39–40
fixed expense, 27
flexible expense, 29
Savings and loans, 40
Section 529 college savings
plan, 104–5, 130
Secured credit, 71–72
Securities, 2
Self-employment
earnings, 133
income, 25
retirement planning, 98,
119–20
tax, 4
tax law changes, 132
SEP. *See* Simplified employee
pension
Series EE savings bonds, 104
Service loans, 73
Shared appreciation mortgage
(SAM), 63
Short-term goals, 12, 13
SIMPLE (savings incentive
match plan for employees)
plan, 98–99
Simplified employee pension
(SEP), 98, 119–20
Single person
financial checkup,
178–79
tax status, 133, 136
Small claims court, 148–49
Social Security
death benefit, 185
disability issues, 183
divorced person, 185

retirement income, 25,
112, 114–15
survivor's benefits, 184,
185
tax, 133
Spend and save programs, 105
Standard deduction, 132
Standard & Poor's 500 Index,
46
State health insurance risk
pool, 89
State income tax, 138
Stock
bonus plan, 97–98
growth, 104
income from, 26
investment strategy, 42–43
mutual fund, 44
options, 25
Stockbroker, 162–65
Straight life annuity, 118
Street name, 163
STRIPS (separate trading of
registered interest and
principal of securities), 104
Student loan interest, 132, 138
Succession planning, 121

T

Tangible personal property
memorandum (TPPM), 122
Tax attorney, 147
Tax planning
alternative minimum tax,
140–41
audits, 142
capital gains/losses, 132,
140
credits, 131, 139–40
divorced person, 184
exemption amount, 132
expense category, 27
40s and 50s age bracket,
174
implications, 129
IRS advice, 129–30
legal deductions, 137–38
married person, 181
medical savings account,
132
refunds, 2, 133
resources, 142–43
return filing, 132–34, 135

Tax planning *continued*
    rollovers, 131
    self-employment tax, 132
    60s+ age bracket, 177
    standard deduction, 132
    standard mileage rate, 132
    strategies, 129, 141–42
    student loan interest, 132
    taxable income, 137
    tax law changes, 130–32
    tax rates, 130, 134,
        136–37
    widowed person, 183–84
Tax preparer, 146–47, 167
Ten-year term certain annuity,
    96
Term insurance, 92
Third-party loss, 83
Thrift savings fund, 118–19
Thrift savings plan, 98
Timeshares, 65
TPPM. *See* Tangible personal
    property memorandum
Transaction fees, 71
Trans Union, 75
Travel expense, 29
Treasury bills (T-bill), 2, 41
Treasury bonds, 104, 142

Treasury securities, 2
Trust
    department, 148
    estate planning, 122,
        124–25
    income from, 25
    types of, 125
Trustee, 121
Truth-in-Lending Act, 72
Tuition expense, 27
12b-1 fees, 44

U

Umbrella coverage, 27, 92
Uniform Gift to Minors Act
    (UGMA), 103–4
Uninsured/underinsured
    motorist, 84
U.S. savings bonds, 2, 104
Universal life insurance, 93
Unpaid taxes, 4
Unreimbursed business
    expense, 29
Utilities, 27–28

V

Vacation expense, 29
Variable annuities, 93

Variable life insurance, 93
Vehicle. *See* Automobile
Vesting rules, 95–96, 98
Volatility risk, 50

W

Walk-away lease, 69
Web sites
    credit resources, 78
    do-it-yourself legal,
        149
    estate planning, 127–28
    financial institutions, 40
    money strategies, 188
    retirement planning,
        127–28
    securities, 2
    tax planning, 143
Whole life insurance, 93
Widow/widower, 133, 182–87
Will, 121–25
Wilshire 5000 Equity Index,
    47
Wirehouse, 163

Y–Z

Yield, 2, 12–13
Zero-coupon bonds, 104

Bulk Pricing Information

For special discounts on
20 or more copies of
*Everyone's Money Book
on Financial Planning,*
call Dearborn Trade Special Sales
at 800-621-9621, extension 4455,
or e-mail bermel@dearborn.com.
You'll receive great service
and top discounts.

For added visibility, please
consider our custom cover service,
which highlights your firm's name
and logo on the cover.
We are also an excellent resource
for dynamic and
knowledgeable speakers.

Dearborn™
Trade Publishing
A **Kaplan Professional** Company